ANCIENT
GREEK
ATHLETICS

Bronze age - 3000 - 1200 BC
(dark ages)
homeric period - 1100 - 800 BC

ANCIENT GREEK ATHLETICS

Stephen G. Miller

YALE UNIVERSITY PRESS   NEW HAVEN AND LONDON

Designed and typeset by Gregg Chase and set in Albertina.

The Library of Congress has cataloged the hardcover edition as follows:
Miller, Stephen G.
Ancient Greek Athletics/Stephen G. Miller.
p. cm.
Includes bibliographical references and index.
ISBN 0-300-10083-3 (alk. paper)
1. Athletics — Greece — History.   I. Title.
GV21.M55 2004
796'. 09495 — dc22   2003016875

A catalogue record for this book is available from the British Library.

The paper in this book meets the guidelines for permanence and durability of the Committee
on Production Guidelines for Book Longevity of the Council on Library Resources.

ISBN-13: 978-0-300-11529-1 (pbk. : alk. paper)
ISBN-10: 0-300-11529-6 (pbk. : alk. paper)

10 9 8 7 6 5

CONTENTS

PREFACE

ANCIENT GREEK ATHLETICS as a field of study does not suffer from overpopulation. Those who might be most interested in the subject may not have the necessary training to handle the primary evidence, and those who have it may not want to spend time on what seems a nonacademic area. Aristotle researched the history of athletics, but many modern classical scholars have shunned it. Plato spends long discussions on the place of athletics in education and society, yet modern books on such topics as ancient Greek history and Athenian democracy can be completely silent about athletics. This blind eye, however, means that the field has been fallow and is now fertile for research. The wealth of ancient written and visual sources that tell us about athletics has never been fully exploited, and that has turned out to be a challenge and a joy to people like me.

A happy development is that during the past three decades many scholars have emerged whose research into various aspects of Greek athletics has enriched our knowledge dramatically. Albanidis, Aupert, Bernardini, Bouvrie, Crowther, Decker, Ebert, Gebhard, Glass, Golden, Kefalidou, Kennell, Kyle, Larmour, Lee, McDonnell, Moretti, Morison, Neils, Pleket, Poliakoff, Raschke, Reed, Rieger, Romano, Sansome, Scanlon, Serwint, Siewert, Sinn, Spathari, Swaddling, Yalouris, Young, Ulf, Valavanis, Vanhove, Wacker, Weiler, and Welch, among others, have produced significant contributions on athletics, and most of them are still doing so.

Equally happy, but more personal, was the suggestion in 1975 from the chair of my department at the University of California at Berkeley that I devise and implement an undergraduate course on ancient athletics. The impetus for the suggestion came, at least in part, from my experience in excavating the ancient stadium at Nemea; it was felt that my firsthand knowledge of evidence that was just coming out of the ground would inspire the students. That assessment has proven to be correct. To the constant cross-fertilization and stimulus among the scholars just mentioned was added the curiosity and enthusiasm of the undergraduate students which has provided me with both a prod and a check.

A recurring problem in the classroom, however, was the lack of a text that could serve as a framework for the material, especially since I believe that students need to confront the primary evidence—to know what we know and how we know it, and to learn how to deal with fragmentary and contradictory data. My first response to this need was a collection of translations of ancient written sources which became

Arete: Greek Sports from Ancient Sources (1979). As my knowledge has grown and I have found more and more material, the collection has grown as well; it is now forthcoming in a third, much-expanded edition (2004). The evidence from that book can be helpful to readers of this one as well, and I have therefore appended cross-references to these translations (marked *A* followed by the selection number) to my references to ancient sources.

Equally important is the visual evidence that survives. That evidence has been made available in part through the World Wide Web, where we have created a site for students (*http://socrates.berkeley.edu/~cls180/*). But this material, helpful as it is, does not take the place of a handbook, and the wish to bring such a book to every interested reader, including those outside the formal boundaries of the university classroom, has driven me to write the work you are now reading. The choice of illustrations has not always been easy, and a part of me would like to present a photograph of every single vase painting of athletes and every single statue base of an athlete so that the full set of evidence would be readily available. Such a project, aside from economic realities, would relieve me of the need to make choices but would be a denial of my responsibility to present the most significant works so as to save the general reader from wading through redundancies. Although every illustration presented here shows a detail that is distinctive and necessary for an understanding of the subject, there are still a great many pictures. I feel particularly fortunate that Yale University Press, alone of all the presses with which I had contact, agreed to undertake the publication of a book that would involve hundreds of illustrations, many of them in color. The support of my editors, Larisa Heimert, and of my manuscript editor, Susan Laity, in this production was critical.

Many other people have lent assistance in various ways. Chief among them is Frank Cope of the Nemea Archives at the University of California. I thank him. Others who have given important help and advice are Jenny Bouyia, Joan Mertens, Paul Royster, Athena Trakadas, and Christiane Tytgat. The anonymous reader for the Press saved me from several errors and forced me to strengthen some arguments; I am grateful for that. Bob Mechikoff read large parts of the manuscript, and Effie Miller read the whole. I especially thank her for the needed encouraging word, and for the questions that revealed problems in my exposition. Indexing was aided by Gloria Bath, Jini Kim, and Clarice Major. I also thank John Camp and John MacAloon for their encouragement, and the International Olympic Akademy and its president and rector, Nikos Filaretos and Costas Georgiades, for a chance to revive. The University of California has provided crucial support and library facilities, as has the American School of Classical Studies at Athens. For their inspiration, I thank the hundreds of students and the private donors who support the Nemea Excavations. Their faith in me over the years is humbling.

A NOTE ON TRANSLITERATIONS
AND MEASUREMENTS

The transliteration of Greek words into English has always produced anomalies. This book has its share, and many of them derive from personal comfort and discomfort. The Greek kappa may be the most obvious case in point. We derive many of our visual familiarities with Greek through transliterations made by the Romans, who had no letter k in their alphabet. Hence, *Socrates* has been the received form of *Sokrates,* even though the latter, it has seemed to me, should be the proper way for us, who do have a "k," to write that name. We thereby avoid possible confusion deriving from the use of a potentially soft "c." Using the "k" instead of the "c" is not particularly distressing with words that are unfamiliar in English like *akon, ankyle, didaskalos,* or *Kroton.* In addition, it immediately will be apparent that unfamiliar words with a "c" are not Greek, for example *caestus* and *curia.* There are, however, a few words that—for me—are so familiar with a Latin "c" that I find the "proper" transliteration distressing. I cannot, for example, see *Corinth* as *Korinth* without a twinge. Hence, I must ask the reader's indulgence and trust that the message will not be corrupted by these personal inconsistencies.

Measurements are another source of potential confusion. As an archaeologist working in an international discipline I have long made it a habit to use metric measurements. But the Greeks used a basic unit of measurement called a foot. It was not, however, a standard size but varied from place to place. Thus, for example, the foot used in the stadium at Olympia was about 32 centimeters long, while that used at Nemea was about 29.6 centimeters. To translate a measurement expressed by a Greek source as a number of feet into an absolute number of meters would thus be incorrect more often than not. Therefore, I supply the measurement in ancient feet, offering a rough metric equivalent, comfortable in the knowledge that whatever the precise length of that ancient foot at a given place and time it was not far from 12 inches.

EDITOR'S NOTE: For ease of readability, foreign words are set in italics or defined only at the first usage in each chapter. To assist readers unfamiliar with Greek, plurals are given following new words. A glossary is located at the end of the text. Angle brackets on page 188 indicate restored text.

1

INTRODUCTION

WILL ANTIGONE bury her dead brother or leave his corpse as carrion for the crows — will she obey the dictates of her conscience or the orders of the state? The dilemma of Sophokles' heroine resonates with us as an example of how the rights of the individual and the needs of society can conflict.

Is the Athens of Thucydides' Perikles a monument to the accomplishments of ancient Athenians — an inspiration to generations unborn — or do the Athenians of the Melian dialogue teach us a brutish, might-makes-right lesson?

Can we sympathize with, even as we laugh at, Aristophanes' sly Strepsiades, a man on the verge of bankruptcy thanks to his spendthrift son, who begs Sokrates to teach him how to cheat his creditors by use of a neat auditing trick?

Does the Sokrates of Plato speak to all that is most noble in us when he chooses to die rather than abdicate his principles?

Do Aristotle's concerns about education — its nature and content, whether it ought to be private or public — remain timely and timeless?

The Greeks of two-and-a-half millennia ago recognized and wrestled with so many of the difficult issues of what it is to be human that they stand as one of the highest points in our struggle to understand ourselves — to be civilized. In architecture and sculpture, painting and literature, drama and philosophy the ancient Greeks defined and developed various components of a culture that we still understand as fundamental to our own.

It is the purpose of this book to explore another aspect of Greek culture: athletics. For athletics was integral to the life of the Greeks — especially and most obviously (but not exclusively) for Greek men. My exploration will, of necessity, go into the details of competitions and may sometimes remind the reader of the sports section of a modern newspaper. But once we have examined those details, we can set athletics in the broader framework of ancient society. It is my hope that you, the reader, will come away not only learning something about ancient Greek athletics and its role in society but also understanding something more about our own world.

As much as possible I shall approach this study through the words and the artifacts that have been preserved from antiquity—let the Greeks speak for themselves. No matter how experienced or knowledgeable a modern scholar may be, the primary sources must always be the point of departure. I shall try to differentiate between certain knowledge and my interpretations of evidence that is frequently fragmentary, ambiguous, or contradictory—or all of the above. This will require you to examine these questions and come to your own conclusions, recognizing that some details are not yet known, and may never be. But I believe that your appreciation of our society's Greek heritage will thereby be enhanced.

Before we begin our investigation, we must set the historical framework. During the second millennium before Christ there flourished a vibrant civilization that we call the Minoan, centered on Crete but documented elsewhere (especially the island of Thera), and in regular contact with Egypt (fig. 1). This culture gave way to one located on the mainland, particularly in the Peloponnesos. Its center, Mycenae, gave this society the name by which we know it today. The myths and legends of historical Greece were largely rooted in these successive Bronze Age cultures. Theseus and the Minotaur, Daidalos and Ikaros, Helen, Agamemnon, Odysseus, Achilles, and Hektor, are only a few of the figures we can understand as representations of some historical truth perceived now only dimly through the discoveries of archaeologists, discoveries that record, as the myths suggested, the disastrous end that befell a brilliant civilization on the brink of developing a written literature.

The causes of that collapse are debated, and were probably diverse, but the ensuing depopulation and cultural depression are visible in the archaeological record and justify the name long given to this era—the Dark Ages. This period (ca. 1100–800 B.C.) was associated in myth with and substantiated in history by the Return of the Sons of Herakles—the Dorian Invasion. By the end of the Dark Ages, the dominance of the Dorians in the Peloponnesos and the Ionians in Attica and the Aegean was established, and it is on this cultural map that the next centuries of Greek development can be plotted.

Greece begins to awaken from the Dark Ages in the eighth century, when Homer reputedly hymned the Trojan War and when—in 776 B.C.—the Olympic Games were traditionally founded. The archaeological record, which details an increasing number of burials, testifying to a population explosion, also shows an increase in the quality of the artifacts discovered in the grave sites (including a clear interest in portraying the human figure), and the beginnings of a substantial architecture. In this period, too, begins the push of colonization as the expanding population sought space in ever larger parts of the Mediterranean: Sicily and Magna

Fig. 1 The world of Greek athletics before Alexander the Great.

Graecia, the coasts of the eastern Adriatic and North Africa, producing over the next two centuries Greek settlements ultimately stretching from the southern coast of France and the eastern coast of Spain to the Black Sea.

This expansion brought the Greeks into contact with older, well-established cultures, especially in Egypt (again), Anatolia, and Phoenicia. From them the Greeks took artistic and architectural forms, as well as an alphabet, but they retooled their borrowings during the "Orientalizing period" of the seventh century and brought them forth in new forms clearly stamped "Hellenic." For example, by about 650 B.C. poetry had advanced to a level of sophistication and wit that allowed Archilochos of Paros to express a literate understanding of human frailty through sardonic self-deprecation:

> Some barbarian is flashing my shield, a perfectly good tool
> That I left by a bush unwilling, but likewise unwilling
> To face death. To hell with that shield!
> I can buy a new one just as good. [fragment 6]

By about 600 we see the first of many forms: large-scale stone temples, lyric poetry, and human figures portrayed in stone at life size (and larger). Most characteristic is the nude young man (*kouros*) standing rigidly with left foot slightly forward and hands clenched at his sides—betraying both his Egyptian inspiration and the block of stone from which he was carved. At Athens, Sparta, Corinth, and the islands, painters developed the black-figure style (see, for example, figs. 3, 4, 5, 32, 69) that allowed them to present more detail, and replaced the fantastic birds and animals of earlier vases with the human form. It is at this time, too, that the Olympic Games were joined by the three other games of the Panhellenic cycle: the Pythian (initiated 586 B.C.), the Isthmian (580 B.C.), and the Nemean (573 B.C.). Also in these years, the Athenian lawgiver Solon both wrote his own poetry and set limits on the prizes given to athletes by the state. The games ran hand-in-hand with Greek cultural development.

By the end of the century these forms had developed dramatically. The statue of a nude youth became a naturalistic rendering in which muscles bulged and the skin betrayed not stone but the flesh and bone beneath it. The new red-figure style of painting (see, for example, figs. 6, 7, 8, 12) replaced the black, and the incised details of the earlier form gave way to brush strokes that offered a greater fluidity and curvilinear naturalism to anatomical details. The search for wisdom—philosophy—was under way, even as Simonides of Keos was beginning the tradition of odes commemorating athletic victories and the exploits of Arrhichion of Phigaleia and Milo of Kroton were launching a specifically athletic mythology.

By 500, a Hellenic cultural identity had come into full existence, an identity that demanded its own political structure. In Asia Minor, where the Persian Empire dominated the Greek cities, the Ionian Greeks launched a revolt in 499–495. It failed, bringing Persian wrath not only on the Ionians but on the Athenians, who had supported them, and in 490 a punitive expeditionary force landed northeast of Athens at Marathon. The unexpected Athenian victory there was justly celebrated, but it led, ten years later, to the assault of a huge Persian force bent on vengeance against them and any other Greeks who got in the way.

Three hundred Spartans were the first to get in the way at Thermopylai at the beginning of August, and their famously futile heroism should be put into the context of another Greek event: the Olympic Games of 480 were in the final stages of preparation even as Leonidas and his Spartan warriors were sacrificing themselves. A few days later, while the Persians were torching Athens, the games took place at Olympia. The athletes, like the crowd as a whole, came from all over Greece: Thebes, Argos, Syracuse, and Rhegion in Magna Graecia; Heraia, Stymphalia, and Mantineia in Arkadia; the islands of Chios and Thasos. That these games went on as Athens was burning tells us much about the position of athletics in Greek society, although no Athenians or Spartans are known to have competed while their fellow citizens were dying at Persian hands, and Phaÿllos of Kroton, a famous pentathlete, gave up his chance at Olympic victory to man his own ship at the Battle of Salamis, contributing to the

Greek victory there. After the games were over, the rest of the Greeks presented a more nearly unified front in the defeat of the Persians at Plateia in 479.

This victory, so unexpected in the face of overwhelming odds, unleashed a newfound Panhellenic pride. In one tangible expression of the new spirit, booty from the defeated Persians was dedicated at Olympia, Delphi, and Isthmia but not Nemea, which was controlled by Argos. Argos had not fought against the Persians, so its games site was not allowed to benefit from the Greek victory. But Pindar and Bacchylides led the poetic celebration of athletic victories at all four sites, while Myron commemorated them sculpturally. Many of the best-known athletes and examples of athletic art date from the period just after the Persian Wars, and for the next generation sources record more competitions between athletes than between city-states.

The political situation had shifted by the middle of the fifth century as the Greek world became increasingly polarized between Athens and Sparta. To be sure, this was also the time when an unprecedented (and still unequaled) eruption of creative energy was occurring at Athens: Aischylos, Sophokles, Euripides, and Aristophanes were setting the Athenian stage, Pheidias was building the Parthenon, and Thucydides was recording the disastrous conflict that eventually consumed the city. But the Athenian brilliance of 440 under the leadership of Perikles had dimmed by 399, when the state condemned Sokrates to death. It is not surprising that athletic performance during this period was overshadowed by political intrigue or that we know more about Sokrates' visits to the *gymnasion* than about Athenian victories at Olympia.

Politically, the fourth century was a struggle for dominance: Thebes entered the picture, but none of the cities held sway for long. Culturally, the fourth century offered refinement rather than innovation. It is telling that the leading men of letters were lawyers and philosophers. Plato gave up an athletic career to pursue the quest for the perfect state, and Aristotle included a revision of the list of Olympic victors among his works and conducted the research that established the list of Pythian victors. But we find no records of famous fourth-century athletes such as existed a century earlier, and no art is tied to these individuals.

The emergence of Philip II of Macedon and the spread of his power and influence changed the situation. The Battle of Chaironeia in 338 established Macedonian dominance in Greece, setting the foundation from which Philip's son Alexander began his own conquests, which are as remarkable for their speed (336–323) as for their endurance, at least in a cultural sense. At Alexander's death the Greeks' known world was under Greek control as far as the Indus; part or all of the modern states of Greece, the Former Yugoslav Republic of Macedonia, Bulgaria, Turkey, Cyprus, Syria, Lebanon, Jordan, Israel, Egypt, Iraq, Iran, Afghanistan, Uzbekistan, Tajikistan, Pakistan, and India were under a single central political authority.

But the Greeks could not hold this world together, and after Alexander's death it was divided into a number of kingdoms. These were all, to some degree, Greek; the old Hellenic world had spread to become a larger, Hellenistic world, where the Greek language and, at least superficially, Greek customs were current. The great libraries in Alexandria and Pergamon provided the basis for the study of early Greece and the fitting of indigenous cultures into a Hellenic framework. For example, a Greek version of the Hebrew Bible, begun in Macedonian Alexandria in about 270, made Hebrew texts available to Greek scholars.

Alexander had taken athletics along with him, and as his empire grew, competitions also proliferated. These required an ever greater supply of athletes, and athletics became a full-time job. It is not a coincidence that the first athletic trade unions appeared at this time.

During the next two centuries Hellenistic successors of Alexander struggled among themselves while Rome rose in the west. The inexorable expansion of the Romans brought defeat and destruction to the Greek world including most notably the utter destruction of Corinth in 146 and only slightly less destructive sack of Athens in 86. With Greece depopulated and denuded of its wealth, athletics fell on hard times in the old Greek world: in 80 only competitions for boys were held at Olympia. It took an endowment from Herod the Great in 12 B.C. to start the Olympic Games toward recovery. With Augustus firmly in control of the Roman Empire (as of 31 B.C.), the Greek world, now part of that empire, began to recover economically, becoming a school, museum, and tourist attraction.

From the time of Augustus to about A.D. 180 the eastern Hellenic section of the empire enjoyed peace and prosperity. Athletics flourished along Hellenistic lines, becoming a vast entertainment industry that finally was established in Rome itself in A.D. 86. As Rome's expansion slowed and attention turned to the administration of the empire, we hear more about pensions and parades, of the organization of athletic guilds, and about the benefits granted them by various emperors. Athletes were as cosmopolitan as any members of their society while nonathletes turned to private exercise and public baths. Specialization was complete.

The advent of Christianity, which had been growing into a major force and was officially tolerated by Constantine in 313, foreshadowed the end of athletic competitions. This was not because of any specifically anti-athletic bias by the Christians but because athletics had always been tied to religion; every game was sacred to some god or goddess in the old Greek pantheon. As the popularity of the gods diminished in the face of the new religious force, so did that of the games. There is no evidence that the Olympic Games were ever officially ended. But when Emperor Theodosios II formally forbade the use of the old pagan religious buildings in 435, games that were tied to buildings like the Temple of Zeus certainly also ended. Greek religion and Greek athletics, already relics, ceased completely to play any meaningful role in society.

Fig. 2 Greece and the Aegean Sea, ca. 300 B.C.

Many factors influenced the long history of ancient Greek athletics, but initially geography was the most important of these (fig. 2). The southern end of the Balkan peninsula is very mountainous, containing only a few well-defined valleys suitable for large-scale cultivation and horse-breeding. In the north, one such valley lay in Macedonia to the north of Mount Olympos and another—the largest of all—in Thessaly on the south side of the Olympos range. Boiotia, the eastern part of Attika, Argos, Sparta, and Elis are smaller productive areas. It is not coincidental that the majority of victories in the equestrian events came from these regions.

The ruggedness of the mountains of the mainland is paralleled by that of the coastline and the islands. These features served to isolate pockets of habitation and were a major reason for the rise of the city-states, political entities based on a well-defined territory and citizen body. The sense of identity (and rivalry) that derived from geography was fundamental to the development of ancient Greek culture, including athletics. The Greeks in Asia Minor, Sicily, and southern Italy lived in regions that were kinder and gentler than the homeland; they also were surrounded by non-Greeks. Furthermore, they were isolated from the centers of Hellenism — especially Olympia and Delphi — and the role they played in the evolution of early Greek athletics, though important, was secondary.

The actual distances between city-states and sanctuaries are not great, and the geographical features that increased those distances were overcome or ameliorated as time passed, but the effect of mountains and sea should never be underestimated in our understanding of Greece and its athletic tradition.

Turning now to the evidence about ancient Greek athletics we see that it can generally be categorized into two types: written and visual. The writings take several manifestations, beginning with the texts of ancient authors that have been passed down to us in the form, usually, of later manuscripts. The copying and recopying of those manuscripts over centuries and even millennia introduces an element of uncertainty: is the text of Herodotus or Euripides we read the one the author composed? Further, the authors themselves may not be interested in athletics as such but rather use stories about athletes to make political or moral points. Can we trust them even if their words have been preserved accurately? Such concerns notwithstanding, these writings form the largest single group of evidence.

One author is of special importance. Pausanias was a Greek of the Roman period who visited the most important historical sites of classical antiquity hundreds of years after their prime. His writing can be dated to about A.D. 175, although his research began much earlier. And two of his ten books concern Olympia, a much greater proportion than he devotes to any other site. (He apparently considered one book more than sufficient to describe Athens.) This is the most compelling evidence we have for the importance of Olympia and its games in the ancient world. Pausanias describes the buildings and monuments of Olympia, offering an architectural outline of the site as a whole. Most important, he saw the statues of hundreds of athletes and read the inscriptions on their bases. His works provide details of names, dates, accomplishments, events, and procedures. I draw upon his accounts extensively in the pages that follow.

Another kind of written evidence has been preserved only rarely and that through serendipity, but it offers firsthand, contemporary ancient testimony. This is papyrus, almost always found in Egypt. A fragment of a wrestling manual or a list of the victors at Olympia or correspondence from a trainer-agent who promises good returns on an investment in a young athlete offers direct, if limited insight into athletic practices and their place in society.

Inscriptions, a third kind of writing, speak directly to us without an intermediary to color their testimony. These can detail laws about the functioning of a gymnasion,

Fig. 3 Runners in the stadion race. Panathenaic amphora by the Eupalets Painter, ca. 520 B.C. New York, The Metropolitan Museum of Art, Rogers Fund, 1914, inv. no. 14.130.12 (photo: © 1998 The Metropolitan Museum of Art).

decrees establishing prizes in games, rules of competition, or simple dedicatory texts from the statue bases and equipment of victorious athletes (see figs. 115, 187, 244). The nature of the medium—hard, expensive to carve stone or occasionally bronze—ensures that the evidence will be presented in a terse, sometimes elliptical, fashion.

Visual evidence also comes to us in many different forms. These include the actual gear—oil jars, *diskoi*, jumping weights—used by ancient athletes in practice or competition (see figs. 13, 105, 116). Akin to these artifacts are the starting lines and turning posts in ancient stadiums (see figs. 36, 66) and the entrance tunnels and undressing rooms used by the athletes (see figs. 175, 197). Other architectural remains, both secular and religious, help us to visualize the setting where the games took place (for example, figs. 184, 193).

More immediate are the all too rarely preserved statues that bring us face to face with the athletes of ancient Greece (see figs. 183, 243). So, too, marble reliefs provide us with details of athletic practices (see figs. 255, 259). The largest single category of visual evidence, however, is the vase painting. These vases are restricted almost exclusively to the sixth and fifth centuries B.C. and therefore must be studied in conjunction with written evidence from other eras. Caution is obviously needed when we examine these two types of chronologically distinct evidence together. It is also difficult, sometimes, to determine whether we are looking at depictions of athletic competitions or practice sessions in the gymnasion. This evidence comes almost exclusively from Attic painters, forcing us to take as a working hypothesis that Athenian athletic customs resembled those of other city-states.

Among the vase paintings, the largest and most important evidence comes from Panathenaic amphoras (figs. 3, 9). These huge vessels, sometimes holding as much as 39 liters of olive oil, were offered as prizes at the Panathenaic Games (see Chapter 7). One side always depicted the goddess Athena, striding forward with shield and spear in defense of her favorite city, frequently with the painted notation "the prize at Athens" (see fig. 217). Sometimes the name of the Athenian official (the *archon,* elected annually) is given, allowing us to date the amphora precisely. On the other side of the amphora is a depiction of the competitive event for which the prize was offered (fig. 3). In some cases, we can be certain that the events were the same as those at Olympia and the other Panhellenic sites. But in other cases, the events clearly were contested only at the games at Athens, not at the four Panhellenic Games. Given that proviso, the Panathenaic amphora is the single most important type of visual evidence for ancient Greek athletics. It was a prize much sought after in antiquity, and there are many examples of Panathenaic amphoras that were carefully repaired, even though they would no longer be able to hold liquids (see figs. 84, 152). Though we do not always know whether the person who was buried with a certain amphora won it in a competition or purchased it, these detailed paintings give us the closest possible link to ancient athletics in those prephotographic days.

2

THE WORLD OF GREEK ATHLETICS

THE WORLD OF GREEK ATHLETICS had a number of features that will seem strange to us but which are essential to an understanding of the subject. Fundamental to the whole study is the word *athlon,* from which the name of our subject derives. *Athlon* is a noun that means, initially at least, "prize" or "reward." This prize can take any form: money, victory crowns, shields, amphoras filled with olive oil. Its value may be real or symbolic, but the athlon is omnipresent in competitions. Its verbal form, *athleuein,* means "to compete for a prize," and the competitor was called an *athletes,* "one who competes for a prize." This basic etymology should alert us to an equally basic aspect of the subject: athletics was not simply about competition; it concerned winning a prize. Sport for sport's sake was not an ancient concept.

A second fundamental aspect of ancient athletics resides in the word *gymnos,* "naked," and its verbal form *gymnazein,* "to perform in the nude." This is the most obvious and striking difference between today's athletes and the ancient Greeks, and we find it not only in the name but in the countless representations of Greek athletics (see fig. 3). It is a custom that invariably makes modern students (particularly males) uncomfortable, but, modesty aside, we now know that the cremaster muscle forces the genitals to contract during exercise so that the danger of injury is less than might first appear.

We do not know the origins of competition in the nude. Pausanias (1.44.1; A 3) attributes the "invention" of nude athletics to Orsippos of Megara, who won the *stadion* (a footrace) at Olympia in 720 B.C. when his *perizoma* (plural, *perizomata;* loincloth) fell off during the race. Another writer, Dionysios of Halikarnassos (7.72.2–3; A 4) also dates the custom to 720 B.C. but attributes it to a Spartan, Akanthos. Thucydides (1.6.5–6; A 5), writing around 420 B.C., likewise ascribes a Spartan origin to nude competition but states that it is "not many years since" the custom began. We do not know what Thucydides intended by that indication of date, but three hundred years do not

Fig. 4 Runners wearing peri- zomata (loincloths), with a single kampter (turning post) and a judge seated beneath the handle. Black-figure amphora by the Michigan Painter, side A, 530–520 B.C. Martin von Wagner Museum, Universität Würzburg, inv. no. L 328 (photo: K. Oehrlein).

Fig. 5 Nude boxers flanked by a jumper and a boxer waiting his turn, both wearing perizomata. Does this represent an accidental omission by the loincloth painter? Black- figure kyathos in the Group of Vatican G.58, side A, ca. 530 B.C. Paris, Bibliothèque nationale de France, inv. no. 354.

seem to be "not many." In other words, the ancients themselves were uncertain about the beginning of athletic nudity.

Augmenting our uncertainty is a series of black-figure vases of the sixth century B.C. that show athletes with perizomata (also called *diazomata*) painted in white over their waists and genitals (the ancient equivalent of the fig leaf; see figs. 4, 5, 102). All these vases were discovered in Etruria, however, and it seems clear that they were made for an Etruscan market that admired Greek art but not nudity in athletics. In most cases the incised details of the genitals can be seen where the white paint was either carelessly applied and so failed to cover them or has since worn off. In one case (fig. 4) the perizoma was painted down the outside of the thigh; the painter seems not to have realized that this runner had his right foot and leg forward, hiding the genitals, so the perizoma's lower flap, which ought to be between the legs, should not have been visible either. Yet these exceptions to the portrayal of athletic nudity actually prove the ubiquity of the custom among the Greeks.

Another custom related to nudity but less well documented and not completely understood is the practice of infibulation, tying up the foreskin of the penis. (The Greeks did not practice circumcision.) Infibulation is mentioned only in late lexico- graphic sources under definitions of *kynodesmai* (dog leashes). An example from Phrynichos (85; A 13) is typical: kynodesmai are "the things with which the Athenians tied up their private parts when they stripped, because they called the penis a dog." The practice is shown, albeit rarely, in depictions of athletics on vase paintings. In one

Fig. 7 Scene from a gymnasion: the athlete on the left is tying the foreskin of his penis while a boy watches. The athlete on the right disrobes in front of another boy, and the athlete at center prepares to throw a diskos while a trainer or judge gestures, apparently at his penis. Red-figure krater by Euphronios, ca. 510 B.C. Berlin Staatliche Museen — Preussischer Kulturbesitz, Antikensammlung, inv. no. F 2180 (photo: Johannes Laurentius).

Fig. 6 Athlete tying foreskin of his penis. His aryballos and stlengis hang on the wall above a stool. Red-figure tondo by Onesimos, ca. 490 B.C. St. Petersburg, The State Hermitage Museum, inv. no. B-1534.

a young man is tying himself while his athletic gear (oil jar and scraper) hang on the wall in front of him (fig. 6). In another one young man ties his penis while another practices the diskos and a third disrobes (fig. 7). In a vase painting of a boxing match the penis of one athlete seems to be tied up (fig. 8), while that of his opponent is not. The use of kynodesmai, then, must have been a personal choice, but the reason for deciding whether to use them is not clear. Did some athletes feel that the practice helped their performance? Did it have a sexual dimension?

The word *gymnos* gave rise to cognates we shall encounter throughout our study. A *gymnastes* could be anyone who did something in the nude, but it came to have the specialized meaning of a trainer of nude activities — an athletics coach. The *gymnasion* was literally a place for nudity, but specifically a place for nude athletes, and finally a place for training the (nude) body and the mind. Even more fundamental is the adjective *gymnikos*, especially when applied to the word *agon*. The original meaning of *agon* was a meeting or assembly, and it came to refer to an assembly to watch games. So pervasive were the competitions that *agon* soon referred to them, and then to the act of competing in the games. The cognate *agonia*, the source of our "agony," referred more exclusively to the struggle for victory that involved *ponos* (pain), regardless of whether a victory resulted.

In a technical sense, *gymnikos agon* referred to the nude competitions: what today we would call athletics. However, since by definition ancient Greek athletics were any competition for a prize, *agon* was modified by other terms as well: *hippikos agon* referred

Fig. 8 Boxers. The penis of the man on the left appears to be tied up, but not that of the man on the right. Red-figure tondo in the manner of Euergides, 510–500 B.C. Bologna, Museo Civico Archeologico, inv. no. 28655.

Fig. 9 Paides racing. The victor talks to judge on the right. Panathenaic amphora by the Achilles Painter, ca. 440 B.C. Bologna, Museo Civico Archeologico, inv. no. 18039.

to equestrian events and *mousikos agon* to musical events, both of which were standard components of the competitive program in many places, though not Olympia.

In addition to being nude, competitors in the ancient gymnikos agon were divided into age categories. At Olympia there were two groupings: *andres* (men) and *paides* (boys). At precisely what age the division occurred is not clear, but the best evidence puts it at about seventeen. The exact age was not as important as the stage of development: a younger but more physically developed athlete might be assigned to the *andres* category. At other sites, there was an intermediate group called *ageneioi* (beardless youths). From vase paintings, we can deduce that these were probably in their late teens, while the paides at such sites were in their early teens. Representations of small youths (fig. 9), clearly not men, should be compared to those of larger, better-developed youths (fig. 10) who are without beards. The latter are the ageneioi. These, in turn, differ from images of youngish men who are bearded (fig. 11), presumably the vase painter's way of signaling the presence of andres. Although physical size and development might be considerations in assigning athletes to a group, there were no weight divisions. In boxing, for example, speed might be set against strength when one competitor was significantly smaller than his opponent.

Given the nudity of ancient athletes, a discussion of their equipment might seem to be brief. But even without a uniform, the ancient Greek athlete, like his modern counterpart, did have a personal kit. The main component was a jar of olive oil, which he rubbed on his body before exercise and competition (fig. 12). The standard oil jar was the *aryballos* (plural, *aryballoi*), a rounded, baseless vessel with a small mouth that could easily be corked. Aryballoi vary in size, but the most common are about the size of a baseball (fig. 13). A cord by which the athlete carried the aryballos or hung

Fig. 10 Wrestling competition for ageneioi. Note that the judge, though young, is starting a beard and therefore not ageneios—beardless. Panathenaic amphora, 420–410 B.C. Athens, National Museum, inv. no. 451 (photo: © Treasury of Archaeological Receipts).

Fig. 11 The stadion race for andres. Panathenaic amphora by the Achilles Painter, ca. 440 B.C. Bologna, Museo Civico Archeologico, inv. no. 18040.

it on a peg was threaded through the handles. Aryballoi are sometimes decorated, especially in the sixth century B.C., but the designs are usually simple repetitive patterns. A variant shape, the *alabastron,* is an elongated aryballos, and the larger surface was sometimes decorated elegantly, often with figures (fig. 14).

Why athletes oiled their bodies has been much discussed, and modern scholars offer many explanations. Some suggest that rubbing the oil in helped to warm up and limber the muscles before exercise, others that the oil protected the skin from the sun and the elements. Another theory is that the oil produced a glistening body which was aesthetically pleasing and desirable, or that the coating of oil prevented the loss of body fluids during exercise. Ancient sources support some of these interpretations. Lucian (*Anacharsis* 24; A 7) suggests that the tone of the skin was improved by the oil in the same way that leather is made more durable, while Pliny (*NH* 15.4.19; A 8) states that oil protected the body against cold. There may also have been a religious connotation: the athlete dedicated himself by the use of oil. There are many examples of oil being used to anoint both iconic and aniconic images of Greek divinities, and the Greek epithet for Jesus, *Christos,* means "the anointed one." These theories are not mutually exclusive, and we may suspect that the custom was so venerable and ubiquitous among the Greeks that they themselves were uncertain of its full range of significance. The Romans had no such doubts—they considered rubbing oil on the body an extension of the same Greek perversion seen in nude athletes.

After exercise, the athlete scraped his body with a strigil (*stlengis*), a curved tool, concave in section, usually made of bronze although iron was sometimes used (fig. 15). Some sources mention reeds that were split to provide the requisite scraping shape. Greek vase painting is full of depictions of the *apoxyomenos,* the scraping off of

Fig. 12 Athlete prepares to anoint himself with oil from his aryballos. Red-figure tondo by the Ambrosios Painter, ca. 510 B.C. Malibu, Calif., The J. Paul Getty Museum, inv. no. 86.AE.298.

Fig. 13 Black-glaze aryballos, 500–480 B.C. Athens, National Museum, inv. no. 12665 (photo: © Treasury of Archaeological Receipts).

Fig. 14 Alabastron showing an athlete fixing a ribbon on his head. An image of Nike appears on the opposite side of the vase. White-ground alabastron, ca. 480 B.C. Berlin, Staatliche Museen — Preussischer Kulturbesitz, Antikensammlung, inv. no. F 2258 (photo: Ingrid Geske).

the body (fig. 16), and one of the more famous statues by Lysippos, court sculptor of Alexander the Great, shows an athlete in this pose (fig. 17). There are also depictions of athletes running a finger or thumb along the inside of the stlengis (fig. 18), presumably to rid it of the combination of oil, sweat, and dust that accumulated on their bodies during exercise or competitions. This mixture was called *gloios* and it was collected in the gymnasion and sold for its (presumed) medicinal value.

In addition to the aryballos and the stlengis, athletes also carried a sponge (*spongos*), which was used to wash up after the scraping was completed. These are depicted frequently as a part of athletic equipment (fig. 19), although the sponge is less often seen in actual use (fig. 20).

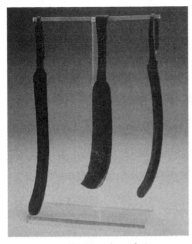

Fig. 15 Bronze strigils (stlengides). Olympia, Archaeological Museum, inv. nos. M 348, M 349, M 281 (photo: © Treasury of Archaeological Receipts).

Fig. 16 Athletes (identifiable by the diskos and the kampter behind the figure at left) scrape themselves off with stlengides. The inscription reads "kalos" (beautiful). Red-figure bell krater by the Kleophon Painter, 430–420 B.C. Oxford, Ashmolean Museum, inv. no. 1922.8.

One other piece of athletic equipment is sometimes portrayed. This is a kind of cap; it does not cover the ears but seems to be used to hold the hair down (fig. 20; see also figs. 122, 141). It is not shown being worn in competitions, only in practice, and should perhaps be understood as a kind of hairnet. It typically appears in scenes featuring pentathletes (when the athletic event can be identified) and may be a way to keep the athlete's hair from becoming entangled with the throwing strap of the javelin.

Lastly, ancient sources describe dust or powder (konis), which athletes used after they were through exercising and cleaning up; gymnasia even had a special room called the konisterion. Philostratos (On Gymnastics 56; A 19) speaks of dust made from clay, from terra-cotta, or from asphalt, but recommends yellow powder as the most attractive. As described, it appears that the powder was thrown up in a cloud to settle evenly on the athlete's body. There are not, so far as I know, any visual representations of this practice nor of konis as part of the athlete's gear, and all references to it are from Roman times. It may have been a later practice.

Another characteristic of ancient Greek athletics that strikes modern readers as alien is the punishment for fouls: flogging. The evidence for the practice is unequivocal. Vase paintings show judges equipped with switches (rhabdoi) throughout the sixth and fifth centuries (see, for example, figs. 5, 43, 81, 88). Usually the switches are simply iconographic props, but sometimes they are shown in use on athletes committing a foul, such as the fighter gouging his opponent's eye in figure 98. References in ancient texts to the custom of flogging are equally numerous. Perhaps the most famous is that of Herodotus (8.59; A 102), describing a scene in 480 B.C. on the eve of the Battle of Salamis. During the debate among the Greek allies about whether and where they

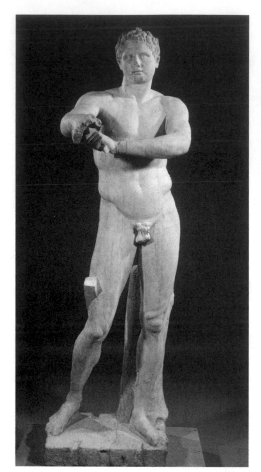

Fig. 18 Athletes after practice; at right, an older youth scrapes his left arm with a stlengis; at center, a younger boy with an aryballos hanging from his left hand looks toward youth at right; at left, an older youth runs his thumb down the inner groove of a stlengis to clean out the gloios. The dipinto above reads, "Euaion the son of Aischylos is kalos." Red-figure oinochoe by the Achilles Painter, 450–440 B.C. Antikenmuseum Basel und Sammlung Ludwig, inv. no. BS 485 (photo: Claire Niggli).

Fig. 17 Athlete engaged in scraping off his body (apoxyomenos). Marble Roman copy of an original statue by Lysippos, ca. 320 B.C. Vatican, Vestibolo Cortile Ottagono, inv. no. 1185 (photo: P. Zigrossi).

would take a stand against the invading Persian forces, Themistokles, in his eagerness to advocate the defense of Salamis, spoke out of turn. Adeimantos, a Corinthian, chided him: "At the games, Themistokles, those who start too soon are flogged with switches." These rhabdoi were typically switches cut from the lygos bush, a kind of willow, which, we can imagine, produced painful welts. Tellingly, it was not permitted to flog an athlete's head.

The willingness of a free man to subject himself to the punishment of a public flogging should be understood not only as a basic part of ancient Greek athletics but also as a fundamental characteristic of ancient Greek society. The notion of equality before the law inherent in this custom may be the most significant contribution of athletics to the ancient world, one to which I shall return in Chapter 15.

A few further points should be mentioned here. They all have to do exclusively

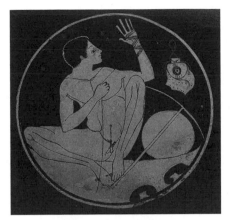 

Fig. 19 An athlete is shown binding his hands for boxing, surrounded by his equipment. Jumping weights (below), diskos, and pick (right) lie beside him, while on the wall an aryballos hangs in front of a sponge. The inscription reads, "Epidromos is kalos." Red-figure tondo by the Epidromos Painter, 520–500 B.C. Hanover, N.H., Hood Museum of Art, Dartmouth College, inv. no. C.970.35; gift of Mr. and Mrs. Ray Winfield Smith.

Fig. 20 An athlete leaning on a basin while squeezing out his sponge. On the wall at left hang an aryballos and a stlengis. Detail from a red-figure mask-kantharos by the Foundry Painter, ca. 480 B.C. Malibu, Calif., The J. Paul Getty Museum, inv. no. 85.AE.263.

with the four *stephanitic* (crown) games, at Olympia, Delphi, Isthmia, and Nemea, and do not apply to the numerous local games held at and by individual city-states. But they are critical to our understanding of ancient Greek athletics because they demonstrate the gulf between ancient and modern ideas about athletics.

First, there were no team competitions. Every event pitted man against man, one on one. In addition, there was no prize for second place. One man won, and everyone else lost. We hear of no one taking solace in being a runner-up. The ideal of *arete*, "excellence," had no room for "nearly." Finally, there was no subjective judging in the gymnikos agon and the hippikos agon (I shall examine the judging in the mousikos agon in Chapter 4). No panel of judges awarded "style points" that could help decide a winner. The winner was chosen by obvious, objective standards: who crossed the finish line first, who hurled his javelin the farthest, who threw his wrestling opponent to the ground. The concern to remove all subjectivity from the competition extended to the adjudication of fouls or the arrangement of pairings that might influence the final determination of the victor. As we shall see, these strict standards resulted in a limited program of competitive events at the games. They also greatly reduced controversy and accusations of favoritism. This adherence to objective criteria in establishing a winner is the fundamental reason why the ancient Olympics thrived, and why the Olympic idea (whatever its reality) still lives today.

3

THE ORIGINS OF GREEK
ATHLETICS

THE DATE ESTABLISHED by ancient scholars for the beginning of the Olympic Games was (in our system) 776 B.C. They arrived at this year by fixing a sequential list of victors at Olympia, after which they counted backward in quadrennial units. The strict historical validity of the 776 date has been the subject of intense debate in modern times; our concern here is more with its general accuracy for the emergence of Greek athletics as a whole. When did the customs described in the previous chapter evolve? Where were they generated?

Scholars have sought the origins of Greek athletics in the older cultures of Mesopotamia and especially Egypt because of the influential contacts between Egypt and Greece that were already present in the Bronze Age. It is clear that the initial inspiration for large-scale sculpture and monumental architecture came to Greece from Egypt in the period around 600, but we look in vain for indisputable evidence of such borrowings in the area of athletics. The art of Mesopotamia and of Egypt certainly shows evidence of sporting activities, but the sense that these are competitions among equals is missing, nor do the events parallel many of the competitions in the Greek program. Most obvious, the men in these depictions of what may be sporting events are clothed. Consequently, Greek athletics have been understood as a peculiarly and uniquely Greek institution.

We may next look for the origins of Greek athletics in Bronze Age Greece. The brilliant Minoan and Mycenaean civilizations of the second millennium B.C. are clearly the ancestors of Greek culture of the following millennium, and the Mycenaeans wrote and spoke an early form of the Greek language. Further, the myths of classical Greece are set in the labyrinths of Minoan Crete and the familial bloodbaths of Mycenae. The Greeks themselves looked back to those civilizations as the source of their own. Were athletics part of those roots? Their presence in the Homeric poems suggest that they were.

Fig. 21 Bull-leaping. Gold signet ring, 1550–1500 B.C. Oxford, Ashmolean Museum, inv. no. AE 2237.

Fig. 22 A bull-leaper clinging to the bull's horn. Terra-cotta figurine, Middle Minoan I (2000–1800 B.C.), Herakleion, Archaeological Museum, inv. no. 5052.

This is not the place to discuss the Homeric Question, starting with whether Homer even existed and including the issue of how he (or she or they) learned about the centuries-earlier events described in the poems. More important is the fact that the prominent place of the funeral games of Patroklos in book 23 of the *Iliad* (A 1) suggests that Homer and his audience could believe that their athletic practices came down to them from the Mycenaean world. So, too, the informal competitions of the Phaeacians portrayed in the *Odyssey* (8.97–253; A 2) reveal a well-developed athletic program. Taken together, the Homeric poems share with the later Olympics competitions in footracing, wrestling, boxing, chariot racing, and the pentathlon events of the javelin, *diskos,* and long jump. There are, to be sure, non-Olympic events as well. The *Iliad,* as befits its military setting, has competitions in archery and an armed duel (*hoplomachia*), while the Phaeacians compete in dancing and singing. The centerpiece of Odysseus's return to Ithaka is an archery competition. Despite these differences, the similarities of the Olympic and Homeric programs are striking.

Archaeology, however, tells a very different story. Minoan culture was clearly much concerned with bull-fighting (also called bull-leaping). This event was portrayed in many different media: wall paintings, carvings on gold rings (fig. 21), terra-cotta figurines (fig. 22). The popularity of the sport is evident, but it is equally evident that it was performed by trained, clothed specialists (at least when it was done correctly; compare figures 21 and 22). It has no relevance to the athletics of classical Greece. In the same vein as bull-leaping, with an equal lack of relevance to our subject, are the depictions of acrobats and tumblers on many Minoan artifacts (fig. 23).

The major event in the funeral games of Patroklos is the chariot race. More space in the poem is devoted to this race than to all the other competitions combined. Bronze Age archaeology certainly confirms the existence of chariots, but they are shown in the context of hunting or warfare (fig. 24). The only depiction that might

Fig. 23 Acrobats performing synchronized handstands. Chalcydony seal stone, 1550–1500 B.C. Oxford, Ashmolean Museum, inv. no. 1938.955.

Fig. 24 Warrior bearing shield and spear riding in a chariot. Haematite seal stone, Late Helladic IIA (1500–1450 B.C.). Athens, National Museum, inv. no. 1770 (photo: © Treasury of Archaeological Receipts).

possibly show chariot racing appears on a fragment of a late Bronze Age amphora (fig. 25). As restored, the scene appears to show a race, but other restorations are possible. It is not incontrovertible evidence for chariot racing in the Mycenaean world.

The Bronze Age archaeology of Greece has produced no depictions of footraces, diskos or javelin throwing, jumping, or wrestling. Possible evidence seems to exist for boxing. This consists of a restored fresco from Thera and of the so-called Boxers' Rhyton from Haghia Triada in Minoan Crete (figs. 26, 27). The rhyton is also heavily restored, but it seems clear that the second of four horizontal bands of decoration portrays bull-leaping, as we would expect to see on an object from Minoan Crete. The third band shows helmeted figures striding forward with their left arms extended in a protective position while their right arms are drawn back to stab an opponent; the ground is strewn with fallen bodies. The bottom band shows striding figures preparing to thrust knives into the bodies of their fallen enemies. None of these have anything to do with the athletics of ancient Greece. The uppermost band, however, portrays men in attitudes that suggest boxing, and even though the evidence is not strong, we might conclude that boxing was known in the Minoan world.

Boxing notwithstanding, there are significant differences between the picture of athletics produced by archaeology and the competitions described in the *Iliad* and *Odyssey*. These can be summarized in tabular form. The Olympic events are listed with the date when each became a part of the program.

Fig. 25 Chariot race? Restored drawing from an amphora from Tiryns, Late Helladic IIIC (1200–1100 B.C.). After S. Laser, *Sport und Spiel: Archaeologia Homerica*, vol. 3:T (Göttingen, 1987), fig 2.

Event	Present in historical era [date at Olympia]	Present in *Iliad*	Present in *Odyssey*	Evidence from Bronze Age archaeology
footrace	x [776]	x	x	o
wrestling	x [708]	x	x	o
pentathlon	x [708]			
javelin	x	x	x	o
diskos	x	x	x	o
jump	x	o	x	o
boxing	x [688]	x	x	x
chariot	x [680]	x	o	?
archery	o	x	x	x
hoplomachia	o	x	o	x
dancing	o	o	x	o
singing	o	o	x	x
bull-leaping	o	o	o	x
acrobatics	o	o	o	x

Fig. 26 Possible depiction of boxing
(top band) on a steatite-carved rhyton
from Haghia Triada, Late Minoan
IA (ca. 1500 B.C.). Herakleion, Archaeological Museum; inv. no. 409.

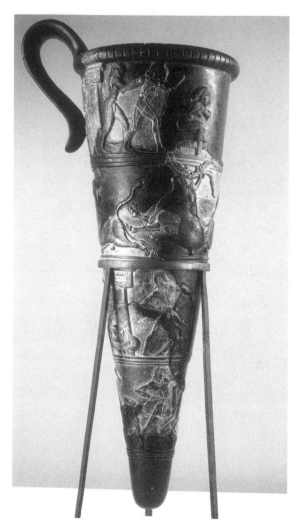

It is clear that athletics in the Homeric poems coincide much more closely with
the program at Olympia than with the events that can be documented archaeologi-
cally in the Bronze Age. Thus, even though the stories of the Trojan War have their basis in the realities of the Bronze Age, Homer's picture of athletics is not accurate for
that period. Indeed, when Achilles sets out prizes to honor his dead friend Patroklos,
he includes for the diskos and archery competitions pig-iron, which will give the winner "a supply of iron for five years, and neither his shepherd nor his plowman will have
to go to the city for iron, but will have it already at home." In other words, we are
alerted to the anachronistic use of iron for tools in a supposed Bronze Age context—
another clue that the athletics of Homer are not those of the Mycenaeans.

In addition, the prizes for the chariot race include a "tripod with ears" and for
the wrestling a "huge tripod to be set over the fire." Tripod cauldrons are well known

Fig. 27 Drawing of the restored Haghia Triada rhyton. Drawing by Ruben Santos.

in vase paintings of the sixth century (see, for example, figs. 32, 162, 164) and are documented in the seventh on a seal matrix (fig. 28) and by the dozens of actual cauldrons found at Olympia. These bronze tripod cauldrons date to the eighth and seventh centuries, the time the Homeric poems were composed, not from the Bronze Age period five hundred or more years earlier that the poems purport to describe. They continue into the sixth century as is documented by, among other evidence, the story of Hippokrates, the father of the Athenian tyrant Peisistratos (see Herodotus 1.59). While at Olympia, Hippokrates had filled some tripod cauldrons with meat and water, which miraculously began to boil before a fire was set under them — an omen for him, an elucidation for us.

We must conclude that the picture of athletes in the *Iliad* and the *Odyssey* reflects the age of Homer himself, not the period of the Trojan War. To be sure, Homer's ath-

THE ORIGINS OF GREEK ATHLETICS

Fig. 28 A tripod cauldron set as the prize for boxing. Seal matrix, 7th century B.C. Oxford, Ashmolean Museum, inv. no. 1895.130.

letes do not compete in the nude, and they are awarded prizes for second and even last place, so the picture does not describe the Classical period. Nonetheless, we can safely see in Homer a depiction of athletics of the eighth and seventh centuries, a period of transition from the depopulated Dark Ages to the creative and productive sixth and fifth centuries.

What happened between the Golden Age of Mycenae and the Homeric period that resulted in the athletic image of the *Iliad*, and the ultimate development of Greek athletics? This is the clue to the origin of Greek athletics, and it lies in the Dorian invasion that followed the fall of Mycenae. We know very little about the Return of the Sons of Herakles, as the ancients called this event, and scholars have expended much energy and ingenuity trying to understand it. At the least, we can say that one result of the Dorian invasion was that the Mycenaean Greeks migrated to Ionia on the west coast of Asia Minor, while the whole of the Peloponnesos was converted into a Dorian peninsula. These Dorians in general, and the Spartans and Arkadians in particular, were reckoned to be exceptionally vigorous and warlike, with a highly developed sense of competition. It is surely no coincidence that three of the four Panhellenic centers—Olympia, Nemea, and Isthmia—are in the Peloponnesos, and the fourth, Delphi, is in another Dorian area (see fig. 2). Athletics did not grow up among the Ionians, who were originally Mycenaeans, and were never as popular in the Greek east as in the west.

Greek athletics, therefore, were born under strong Doric influence during the Geometric period. This was the time when the unbroken chain of depictions of athletics begins (fig. 29). It was also the time when a population explosion on the Greek mainland resulted in the colonization of other parts of the Mediterranean, especially

Fig. 29 Wrestling. Amphora, Late Geometric (ca. 750 B.C.). Argos, Archaeological Museum, inv. no. G 209 (photo: author).

in Sicily and Magna Graecia. Most of those western colonies were Doric, and they were heavily represented at the Olympic Games.

At the same time athletics and colonization were developing, so was the polis. The city-state was to become the fundamental political unit of the Classical Greek world, and was essential to the development of the Panhellenic athletic festivals.

The Homeric poems give us an image, incomplete and not in full focus, of those earliest athletic competitions. We see that they are local and informal. They are not part of a recurring festival, but take place occasionally and in response to a particular stimulus. The stimulus can be a funeral, like the games of Patroklos. Funeral games represent a reaffirmation of life in the face of death, a revival that provides the underlying religious basis for all such games. But the stimulus can simply be a more general expression of life, the desire of youth to exercise its vigor that we see in the informal "pickup" games of the Phaeacians in the *Odyssey*. In both cases, athletics represent a relaxation, a rest from the daily routine of work or war; they are not a training for battle in any sense. Just as with the voluntary subjection to flogging and its implicit acceptance of equality before the law, this quality of ancient Greek athletics shows, and perpetuates, something of the national character.

If the Homeric poems describe at least part of the nature of competitions in the Geometric and Orientalizing periods, they also indicate that athletics had not yet evolved into the form we shall see in later times. I noted that all the competitors received prizes. These prizes are significant, for they reveal the relative social status of the competitions. We have seen that more space in the *Iliad* is devoted to the chariot race than to all the other competitions put together, and it is not surprising that the collective value of the prizes for the chariot race is greater than that for the other competitions. These facts stem from a fundamental aspect of chariot racing: it cost more than the other competitions and so was open only to the wealthy. As we shall see, it always retained a flavor of aristocracy, which was never very strong in the *gymnikos agon* and which quickly disappeared almost entirely. Indeed, it is telling that Odysseus, who is clearly one of the poorer Greek kings at Troy and must rely more upon his wits than his wealth, does not participate in the chariot race but does compete in (and win) the footrace and the wrestling. Men from any social or economic background could compete in those events.

The prizes, the *athla,* in the games of Patroklos can also be understood as less important in and of themselves and more a means by which Achilles honors and glorifies the memory of his fallen comrade. The prizes serve as reminders of Patroklos and will give him a kind of immortality. At the same time, the prizes are not a means of livelihood for the competitors, whose socioeconomic status does not depend upon winning games. Indeed, although the five prizes offered by Achilles for the chariot race reveal something of their perceived value in that society, they also have a symbolic value:

> 1st prize – "a woman faultless in her work and a tripod
> with ears holding twenty-two measures";
> 2d prize – "a six-year-old unbroken mare carrying an
> unborn mule foal";
> 3rd prize – "a beautiful unfired cauldron holding four
> measures, still new and shiny";
> 4th prize – "two gold talents";
> 5th prize – "a two-handled unfired bowl."

We would probably not rank these prizes the same way Homer did. The two talents of gold, for example, by the standards of the sixth century B.C. must have weighed about 52 kilograms. Whatever the value, real or relative, the prizes are most important as a reflection of the skill and *arete* (virtue or excellence) of the athlete. Note the actions of Antilochos, the second-prize winner in the chariot race. Achilles proposes that Eumelos, who came to grief when his chariot crashed, be awarded the second prize as a consolation. Antilochos responds, "Give him a prize, Achilles, whatever you want, even better than mine, but I'll fight the man who wants to take my mare away from me." Antilochos demands the prize not because of its economic value but because it is rightfully his and represents his skill as a charioteer. After he gets the mare, he turns around and gives her to Menelaos. The prize is his to dispose of as he wishes, but the glory symbolized by the prize remains with him.

Throughout the games described in the *Iliad,* the general impression emerges of a society that lived outdoors, possessed vigorously good physical condition, and delighted in displaying physical abilities as an expression of arete. There are no team events (also a fundamental characteristic of later Greek athletics): the emphasis is exclusively on the individual and his competitive capabilities. We should also note the informality of these games. They are not highly organized and make use of no special equipment or uniforms. A tree stump is used for a turning post and a road filled with ruts becomes a chariot course. The footrace course is covered with animal dung, and the diskos is an amorphous lump of iron. In the games of the Phaeacians, Odysseus throws a diskos that is larger than his competitors'. There is no standardization.

And a human quality pervades these competitions as well. These competitors could be competitors anywhere, at any time. We see it in the dangerous driving of Antilochos, who forces Menelaos off the road after "encouraging" his horses with the threat of turning them into dog meat. Likewise, the bickering of Ajax and Idomeneus over who was in the lead as the horses came out of the far turn can be heard in sports bars today:

Idomeneus stood up and called to the Argives, "Friends, am I the only one who sees the horses, or do you see them too? It seems to me that other horses are leading, another charioteer ahead. The mares of Eumelos must have come to grief on the plain, for I saw them running in front around the *terma* [turning post], but now they are nowhere to be seen, and I have looked over the whole Trojan plain. Perhaps the reins slipped away from the charioteer, and he could not hold them around the terma, and did not make the turn. I think that he must have been thrown out there and his chariot wrecked, and his mares bolted away wildly. But do get up and see for yourselves, for I cannot make it out clearly. I think that strong Diomedes is in the lead."

And swift Ajax, son of Oileus, spoke shamefully to him, "Idomeneus, can't you hold your wind? The horses are still far out on the plain. You are not the youngest of us, and your eyes are no better than ours, but you must always blow on and on. There is no need for your wind since there are others here better than you. Those are the same mares in front as before, and the same Eumelos who holds the reins behind them."

Then the lord of the Cretans angrily answered him to his face, "Ajax, although you are the best in abuse and stupidity, you are the worst of the Argives with that donkey's brain of yours. Now put your money where your mouth is and bet me a tripod cauldron. We'll have Agamemnon, son of Atreus, hold the bet so that you will pay up when you find out which horses are in front."

So he spoke, and swift Ajax jumped up again in anger to retort, and the quarrel would have gone on had Achilles not risen and said to them, "Ajax and Idomeneus, be quiet. This is not becoming, and if others were acting like you, you yourselves would be angry with them. Sit down with the others and watch for the horses. They are into the stretch and will be here soon, and then you can see for yourselves which are first and which are second."

Note that their bet was not on the outcome of the race but on the accuracy of their eyesight. This is another characteristic of ancient Greek athletics: gambling by spectators over who will win is nowhere attested in our sources. A man might gamble on his own skill or his own arete, but not on that of another. Each man has something to say about his own performance, but he will not trust another man and has no faith in another's arete.

Again, the human quality of athletics, its emphasis on the individual, appears in the footrace:

> Ajax was in front, but Odysseus was running so close behind that his feet were hitting Ajax's tracks before the dust could settle back into them, and his breath was hitting the back of Ajax's neck. All the Achaians were cheering his effort to win, shouting for him to pour it on. But when they were in the stretch, Odysseus said a silent prayer to the gray-eyed Athena, "Hear me, Goddess; be kind to me, and come with extra strength for my feet."
>
> So he prayed, and Pallas Athena heard him, and lightened his limbs, feet and arms too. As they were making their final spring for the prize, Ajax slipped and fell (Athena tripped him) where dung was scattered on the ground from bellowing oxen, and he got the stuff in his mouth and up his nose. So Odysseus took away the mixing bowl, because he finished first, and the ox went to Ajax. He stood with his hands on the horns of the ox, spitting out dung, and said to the Argives, "Oh, shit! That goddess tripped me, that goddess who has always stood by Odysseus and cared for him like a mother."
>
> They all roared in laughter at him, and then came Antilochos to take the prize for last place, and grinned as he spoke to the Argives, "Friends, you all know well the truth of what I say, that still the gods continue to favor the older men. Look here, Ajax is older than I, if only by a little, but Odysseus is out of another age and truly one of the ancients. But his old age is, as they say, a lusty one. I don't think any Achaian could match his speed, except Achilles."

The funeral games of Patroklos celebrate life in the face of death, but more than anything else they express a basic joy of living. As the individual athlete exerts himself physically, mentally, and emotionally in the competition, a statement is made: "I am alive!"

Perhaps this is the origin of Greek athletics.

4

THE CROWN COMPETITIONS:
THE EVENTS AT OLYMPIA, DELPHI,
NEMEA, AND ISTHMIA

ALTHOUGH GREEK ATHLETICS were emerging and beginning to take the shape they would have in the sixth and fifth centuries by 776 B.C., it was not until 586–573 that they took on sharper definition. These dates mark the establishment of the Pythian Games at Delphi and the Nemean Games, respectively, as participants in the Panhellenic athletic festival cycle. The Isthmian Games were established between these two, in 580, and the three festivals, along with the Olympic Games, became the *stephanitic*, or crown, games of ancient Greece, the central focus of ancient athletics. I shall use the Olympic program as the standard competition program for the stephanitic games, noting variations among the other three as I proceed.

The Gymnikos Agon (Nude Competitions)
THE FOOTRACES

From the beginning the *stadion* race was the premier event of the gymnikos agon. The term *stadion* originally denoted an ancient unit of measurement: one stadion was 600 ancient feet. The race of that distance acquired the same name; its modern equivalent is the 200-meter sprint. Since ancient depictions of footraces are rarely labeled, we must examine the gaits of the runners for features that will help us differentiate the various races. In the stadion, runners will have their knees high and their arms extended as they sprint down the track (see figs. 3 and 11). The stadion was the only event at the Olympic Games from 776 until 724, and the victor gave his name to the entire four-year Olympiad. We thus know the names of nearly every ancient Olympic stadion winner because the ancient Greeks used Olympiads to reckon time. For example, we say that the Battle of Marathon took place in the late summer (September 12) of the year 490 B.C., but ancient Greeks would identify that year as the third year of the Olympiad in which Tisikrates of Kroton won the stadion for the second time.

Fig. 30 Runners in the stadion or (more likely) the diaulos; the leader looks back to check on the competition. The graffito scratched later across the heads of the two losers is probably a person's name. Panathenaic amphora by the Kleophrades Painter, ca. 500 B.C. Paris, Musée du Louvre, inv. no. F 277, Réunion des Musées Nationaux / Art Resource, New York (photo: Herve Lewandowski).

Fig. 31 Diaulos runner, identified by painted inscription reading, "I am a diaulos runner." Fragment of a Panathenaic amphora by the Painter of Boston C.A., ca. 550 B.C. Athens, National Museum, inv. no. 2468 (photo: © Treasury of Archaeological Receipts).

The first addition to the Olympic program was the *diaulos,* or double-stadion, race in 724. This race, the functional equivalent of the modern 400–meters, is difficult to identify on the vase paintings, because the runners' gait is similar to that of stadion runners. By comparing runners whose knees are slightly lower than others' (contrast the knees in figures 3 and 11 with those in figure 30), we may be able to distinguish between the two events. The only depiction of the diaulos of which we are certain, however, is on a fragment of a Panathenaic amphora labeled, "I am a diaulos runner" (fig. 31).

At the next Olympiad, in 720, a long-distance footrace called the *dolichos* was added to the program. The sources are not unanimous about the length of this race: some claim that it was twenty laps of the stadium track, others that it was twenty-four. It may have differed from site to site, but it was in the range of 7.5 to 9 kilometers. We can identify a dolichos in paintings where the runners' knees are low and barely bent, with the arms drawn in close to the sides (see fig. 65).

The programs of the four stephanitic games were not exactly the same. Nemea had a footrace that was not contested at any of the other crown games called the *hippios* (*ephippios* in some sources), or "horsy" race. It was a quadruple stadion in length, or about 800 meters, but no other details are known, and there are no certain depictions of it in art.

The last footrace added to the Olympic program came two hundred years later, in 520. This was the *hoplitodromos* (sometimes called the *hoplites*), or race in armor. Like the diaulos, this was two stadia in length. The competitors carried shields and wore helmets and, originally, bronze shin guards or greaves (fig. 32). Later, the greaves were omitted (fig. 33). Our sources do not specify whether the equipment was standard-

Fig. 32 Runners in the hoplitodromos approach the judges (left). The victory prizes, tripod cauldrons, are on the right. Black-figure amphora by a painter in Group E(xekias), ca. 540 B.C. Munich, Staatliche Antikensammlungen und Glyptothek, inv. no. 1471.

Fig. 33 Runners in the hoplitodromos. Panathenaic amphora, 323/2 B.C. Paris, Musée du Louvre, inv. no. MN 704, Réunion des Musées Nationaux / Art Resource, New York (photo: H. Lewandowski).

ized. It is perhaps to be expected that helmets, made to fit the individuals' heads, might vary, but did each competitor carry a shield of exactly the same size and weight? We do hear of shields being set aside and stored for the hoplitodromos race, perhaps an indication that they were all the same. So, too, in some vase depictions, each shield has the same decoration or device, suggesting that the shields were uniform. But it is rare for every shield in a vase painting to have the same device. Even when the decoration is the same, such as the star that appears on the three shields of a Panathenaic amphora (fig. 33), there can be differences; in this amphora one of the shields is painted white. Was it made from a different metal, or did it have a different surface finish, or was the painter simply varying the decoration to suit his own artistic sense?

We don't know why the hoplitodromos was added to the Olympic program, although we do know that it took place at the end. We also know that it required a different kind of runner from the diaulos racer, for even though it was the same distance as the diaulos, and must have been run in separate lanes like the diaulos, it is rare to find an athlete who won both the diaulos and the hoplitodromos. Special techniques must have been necessary for each event.

The track was usually about 30 meters wide and 600 ancient feet in length. Since the length of the foot differed from site to site, so did the length of the track. The foot used in the stadium at Olympia was one of the longest, 0.3205 meters, giving a total length of more than 192 meters (fig. 34). The track at Delphi (fig. 35) was one of the shortest, fewer than 178 meters, because it used a short foot of 0.2965 meters. This difference underlines a basic feature of ancient athletics. There was no concern with standardization from place to place, for no time records were kept for comparison.

Fig. 34 Aerial view of the stadium at Olympia from the east, showing the Hellanodikaion (H; judges' stand), the Altar of Demeter Chamyne (D) and the krypte esodos (KE; entrance tunnel to the stadium) (photo: © H. R. Goette, Berlin).

Fig. 35 View of the stadium at Delphi from the west with the western starting line (balbis) across the track in the foreground. The wine inscription (see fig. 187) is on the retaining wall near the second cypress tree on the right (X) (photo: author).

Fig. 36 Balbis at the eastern end of the stadium at Delphi, seen from the south (photo: author).

Fig. 37 Balbis at the western end of the stadium at Olympia showing placement of the toes in the grooves, seen from the south (author's feet).

Fig. 38 Runner in the starting position, with his toes placed in the balbis (not visible). The kampter (turning post) is in front of him and a stlengis hangs on the wall. Red-figure krater, first quarter of 4th century B.C. Athens, National Museum, inv. no. 19392 (photo: © Treasury of Archaeological Receipts).

Fig. 39 Runner in the starting position. Bronze figurine, ca. 500 B.C. Olympia, Archaeological Museum, inv. no. B 26 (photo: © Treasury of Archaeological Receipts).

Fig. 40 Hoplitodromos runner in the starting position. The column in front with the three apparent holes from which strings hang down may be a starting mechanism. Red-figure tondo by the Alkimachos Painter, ca. 470 B.C. Leiden, Rijksmuseum voor Oudheden, inv. no. PC 89.

The important record for comparisons was the name of the winner, especially if he won multiple times and his name appeared frequently. But the winner was determined on a specific day at a specific place where all the athletes competed together under the same conditions on the same track.

Each end of the track was marked, at least by the fifth century, by a stone starting line, or *balbis* (plural, *balbides*). In its most advanced stage chronologically, the upper surface of the balbis contained a set of double grooves, roughly 10–12 centimeters apart, in which the runner placed his toes, with one foot of necessity slightly in front of the other (figs. 36, 37). The front edges of the grooves were beveled while the back edges were vertical to give the runner's foot leverage. In the case of right-handed athletes (and I know of no examples of ancient left-handers), the left foot would be the natural forward one.

This positioning of the feet is seen in scores of vase paintings (fig. 38) and statuettes (fig. 39) in which the runner stands with left foot in front, leaning forward with

Fig. 41 Runner in a four-point starting position at the kampter being regarded by another young man. Red-figure stemless cup, side A, 430–420 B.C. Leiden, Rijksmuseum voor Oudheden, inv. no. GNV 71.

Fig. 43 Judge stopping the hoplitodromos runner shown on the other side of the same vase (fig. 42).

Fig. 42 Hoplitodromos runner in a three-point stance at the start of the race. Note the column behind him; like the one in figure 40, this may be part of the starting mechanism. Red-figure skyphos, 440–420 B.C. Hearst private collection, California (photo: A. Raubitschek).

outstretched arms. We can almost feel the rocking motion that will bring the weight forward at the signal. This is also the position shown for the start of the hoplitodromos, although the athlete would have had to make an adjustment for the weight of the shield (fig. 40). The placement of the feet is also implicit in the words used to tell the runners to get ready. The ancient equivalent of our modern "on your mark" in "on your mark — get set — go!" was *poda para poda* (foot by foot) . . . *apite* (Go!).

Modern runners do not like this upright stance, and some insist that the four-point starting position must have been used. There are, in fact, two depictions from antiquity that seem to document the use of the modern position. One of these shows a runner at the *kampter*, or turning post (fig. 41). But the artist has been careful to show the bent, cramped position of the right leg that results from the placement of the toes in the grooves, and the robed figure to the left is looking at the runner in a quizzical way, making a motion with his right hand as if to comment on the runner's unusual starting position.

Fig. 44 The start of the 200–meter race at Athens in the first modern Olympics, 1896.

The second depiction shows a hoplitodromos racer poised at the kampter in a three-point position; the shield on his left arm prevents a full four-point stance (fig. 42). We can be reasonably certain, however, that he has simply fallen forward and is not in his starting stance; on the other side of the vase a judge, armed with his *rhabdos* (switch), motions to the runner to stop (fig. 43). The evidence of these two paintings, then, demonstrates that the four-point stance was not allowed. In any event, after the starting mechanism began to be employed, the stance would have been impossible. As we shall see, the barriers of the starting mechanism were placed in front of the runners at knee and waist height, making it impossible to crouch (see figs. 50, 55).

The upright starting position can be regarded as proven. It may be some solace to those who find this position uncomfortable to look at the start of the 200–meter race at the first modern Olympics in 1896 (fig. 44). The variety of stances include some that resemble the ancient position, and only one runner uses the four-point stance. However, this runner, Thomas Burke, won the race, and his stance was soon adopted by all sprinters.

The balbis with the double grooves filling the space between the postholes marking the lanes was standard by the fourth century B.C., but there were earlier versions as well. In Nemea we find the earliest balbis blocks so far recognized, dating to around 500 (fig. 45). These are characterized by a single toe groove about 10 centimeters wide set back about 10 centimeters from the front edge of the block. As in the later blocks, the grooves were beveled toward the front with a vertical edge to give the toes purchase at the rear. Apparently the runner hooked the toes of his front foot over the edge of the block and put the toes of his rear foot in the groove. At the end of each block is a socket for a post to mark the lane divisions, and in front of these postholes are letters to denote lane numbers. The use of the twenty-second letter in the alphabet (chi) suggests that there may have been as many as twenty-two lanes in the stadium during this period. The lanes varied from 88 to 92 centimeters wide. This series of bal-

Fig. 45 Early balbis block from Nemea with a single foothold and posthole at the end of each block to mark the lanes. Nemea inv. no. A 402 (Photo: author).

Fig. 46 Later balbis block from Nemea (a later posthole and cuttings at the far end indicating reuse as a threshold have been edited out). Nemea inv. no. A 100. (Photo: author).

bis blocks was found in a reused situation, so it is impossible for us to understand every detail of how they functioned, but it is clear that the position of each runner within his lane was specified and that there was only one runner per lane. The later balbis with longer (frequently continuous) grooves clearly allowed greater flexibility in the arrangement of runners.

A series of balbis blocks from a later phase has also been found at Nemea, although they are still earlier than the double-groove balbis typical of the Hellenistic period. These blocks have a single continuous groove 6 centimeters from and parallel to the front edge of the block, but the single foothold grooves behind are spaced at intervals of 1.02 meters, which must therefore be the width of each lane (fig. 46). The flexibility provided by the continuous groove was canceled out by the single foothold grooves: the runner was fixed in a specific place. These balbis blocks were all discovered in later, reused situations. They seem to represent an idea that did not work, so they were removed from their stadium.

In addition to the balbis, ancient stadiums were also equipped with a starting mechanism, the *hysplex*, at least by the fifth century. The earliest form of the hysplex (hysplex I) comes from Isthmia, where a triangular area is paved with stone (fig. 47). The runners stood at the base of the triangle facing away from it, with the starter positioned in a manhole at the apex of the triangle (fig. 48). A series of postholes are cut into the starting line about 1.05 meters apart, from which grooves have been carved in the triangular paving beginning at each post and ending at the manhole, bounded on

Fig. 47 Hysplex I at Isthmia, seen from the north. The starting line faces east and is punctuated by holes for posts that divided the lanes (photo: author).

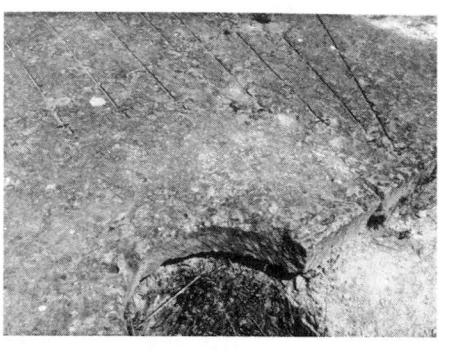

Fig. 48 Manhole for the starter in the Isthmia hysplex. Grooves with bronze staples for release cords radiate from the manhole area to the starting line postholes, seen from the southwest (photo: author).

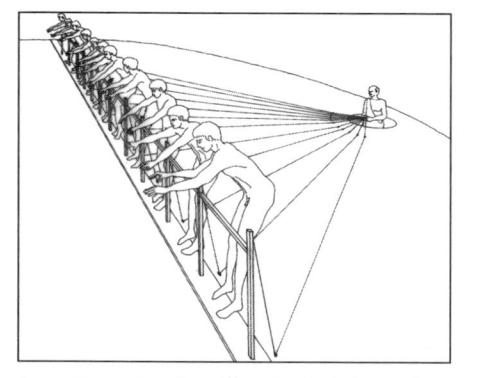

Fig. 50 Reconstruction of hysplex I at Isthmia: the starter in his manhole releases the individual gate for each runner. Drawing by Ruben Santos.

Fig. 49 Detail of a posthole at the starting line of the Isthmia hysplex with a bronze staple at the end of the groove for the release cord connected to this post, seen from the north (photo: author).

each end by a thick bronze staple (fig. 49). The whole system has been reconstructed as a series of individual hinged gates that served as barriers for the runners. Each gate would be controlled by a cord that began at the gate and ran down to the staple at the base of the post, along the groove in the pavement, and up through the staple at the manhole into the hands of the starter (fig. 50). By either pulling on the cord or simply releasing it, the starter caused the gate to fall, allowing the runner to take off down the track.

The potential for problems with this mechanism is clear. The difference in the lengths of the grooves and therefore the cords for the central lanes and those for the outside lanes is more than 7 meters, causing a resulting difference in friction and resistance that must have made the outer gates less responsive than the central ones. Runners in the inner lanes had a distinct advantage. In addition, there was the possibility that a cord could become snarled, accidentally or deliberately, delaying a runner's start. This first type of hysplex has not been found at any site other than Isthmia, and it seems to have been an experiment that failed. Soon after its construction, the

Fig. 51 Balbis of the stadium at Nemea showing added hysplex base projecting northward, seen from the west, 300–280 B.C. University of California at Berkeley, Nemea Excavations Archives, no. STAD 78.34.

Fig. 52 Runners in the hoplitodromos approaching the starting line. Their feet are not yet in the "poda para poda" position, and they are staring at one another rather than the track. Two horizontal barrier cords pass in front of them. Panathenaic amphora, 344/3 B.C. Athens, Third Ephoreia of Classical Antiquities, inv. no. A 6374 (photo: courtesy of Panos Valavanis).

triangular pavement was carefully covered with layer of hard whitish earth and a single-groove balbis installed, without a hysplex.

About a century was to pass before another attempt was made to use a hysplex in a stadium. The new hysplex (hysplex II) was more widespread, used for the stadiums at Nemea, Isthmia, Epidauros, and Corinth (and probably elsewhere). These may all have been the work of one man, Philon of Corinth, who was fined for his failure to install the hysplex at Epidauros within the time specified by his contract (*IG* IV^2 1.98; A 82). Each hysplex was set on a pair of projecting stone bases added to the ends of a preexisting balbis (fig. 51; see also fig. 58). A central area was cut down to hold a wooden frame while another area was cut down on the side away from the track. At the rear a semicircular hole was cut into the balbis. How this new hysplex system worked can be reconstructed from a recently discovered Panathenaic amphora that shows the preliminaries of a hoplitodromos (fig. 52).

On the amphora the runners approach the starting line, where two cords are stretched in front of them as barriers, one at knee, the other at waist height. The cords end at the left at a post set between two square objects connected by what appears to be a horizontal rod or other element (fig. 53). At the right the cords also end at a post, which is in front of another, massive post, also set between two square objects connected by a horizontal rod.

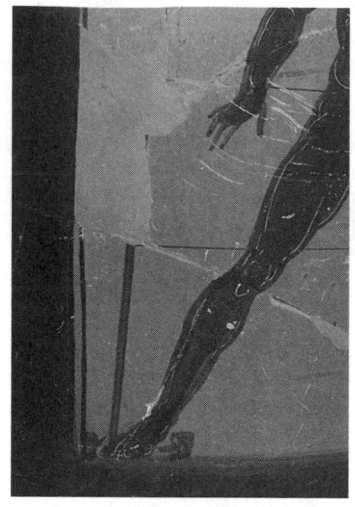

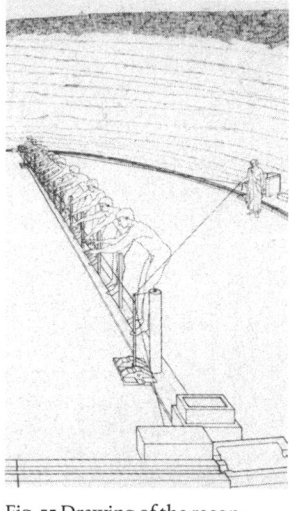

Fig. 53 Detail of the left side of figure 52. The two barrier cords end at a post (whose upper portion is broken and missing), which ends behind the right foot of the runner between two square objects tied together by a horizontal element (probably a rope) (photo: courtesy of Panos Valavanis).

Fig. 54 Reconstruction of the hysplex II machine set into a base projecting from the balbis at Nemea, seen from the north. University of California at Berkeley, Nemea Excavations Archives, no. STAD 93.29.

Fig. 55 Drawing of the reconstructed hysplex II at Nemea. University of California at Berkeley, Nemea Excavations Archives, no. PD 93.5a. Drawing by Ruben Santos.

Considered in tandem with the vase painting, the cuttings in the projecting bases allow us to reconstruct the mechanism: the post is the elbow (as it was called) that threw the barrier cords down to start the race (fig. 54). The massive post seen on the right of the vase painting would have been set into the semicircular cutting in the balbis, where it would anchor the elbow until its release. The square objects are the ends of the wooden frame between which was a twisted rope (the horizontal rod). The names of individual parts of the hysplex listed in inventories from Delos (*ID* 1409 Ba II 43–45; A 22) are the same names used for the individual parts of ancient catapults. This suggests that the rope was twisted to provide the torsion which would throw the elbow, with the barrier ropes attached, to the ground just as a catapult hurls a missile into the air.

The whole system can be reconstructed on paper (fig. 55). The starter stands at the apex of a triangle, with the runners lined up along the balbis at the base. This resembles the first hysplex system from Isthmia, but now only a single barrier prevents the runners from starting, and that barrier is automatically released in a single action. Note as well that the military technology of the catapult, which was invented about a decade earlier than the date of the Panathenaic amphora in figure 52, was used for athletic purposes. Just as military technology was adapted to athletics in the fourth century B.C. so in recent years we have adapted military technologies like the starter's pistol and lasers for our athletic competitions.

Fig. 56 Hysplex system II in use at a revival of the Nemean games. The starter has just shouted, "Apite!" and the barrier cords are falling, but the athletes have not yet reacted. University of California at Berkeley, Nemea Excavations Archives, no. Nemea Game 96.150.

Fig. 57 The athletes have now reacted to the starting call and the fall of the barrier cords. Note that even those runners whose feet land on the cords are not tripping on them. University of California at Berkeley, Nemea Excavations Archives, no. Nemea Game 96.152.

One objection to hysplex II is that the feet of the runners could become tangled in the cords. When a reconstructed hysplex was used at Nemea, however, it was discovered that no such problem exists in practice (figs. 56, 57). For most runners the first footfall comes naturally short of the near cord, and the second just beyond the farther one. Even when a foot lands on the cord, the tension of the system holds the cords hard on the ground, and the foot will not slide under them unless the runner has started too soon—a floggible offense.

In later Hellenistic times, a third hysplex came into use. Now monumental architectural frames divide the lanes, while intricate pulleys, cords, and metal springs release the barriers and start the race. In some cases, as at Epidauros, this new system was added to a preexisting hysplex II (figs. 58, 59). Columns with grooves on the back surface marked the lanes while serving as the frame for the hysplex mechanism. The best-preserved hysplex III is on Kos, where a double row of stones with a space be-

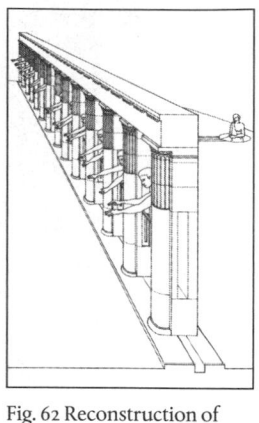

Fig. 58 Balbis in the stadium at Epidauros seen from the north, with the projecting base for a hysplex II system in the foreground. In the background, parallel to the balbis, are individual bases and half-columns for the hysplex III (photo: author).

Fig. 59 Detail of the back of a half-column from the hysplex III system at Epidauros, viewed from the east. The vertical groove and its answering slot in the base held the hidden cords that released the barrier of the mechanism (photo: author).

Fig. 60 General view of the hysplex III system at Kos (photo: author).

Fig. 61 Top and sides of two half-columns of the hysplex III system at Kos (photo: author).

Fig. 62 Reconstruction of hysplex III system at Kos. From his manhole the starter controlled the individual gates by single release cord. Drawing by Ruben Santos.

tween served as the base for a series of half-columns (fig. 60). Apparently the spaces were for ropes, which must have been covered by the typically grooved balbis, although no example survives. The columns are unfluted toward the bottom, as is typical of the Hellenistic period, and hollow in the center (fig. 61). The lower part consists of two blocks with an empty space between them, and cuttings and iron rings located in these spaces help us reconstruct the mechanism. Operated by a system of cords and pulleys, it made use of a simple metal spring, pulled and cocked by one cord and released by another. The whole system could be operated by a single starter pulling on a single release cord. The invention of the spring led to this technological advance, while the monumental gates reveal the theatrical quality that had come to the stadium (fig. 62).

The evolution of the hysplex shows a continuing concern with an issue that was fundamental to the gymnikos agon: the desire to remove all possibility of influencing the outcome of the races, either by faulty equipment or prejudicial behavior by the judges. If a runner started too soon, he would fall against the gate or become tangled in the barrier cords. It would be clear to everyone that he had made a false start, and a judge could neither deny that he had done so nor arbitrarily declare a false start and flog an innocent runner. This concern accords with the ancient principle that the only acceptable competitions were ones in which the winner was determined by strictly objective criteria.

Fig. 63 Early Hellenistic stadium at Nemea with lanes marked for the diaulos and a base for the judges' stand (Hellanodikaion) at right near the balbis. Note the single turning post in front of the balbis to the left of center. University of California at Berkeley, Nemea Excavations Archives, no. STAD 93.3.

Fig. 64 Modern runner in the diaulos at Nemea after rounding the turning post (kampter) in the other half of his lane. University of California at Berkeley, Nemea Excavations Archives, no. STAD-ded 94.73.

The finish of the footraces offered another point at which subjective judgment might enter, although in practice the first runner across the line was usually self-evident. Nonetheless, to make the winner more obvious to the crowd, a balbis also marked the *terma,* or end, of the race. Every stadium was thus equipped with two balbides, located at opposite ends of the stadion-long track. The stadion race would start at one end of the track and end at the other. The diaulos, on the other hand, began and ended at the same balbis. As a consequence, the best seats were near that balbis. When a stadium had a single closed end, such as the one at Nemea (fig. 63), the finish line would be at that closed end. In stadiums like the one at Olympia (see fig. 34), the balbis that served as the finish line can be identified by the proximity of the *Hellanodikaion* (judges' stand).

As indicated by the name, runners in the diaulos ("double channel" or "double pipe") ran in lanes, which were marked by lime, and turned around individual turning posts (kampteres; fig. 64). Thus ancient authors would compare running the race to plowing a field, where the oxen pull the plow back and forth. Spectators on the side of the stadium, however, would see a line of runners surge down the track, turn, and run back toward them. Euripides could therefore use this image in his description of a corpse washed back and forth on the shore by the "many diauloi of the waves" (*Hecuba* 28–30; A 148) and refer to Hades as *adiaulos,* "a place of no return" (Fragment 868; A 148).

In the long-distance dolichos, runners rounded a single kampter, as we see in vase paintings and read in the written sources (fig. 65; compare fig. 4). Nemea is cur-

Fig. 65 Runners in the dolichos approaching the single kampter. Panathenaic amphora by the Berlin Painter, 480–470 B.C. Lent by Trade Arts Investment, Inc. (photo: © 2001 The Metropolitan Museum of Art).

Fig. 66 Base for a single kampter in the stadium at Nemea, seen from the northeast. The balbis and projecting base for the hysplex are behind to the left. University of California at Berkeley, Nemea Excavations Archives, no. STAD 76.4.

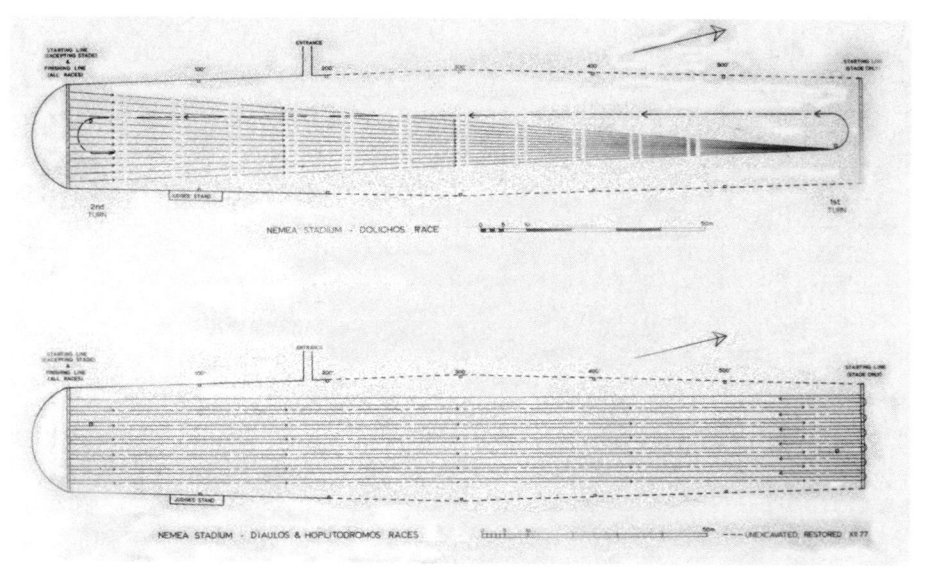

Fig. 67 Sketches for the paths of the dolichos and diaulos races. University of California at Berkeley, Nemea Excavations Archives, no. PD 77.16.

rently the only stadium in which a base has been found for this single turning post (fig. 66). It stands off-center, away from the balbis, presumably to avoid the necessity of crossing the balbis at every turn (see fig. 63). On their approach the runners would come as close to the kampter as possible, for a tight turn, inevitably swinging out farther as they rounded it; with the off-center kampter the center of the turn would be more or less in the center of the track (fig. 67). As in today's races, the shorter distances were run very differently from the longer ones.

Before we leave the footraces, a word should be said about the modern marathon, which bears the name of the site and the battle that were so important to ancient Greece, leading many to assume that the marathon was an ancient competition. The ancient basis for the marathon is, however, itself an illusion. The old story re-

lates that an Athenian warrior named Pheidippides ran from Marathon to Athens to report the resounding victory over the Persians. As he entered the Senate house, he shouted out, "Be happy! We have won!" and then fell down dead. This stirring story inspired the eminent French philologist Marcel Bréal to offer a trophy for the winner of a reenactment of the run from Marathon. Added to the first modern Olympics in 1896, the race was won by a Greek runner named Spyridon Louis, the only track-and-field winner from the host country. Louis's victory was reported around the world, gripping the popular imagination. Thus the marathon became a popular event and now has a life of its own outside the Olympics at regular track meets.

But it is clear that the original "marathon" never happened. Herodotus, who based his history of the battle on interviews with eyewitnesses, does not mention anyone running from Marathon to Athens after the battle. Indeed, hundreds of years passed before the story first appeared, and even then the runner was not named Pheidippides (Plutarch, *Moralia* 347C; A 29). Herodotus does mention an Athenian courier (a *hemerodromos*, "day-long runner"), called Pheidippides in some of the manuscripts and Philippides in others (6.105–106; A 28). But this man, according to Herodotus, ran from Athens to Sparta on the eve of the battle to ask for Spartan help against the Persians. He covered the distance in less than two days, arriving in Sparta the day after he left Athens. This was no mean feat, but it is creditable. The winners of the modern Spartathlon that annually (since 1983) reproduces this run cover a distance of 250 kilometers in an average time of just under twenty-four hours. However, the connection between Pheidippides/Philippides and the Battle of Marathon is clearly an ancient myth. A famous event comes to be associated with the name of someone who accomplished an extraordinary feat, even though the event and the feat were different. Indeed, the official distance of the modern marathon (42.2 kilometers, or 26 miles, 385 yards) is not the distance between Marathon and Athens, and was not established until the 1908 Olympics. It was the distance from Windsor Castle to London's Olympic stadium.

Finally, we should note the addition to the Olympic program in 632 B.C. of a stadion race for the *paides*. It is curious that this was the only footrace for boys at Olympia, whereas the diaulos and the dolichos for this age group were competed at other sites. As we shall see, this was only one of several differences between Olympia and the rest of the ancient athletic world.

WRESTLING

The first event that was not a footrace to be added to the Olympic program was wrestling, or the *pale*, in 708 B.C. Use of the adjective *orthe* (upright, erect) to modify *pale* is to be understood as a reference to the basic feature of ancient wrestling: beginning from a standing position, the object was to throw one's opponent to the ground. The notion of "pinning" an opponent did not exist, and the modern practice of what purports to be ancient "ground wrestling" stems from a confusion of wrestling with the *pankration*, as we shall see.

Fig. 68 The systasis position at the start of the pale. Nike watches from the kampter, waiting to award the victory. Red-figure skyphos by the Penelope Painter, ca. 440 B.C. Oxford, Ashmolean Museum, inv. no. 1890.35.

Fig. 69 Grappling from the systasis position at the start of the pale. Black-figure stamnos, ca. 510 B.C. Paris, Musée du Louvre, inv. no. F 314, Réunion des Musées Nationaux / Art Resource, New York (photo: Herve Lewandowski).

Fig. 70 Wrestlers hold each other in a waist hold, with the advantage still in doubt. Each is in a position, with the right leverage, to lift the other into the air and throw him down. Black-figure amphora, ca. 520–510 B.C. Tarquinia, Museo Archeologico, inv. no. 5654.

Fig. 71 Grappling from the systasis position at the start of the pale. The athlete on the left has managed to seize the left leg of his opponent behind the knee. Silver stater of Aspendos, 420–400 B.C. Athens, Numismatic Museum, inv. no. 1904/5 ΙΣΤ´139 (photo: © Treasury of Archaeological Receipts).

Fig. 72 Wrestlers, each with a potentially decisive hold; one grasps his opponent around the neck, the other holds him behind the knee. Bronze statuette, Hellenistic period. Jerusalem, Borowski collection (photo: owner).

The starting stance was called the *systasis*, or "standing together," and is frequently portrayed in vase painting (fig. 68) and sculpture (see fig. 143). The wrestlers lean into each other with their foreheads touching, a stance likened by Homer to the way the rafters meet in a house (*Iliad* 23.30; A 1). From that position, the athlete would endeavor to throw his opponent to the ground. He might lunge forward and try to grab the other by the shoulders (fig. 69), and then reach further around in a bear hug that might end up with him holding his opponent around the waist from below and above (fig. 70). Another sequence following the systasis might see the wrestlers avoid close contact, "chicken fighting" with their hands to gain a grip on arms or legs (fig. 71). Each might gain a hold simultaneously, and again leverage and inertia of weight would determine who would manage to throw the opponent (fig. 72). Sooner or later, one would achieve the hold that gave him the throw.

Fig. 73 A wrestler holding his opponent by the waist from behind while the opponent pries at his fingers. At the left a palm branch awaits the victor. Panathenaic amphora, 340–330 B.C. Paris, Bibliothèque nationale de France, inv. no. 247.

Fig. 74 A wrestler with a waist hold has picked up his opponent and is about to throw him down. Bronze figurine, Hellenistic period. Athens, National Museum, inv. no. aig 2548 (photo: © Treasury of Archaeological Receipts).

One popular hold was the *meson echein,* or *labein,* "to have" or "grab the middle" (waist) (fig. 73). The wrestler on the defensive in this hold could do little but hope to break it by shifting his weight or try to pry the other's fingers loose. He was liable to find himself picked up and heaved head over heels to the ground (fig. 74). Another hold mentioned in the sources is the *trachelizein,* which was a kind of neck hold in which leverage was exerted against the upper body. In other cases the legs were used to trip or lever the opponent off balance (fig. 75), perhaps the move implicit in the verb *ankyrzein,* "to catch with a hook" or "to hook." The *hedran strephein* was a common move, in which one wrestler would aim, literally, "to turn the rear" into his opponent, trying to throw him over his hip (fig. 76). One defense against the move was to grab the opponent by the waist so that, at worst, both fell together, resulting in a no-throw (fig. 77).

A variation on the hedran strephein was the flying mare, whose ancient name is unknown. Perhaps it was considered a hedran strephein since it also involved turning the back, although the shoulder rather than the thigh became the fulcrum for the throw (fig. 78). Slamming the body of one's opponent to the ground was highly dramatic; that it could also cause the offensive wrestler's knee to touch the ground was clearly acceptable. There are many vase paintings showing a wrestler in the act of throwing his opponent while his knee is touching the ground and a judge is scrutinizing the action. Perhaps the judge's attention was owing to a rule that only one knee was allowed to touch, but the written sources are silent on this point. The knee is also seen to be touching in other

Fig. 75 The wrestler on the right uses his hands and left leg to unbalance his opponent, who counteracts with his left leg. Red-figure psykter by Phintias, 520–510 B.C. Archaeologisches Institut der Universität Zürich, inv. no. 4039b (photo: Silvia Hertig).

Fig. 77 The wrestler on the right, holding his opponent's neck turns his rear in an attempt to throw his opponent over his hip, while the wrestler on the left responds by hooking his left leg around the right knee of his opponent. Panathenaic amphora by Exekias, 540–530 B.C. Karlsruhe, Badisches Landsmuseum, inv. no. 65.45.

Fig. 76 Wrestler on left turns his rear (hedran strephein), attempting to pull his opponent forward over his hip. Red-figure tondo by the Codrus Painter, 430–420 B.C. Rome, Villa Giulia, inv. no. 27259.

Fig. 78 A wrestler with his knee on the ground throws his opponent over his shoulder while a judge watches. Red-figure tondo by Onesimos, 490–480 B.C. Paris, Bibliothèque nationale de France, inv. no. 523.

moves, such as the use of a waist hold to throw the opponent (fig. 79). Probably the initiator of the throw was credited as long as he did not also fall to the ground.

The wrestling took place in an area known as the *skamma*, or "dug-up place." The same word was used for the site of the boxing and the pankration, and for the area in which the jumpers landed in the pentathlon. The skamma was probably an ad-hoc arrangement created at the time of the competition by digging a place in the stadium track, for no traces of a skamma have been discovered. Representations of wrestling matches that show the kampter in the background (for example, fig. 68) suggest that it was located near the end of the track (see figs. 63 and 65). We do not know the size and shape of these skammata; given the idiosyncrasies of each site (such as the unequal length of race tracks), we cannot even assume that they were standardized.

The competitors were sorted into pairs by drawing lots (*kleroi*; singular, *kleros*).

Fig. 79 The wrestler on the left with his knee on ground uses a waist hold to throw his opponent. Red-figure psykter by Phintias, 520–510 B.C. Archaeologisches Institut der Universität Zürich, inv. no. 4039a (photo: Silvia Hertig).

Lucian tells us that these lots were about the size of a bean, each marked with a letter; there were two lots for each letter (*Hermotimos* 40; *A* 97). The kleroi would be mixed up in a pitcher, and each athlete would draw one. Athletes who pulled out the same letter would wrestle each other: alpha against alpha, beta against beta, and so on. If there were an odd number of athletes, the last letter would appear on only one kleros, and the athlete who drew it would not compete in the first round. He was described as *ephedros,* or "on the seat." A victor who had not received such a bye would proudly refer to himself as *anephedros* (see, for example, *IvO* 225; *A* 98).

The wrestler who threw his opponent three times without first suffering three falls himself was the winner. We know this from a number of sources, including the custom of calling the victor a *triakter,* "thricer." Even more graphic is the story of Milo of Kroton, a larger-than-life strongman of the sixth century B.C. (*Anthologia Graeca* 11.316; *A* 33). In one Olympic competition, probably the games of 520, Milo was the only wrestler who showed up. Apparently no one wanted to compete against him. As he was coming forward to claim his uncontested victory, he slipped and fell on his back: "The crowd shouted that he should not be crowned since he fell down all by himself. Milo stood up in their midst and shouted back, 'That was not the third fall, I fell once. Let someone throw me the other times.'"

Milo's victory in those Olympic Games had another distinction, at least until he tripped and fell. It would have been an *akoniti* victory, a "dustless" win; originally a victory without a fall, the word came to mean any victory won without a fight or competition. There is, finally, the curious case of Leontiskos of Messene, a two-time Olympic wrestling champion who is said to have been a poor wrestler but a good finger-bender (Pausanias 6.4.3; *A* 34). He must have known exactly how far he could go, for the rules at Olympia included a prohibition against breaking fingers by the wrestlers (*SEG* 48.541; *A* 101).

The pale for the category of paides was added to the Olympic program in 632, at the same time as the *stadion paidon* (boys' footrace). In many ways this reflects the esteem those two competitions enjoyed. The wrestling and the sprint were regarded as the best expressions of strength and speed, respectively. They are represented mythologically by Herakles and Hermes, the two divinities most worshiped in the gymnasion.

Fig. 80 These boxers have given each other bloody noses, although only the dribbles of blood on the abdomen of the right-hand boxer are visible. Black-figure amphora, 510–490 B.C. Brussels, Musées Royaux d'Art et d'Histoire, inv. no. R 336 (photo: museum).

BOXING

The *pyx* (or *pygme* or *pygmachia*) was introduced to the Olympic Games in 688, twenty years after the wrestling. In Roman times, Philostratos maintained that boxing had been invented by the Spartans because "they had no helmets, nor did they think it proper to their native land to fight in helmets. They felt that a shield, properly used, could serve in the place of a helmet. Therefore they practiced boxing in order to know how to ward off blows to the face, and they hardened their faces in order to be able to endure the blows that landed" (*On Gymnastics* 9–10; *A 37*). Whether or not we take this statement at face value, the evidence for blows to the head, bloody noses, and other cuts is omnipresent; I show here only one example from the dozens that exist (fig. 80).

Blood is not the only feature that identifies boxers in ancient art. Even more characteristic are their "gloves." These were called *himantes* (singular, *himas*) and consisted of leather strips wrapped around the hands (fig. 81). By examining depictions of the himantes during the wrapping process and calculating their length in relation to size of the human figure, we can estimate that they were about 4 meters long (fig. 82; see also fig. 19). Although they were made of oxhide that had been tanned and softened to some extent with oil, their nickname was *myrmikes* (ants) because they stung and left nicks and abrasions on the boxers. Pigskin was specifically not allowed because it left wounds that were particularly painful and slow to heal.

The himantes were wrapped around the wrist and knuckles, apparently to reinforce the former and protect the latter. (There was no thought that they might serve as protection for the opponent.) The fingers were left free so that the boxer could clench his fist to deliver a blow, and open his hand to catch a punch. Both these attitudes of

Fig. 81 The boxers on left wrap himantes around their hands under the watch of a young (assistant?) judge; the boxers on right fight under the watch of an older judge. Note the blood flowing from the face of one fighter and the abraded cheek of the other. Red-figure kylix by the Triptolemos Painter, ca. 490 B.C. Toledo, Ohio, Toledo Museum of Art, inv. no. 1961.26, gift of Edward Drummond Libbey.

Fig. 82 A boxer prepares to wrap a himas around his hand. Red-figure tondo by the Antiphon Painter, ca. 490 B.C. St. Petersburg, The State Hermitage Museum, inv. no. B 1536.

Fig. 83 The boxer on the left clenches his right fist to deliver a blow, keeping his left hand open to ward off blows from his opponent. Meanwhile, his opponent has both hands open and is falling back from his punches. The judge watches on the right while another boxer on the left with his himantes dangling from his left hand waits his turn. Pseudo-Panathenaic amphora by the Antimenes Painter, 520–510 B.C. Berlin, Staatliche Museen—Preussischer Kulturbesitz, Antikensammlung, inv. no. F 1831.

the hands—offensive and defensive—are frequently seen in the portrayal of boxing matches, and both are often displayed by a single boxer (fig. 83).

By the middle of the fourth century this "soft" himas was replaced by the *oxys*, or "hard" himas. The earliest depiction of this new type seems to be the one on a Panathenaic amphora of 336/5 B.C. (fig. 84), but it is best seen—albeit in a later, more developed form—on statues (figs. 85–87). A piece of fleece-lined leather covered most of the forearm, wrist, and hand up to and including the knuckles. A hard protruding knuckle guard made of laminated leather strips increased the protection to the knuckles and the damage done to the opponent. The whole was held in place by a leather harness and strips that wrapped around the fleece on the forearm. The offensive and defensive potentials were both increased, and we no longer see depictions of open hands. Rather, the padded forearm is now the defensive "shield" of the boxer.

Blows to the head, seen in the earlier vase paintings, continue to be the essential tactic of the boxer. The famous bronze statue of a boxer in Rome shows no signs of

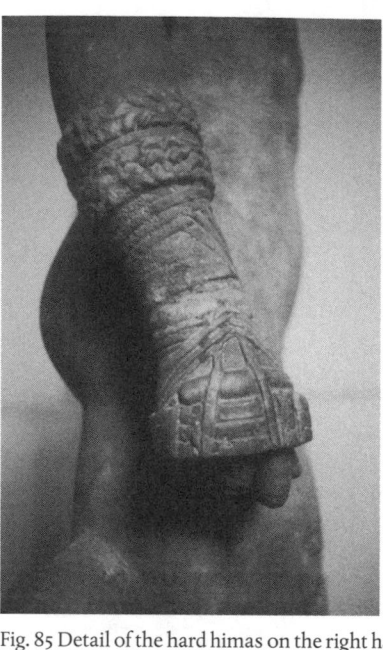

Fig. 84 Boxing match with the hard himantes. At the right the white hand of Nike holds the palm branch of victory that will go to the winner. Note the holes in the surface of the vase. It was broken in antiquity and repaired with lead strips that were passed through the holes to hold together the adjacent fragments. Panathenaic amphora of the Nikomachos Series, 336/5 B.C. London, The British Museum, inv. no. B 607 (photo: © The British Museum).

Fig. 85 Detail of the hard himas on the right hand of a boxer. Marble statue, ca. 200 B.C. Naples, Museo Nazionale, inv. no. 119917 (photo: author).

Fig. 86 Torso of boxer wearing the hard himantes. Bronze statue, ca. 150 B.C. Rome, Thermi, inv. no. 1055 (photo: A. M. Sommella, E. Talamo, and M. Cima, eds., *Lo sport nel mondo antico: "Athla" e atleti nella grecia classica* [Rome, 1987], no. 9).

Fig. 87 Detail of the right side of the head of the boxer in figure 86; copper inlay portrays blood dripping from wounds in the forehead, nose, cheek, and ear.

Fig. 88 A boxing match being watched by several onlookers. At least three can be identified as judges by their rhabdoi, and at least three can be identified as boxers by their himantes. The two onlookers at the right, however, may be waiting their turn to wrestle, not box (see fig. 69 for more of the vase). Black-figure stamnos, ca. 510 B.C. Paris, Musée du Louvre, inv. no. F 314, Réunion des Musées Nationaux / Art Resource, New York (photo: Herve Lewandowski).

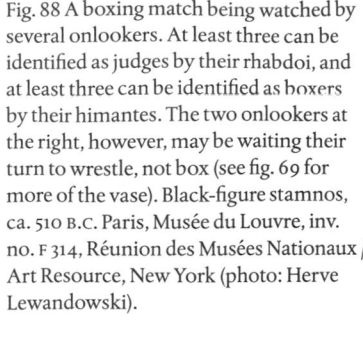

Fig. 89 On the back of the stamnos pictured in figure 88 two boxing matches are in progress, watched by several onlookers. At least two of the onlookers can be identified as judges by their rhabdoi, and at least one as a boxer by his himas.

wounds or blows to his body (fig. 86), but his head has at least a dozen fresh, bleeding wounds (fig. 87). It is no wonder that by the early Roman period we hear of a Greek boxer named Melancomas of Caria who was able to keep up his guard for two days at a time. "He could force his opponents to give up, not only before he received a blow but even before he had landed one on them" (Dio Chrysostom 28.5–8; A 202). We can appreciate the wisdom of this tactic, especially in the Roman period, when the boxing glove known as the *caestus* came into existence. It was commonly loaded with metal and glass fragments. A single punch could be lethal.

In the earlier periods, however, speed of foot and strength of arm were the desired attributes of the boxer. A lively description of a boxing match by Theokritos (*Idylls* 22.27–135; A 39) shows how the massive Amykos was outwitted by the quicker Polydeukes, who created an advantage for himself by maneuvering Amykos into facing the sun. He also sidestepped Amykos's powerful punches, and the repeated misses left Amykos with tired arms. As his punches dropped ever lower, Polydeukes floated around cutting up his opponent at will. Finally, when the giant was essentially defenseless, Polydeukes delivered the haymaker that knocked him out.

Boxing practice must have emphasized such tactics, and equipment included a punching bag (*korykos*), which was set up in a special room (the *korykeion*) of the gymnasion. Korykoi came in several sizes: lightweight for the boxers, larger and heavier versions for the pankratiasts (Philostratos, *On Gymnastics* 57; A 42). We hear of sparring with padded gloves (*sphairai*; Plato, *Laws* 830a–c; A 40) and shadow boxing, as

Fig. 90 A boxer has been knocked down by another who prepares to hit him again. The judge is about to apply his rhabdos as punishment for the foul, while another boxer waiting at the right gestures with two raised fingers in protest. Panathenaic amphora by the Painter of Berlin 1833, ca. 490 B.C. Berlin, Staatliche Museen — Preussischer Kulturbesitz, Antikensammlung, inv. no. F 1833 (photo: Ingrid Geske).

Fig. 91 The boxer on the ground raises a finger (weakly?) while the next opponent watches from the left. Panathenaic amphora, late 5th century B.C. St. Petersburg, The State Hermitage Museum, inv. no. Ky. 1913.4/389.

Fig. 93 A boxer with a bloody nose runs away from his opponent. The painted inscriptions read, from the left, "he pursues," "he boxes," "he flees." Black-figure skyphos, ca. 550–525 B.C. Paris, Musée du Louvre, inv. no. MNC 332, Réunion des Musées Nationaux / Art Resource, New York (photo: H. Lewandowski).

Fig. 92 A downed boxer signals his defeat to the boxer waiting on the right who relays the message to the judge on the left. Black-figure amphora near the Acheloos Painter, 510–500 B.C. London, The British Museum, inv. no. B 271 (GR 1843.2–14.1) (photo: © The British Museum).

well as of ear-protectors (*amphotidai*; Plutarch, *Moralia* 38B; A 42). But depictions of boxing practice and training equipment are extremely rare.

Boxing competitions, like wrestling matches, took place in a skamma in the stadium. The pairs were also determined by drawing lots. A vase from the sixth century suggests that several preliminary bouts might be held simultaneously while the rest of the boxers stood by waiting to fight the winners (figs. 88, 89). In this vase painting there are at least ten boxers in the competition (perhaps even more) and five judges.

There were no rounds and no time limits, although apparently breaks could be taken by mutual agreement. It seems that one was not allowed to hit a man when he was down (fig. 90). Blows below the belt could hardly be judged precisely, but we can

Fig. 94 Kreugas of Epidamnos lifting his arm to expose his midriff to the fatal blow by Damoxenos. Marble statue by Canova based on the story by Pausanias, A.D. 1801. Vatican, Cortile Ottagono, Gabinetto del Canova, inv. no. 968 (photo: L. Giordano).

Fig. 95 Damoxenos of Syracuse aiming the fatal blow at the midriff of Kreugas. Marble statue by Canova based on the story by Pausanias, A.D. 1801. Vatican, Cortile Ottagono, Gabinetto del Canova, inv. no. 970 (photo: L. Giordano).

assume that certain parts of the body were off-limits. Victory was decided when one of the boxers either would not or could not continue. In the former case, he would signal his defeat by raising a single finger (fig. 91; see also fig. 8). Occasionally, an apparently dazed boxer would signal in the wrong direction, toward the waiting boxer, who would relay the signal to the judge (fig. 92). There are also depictions of boxers who have clearly had enough and are "signaling" their defeat by running away (fig. 93).

Fatalities were known in the boxing but none so infamous as the death at the Nemean Games reported by Pausanias (8.40.4–5; A 38):

The Argives gave the crown of victory at the Nemean Games to Kreugas of Epidamnos [fig. 94] although he was dead, because his opponent, Damoxenos of Syracuse [fig. 95], broke the agreement reached between them. While they were boxing evening came on, and they agreed in front of witnesses that each would allow the other in turn to land a punch. Now at that time boxers did not yet wear the hard himas on the wrist of each hand, but boxed with the soft himantes, which were bound in the hollow of the hand so that the fingers were left bare. . . . Now Kreugas aimed his punch at Damoxenos's head. Then Damoxenos told Kreugas to lift his arm, and when Kreugas had done so, Damoxenos struck him under the ribs with his fingers straight out. The combination of his sharp fingernails and the force of his blow drove his hand into Kreugas's guts. He grabbed Kreugas's intestines and tore them out, and Kreugas died on the spot. The Argives expelled Damoxenos on the grounds that he had broken his agreement by giving his opponent several blows [that is, one for each of his fingers] instead of the agreed-upon single blow. They gave the victory to the dead Kreugas and erected a statue of him in Argos.

The potential for death and serious injury in the pyx makes it all the more extraordinary that there were competitions in this event for boys. The event joined the program at Olympia in 616, only four Olympiads after a stadion and a pale were established for paides, and it was later contested at all the crown games.

THE PANKRATION

The most violent of ancient athletic competitions was the pankration, which combined the pale and the pyx into the "all-powerful" event described by the word. The pankration entered the Olympic program in 648. In artistic depictions it can be distinguished from the pale by the contorted holds that frequently are applied on the ground, and from the pyx by the absence of himantes and flowing blood—although the pankration produced its share of blood through various wounds; bloody fingerprints are smeared on the bodies of the competitors (fig. 96). The most succinct ancient description of the event is given by Philostratos: "The pankratiasts . . . practice a dangerous brand of wrestling. They have to endure black eyes, which are not safe for the wrestler, and learn holds by which one who has fallen can still win, and they must be skillful in various ways of strangulation. They bend ankles and twist arms and throw punches and jump on their opponents. All such practices are permitted in the pankration except for biting and gouging" (*Pictures in a Gallery* 2.6; A 45).

The tendency to try to gouge one's opponent—as well as enforcement of the prohibition against both it and biting—can be seen in the visual documents (figs. 97, 98). The myth of Herakles and the Nemean lion associates that hero with the pankration: because the skin of the lion could not be penetrated, making biting, gouging, and

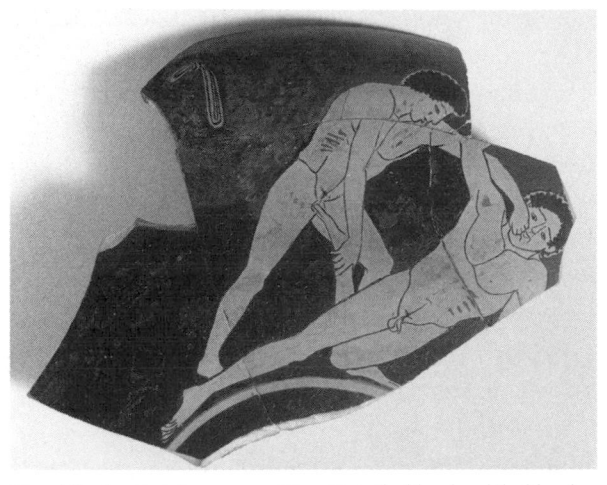

Fig. 96 Pankratiasts in a competition. Note the blood and the bloody handprints on each. Fragment of a red-figure kylix by Onesimos, 500–490 B.C. New York, The Metropolitan Museum of Art, lent by Dietrich von Bothmer, L 2002.21 (photo: © 2002 The Metropolitan Museum of Art).

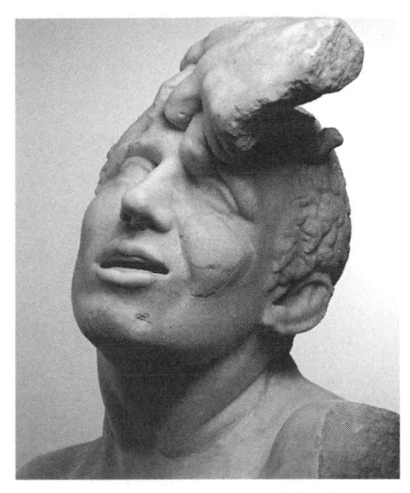

Fig. 97 A pankratiast tries to pull the finger of his opponent out of his eye socket. Fragment of a marble statue, Hellenistic period. Wallmoden Collection, on loan at Göttingen University, Archaeological Institute, no. 20, courtesy of HRH the Prince of Hannover, Duke of Brunswick and Lüneburg (photo: Stephan Eckardt).

Fig. 98 The pankratiast on the right is gouging the eye of his opponent with his thumb and is about to be flogged by the judge for committing the foul. Red-figure kylix by the Foundry Painter, ca. 490 B.C. London, The British Museum, inv. no. E 78 (1850.3–2.2) (photo: © The British Museum).

Fig. 99 Herakles wrestling the Nemean lion, the mythological prototype of the pankration. Poor lion! No biting or gouging allowed. Black-figure amphora, by Psiax, ca. 510 B.C. Brescia, Museo Civico Romano, no inv. no. (photo: M. Rapuzzi).

sharp weapons useless, Herakles was forced to wrestle with the lion, finally strangling him (fig. 99). Herakles, the personification of strength, even brute force, was the patron of pankratiasts.

Brutality was, indeed, a key feature of the pankration. One athlete, for example, specialized in bending fingers—and breaking them if necessary (Pausanias 6.4.2; A 46). Kicking was also allowed in the pankration, as well as various defensive moves against kicking (figs. 100, 101). It has been suggested that pankratiasts could kick each other in the genitals, but the evidence for this is ambiguous (fig. 102). What is clear is

Fig. 100 A pankratiast thwarted in the attempt to kick his opponent. Panathenaic amphora by the Kleophrades Painter, ca. 490 B.C. New York, The Metropolitan Museum of Art, inv. no. 16.71, Rogers Fund, 1916 (photo: © 2001 The Metropolitan Museum of Art).

Fig. 101 A pankratiast about to pay for a failed kick by having his leg yanked up to throw him off balance. Panathenaic amphora by the Kleophrades Painter, ca. 490 B.C. Leiden, Rijksmuseum voor Oudheden, inv. no. PC 6.

Fig. 102 The pankratiast on the left kicks his opponent (in the genitals?) while the judge prepares to flog him. White-ground kyathos in the Group of Vatican G.58, 530–520 B.C. Rome, Villa Giulia, tomba 371 Recinto.

that the victor was determined, as in boxing, by the inability or unwillingness of one of the competitors to continue. The point is demonstrated graphically by one of the most famous athletic stories from ancient Greece, a version of which appears in Philostratos's *Pictures in a Gallery* (2.6; A 45). Arrhachion of Phigaleia, the pankration victor at Olympia in 572 and 568, returned for a third try in 564. In the final bout,

> Arrhachion's opponent, having already a grip around his waist, thought to kill him and put an arm around his neck to choke off his breath. At the same time he slipped his legs through Arrhachion's groin and wound his feet inside Arrhachion's knees, pulling back until the sleep of death began to creep over Arrhachion's senses. But Arrhachion was not done yet, for as his opponent began to relax the pressure of his legs, Arrhachion kicked away his own right foot and fell heavily to the left, holding his opponent at the groin with his left knee still holding his opponent's foot firmly. So violent was the fall that the opponent's left ankle was wrenched from his socket. The man strangling Arrhachion . . . signaled with his hand that he gave up.

Fig. 104 Pentathletes with diskos, halteres, and a pick to dig the jumping pit. Javelins lean against the wall at the center, and a flute player provides a rhythm for the jumper. Red-figure kylix by the Carpenter Painter, ca. 510 B.C. Malibu, Calif., The J. Paul Getty Museum, inv. no. 85.AE.25 (photo: Ellen Rosenbery).

Fig. 103 Pentathletes with diskos, akon (javelin), and halteres (jumping weights). Panathenaic amphora by the Euphiletos Painter, ca. 530 B.C. Leiden, Rijksmuseum voor Oudheden, inv. no. PC 8.

Thus Arrhachion became a three-time Olympic victor at the moment of his death. His corpse, like that of the boxer Kreugas, received the victory crown.

The Olympic pankration was open to the paides age group only as of 200 B.C., but no tender sensibilities delayed the organizers of the other games. The pankration for boys became an event at Delphi, for example, in 346, just at the time when athletics was developing into an entertainment business.

THE PENTATHLON

The name of this event suggests that there were five prizes, but as in today's pentathlon a single winner collected one prize for the five competitions, which joined the Olympic program in 708 along with the pale. Two of the five competitions were contested both as pentathlon and as independent events: the stadion race and wrestling. The other three were contested only as a part of the pentathlon: the diskos throw, the *halma* (jump), and the *akon* (javelin throw). Although we do not know the exact criteria for victory in the pentathlon, it is clear that as in multi-event competitions today winners had to be good in more than one sport. The best diskos thrower, for example, had no chance to become an Olympic victor if he could not perform at least two other events well. Perhaps because of the equipment involved, the pentathlon was a favorite of ancient vase painters, who frequently showed the three specialized competitions together (figs. 103, 104).

The diskos throw was not unlike the modern competition, although the degree to which the diskos was standardized is not clear. There are stone and iron diskoi, but the most common material is bronze, and the most common size is about 21 centimeters in diameter with a weight of about 2 kilograms, the same as the modern discus

Fig. 105 Diskos from Aigina with incised depictions of a javelin thrower and (on the other side) of a jumper. Diameter: 21 cm; weight: 1.984 kg. Bronze, ca. 450 B.C. Berlin, Staatliche Museen — Preussischer Kulturbesitz, Antikensammlung, no. FR 1273 (photo: Ingrid Geske-Heiden).

Fig. 106 Diskos with the name Flavius Scribonianus as chief of security (alytarches) during the 255th Olympiad; the other side bears the name of the dedicator Popl(ios) Asklepiades from Corinth. Diameter: 34 cm; weight: 5.707 kg. Bronze, A.D. 241. Olympia, Archaeological Museum, inv. no. M 891.

Fig. 107 Pentathlete holding a diskos with an owl depicted on it. Hanging on the wall is his kit: aryballos, stlengis, sponge. Red-figure column krater by Myson, ca. 500 B.C. Oxford, Ashmolean Museum, inv. no. G 297.

(fig. 105). An extremely heavy diskos from Olympia was dedicated by a successful pentathlete, but it was surely not used in competition; it was probably just a thank-offering to Zeus (fig. 106). Pausanias (6.19.4; A 56) states that three diskoi, "the number that are used in the pentathlon," were kept in the treasury of the Sikyonians at Olympia. This should be understood to mean that each athlete threw each diskos once, but it is not clear that the three diskoi were the same size or weight. A series of Attic vase paintings show diskoi decorated with an owl, presumably signifying that they belonged to the state of Athens, but the sizes of the diskoi vary significantly, and vase painters may always be charged with inaccuracy (compare figs. 107 and 108, also figs. 110 and 112). Nonetheless, we cannot exclude the possibility that athletes competed with a graduated set of diskoi, using larger, heavier diskoi as they advanced through the competition.

The starting position of the diskos throw is frequently shown by vase painters, who could most easily capture that moment of immobility. The athlete stands with his weight on his right, rear leg, holding the diskos at head level in a vertical position; the left hand supports the weight of the diskos while the right, throwing hand grasps the top edge (fig. 108). (Again, all our examples show right-handers.) This stance is verified not only by its frequent portrayal but by an amphora showing an athlete being corrected because he has the wrong foot forward (fig. 109). In the vase paintings it is not clear whether the athletes in the starting position are looking down the track of the stadium in the direction they are about to throw or have their backs to the track, so we don't know whether they simply twisted their bodies to throw or twisted and spun a half-turn like today's discus throwers before releasing. We do know that the balbis acted as the foul line.

Fig. 108 Pentathlete positioned to start the diskos throw, watched by a judge holding his rhabdos at right. Behind the judge is a pick, used to dig the pit for the jump. Red-figure krater by the Kleophrades Painter, 500–490 B.C. Tarquinia, Museo Archeologico, inv. no. RC 4196 B.

Fig. 109 A pentathlete prepares to start the diskos throw, but he has placed the wrong foot forward. His colleague to the left and the judge to the right both express their disapproval. The once-legible inscription beneath the left arm of the diskobolos read, "Phaÿllos"; that beneath left arm of the youth read, "pentathlon"; the one diagonally down from the head of the judge read, "Orismenes." Red-figure amphora by Euthymides, ca. 500 B.C. Munich, Staatliche Antikensammlungen und Glyptothek, inv. no. 2308.

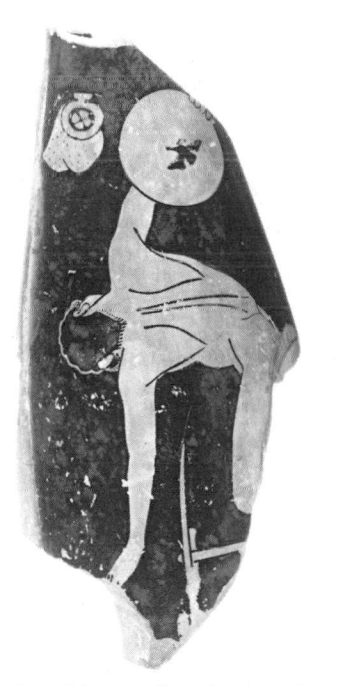

Fig. 110 Pentathlete seen from the rear swinging his arm back, picking up his left leg (note the bent knee), and bending down to coil his body in preparation for the throw. Note the flying owl on the diskos, the pick below, and the aryballos and sponge on the wall. Fragment of red-figure alabastron by Onesimos, ca. 490 B.C. Martin von Wagner Museum, Universität Würzburg, inv. no. L 545 (photo: K. Oehrlein).

Fig. 111 A spinning pentathlete about to shift his weight to the left foot. The inscription reads, "the boy is kalos." Red-figure tondo, ca. 480 B.C. Athens, American School of Classical Studies, Agora Excavations, inv. no. P 2698 (photo: Craig Mauzy).

Fig. 112 A pentathlete (in the ageneios category?) at the point of release in the diskos throw, watched by a judge at the right. The athlete's left foot should have been shown forward, producing the thrust. Panathenaic amphora by the Achilles Painter, ca. 440 B.C. Naples, Museo Nazionale, inv. no. 81294.

Fig. 113 A diskos thrower reaches out toward his semeion. The inscription reads, "Kalos is the boy." Red-figure kylix by Pheidippos, ca. 510 B.C. Martin von Wagner Museum, Universität Würzburg, inv. no. L 467 (photo: K. Oehrlein).

The depictions of diskos throwers twisting their bodies make it clear that as the throwing arm came back, the athlete would bend over to prepare the torsion of his body for the throw, keeping his weight on his right leg (fig. 110). As he started his throw, he would spin around in the opposite direction, shifting his weight to the left foot (fig. 111). He would then extend his body; as the torsion was released, the left leg would provide the extra thrust to help propel the discus (fig. 112; see also fig. 284). The *diskobolos* (diskos thrower) was a favorite of sculptors, whose interest in anatomy and in the suggestion of motion was best satisfied by this competition (see figs. 286 and 287).

The athlete who threw the farthest won. Vase painters frequently show an athlete with a diskos marking his throw with a small peg, or *semeion* (fig. 113). It is likely that each athlete labeled his peg in some distinctive way and moved it after each throw that improved his distance. Although he may have been permitted three throws at Olympia, there is some evidence from the island of Rhodes that five throws were allowed; the rules may have differed at different sites (*SEG* 15.501; A 52).

Contestants in the long jump (halma) used weights called *halteres* (singular, *halter*), which came in two basic types identified by modern scholars as the spherical and the long. There was no chronological progression from one type to another: they appear on vases being used in the same competition (fig. 114). The spherical halter was made of stone and carved to fit the hand. A pair of halteres would be created specifically with a grip for the fingers on one side and a hole for the thumb on the other (figs. 115, 116; see also figs. 124, 125). There are also examples where the stone was carved with a seat for the hand around the exterior but a finger hole through the halter itself. The so-called long halteres were simple weights made of lead. The earliest of these is rectangular and only slightly reduced in size at the center for the hand (fig. 117). If it were not inscribed as the dedication of an athlete, we would probably not know that it was a halter.

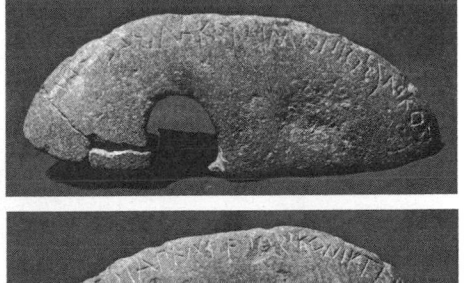

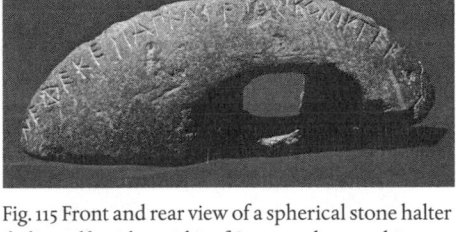

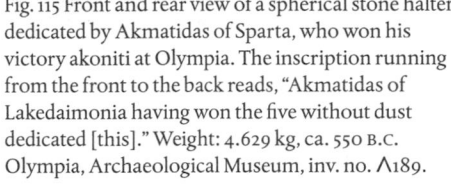

Fig. 114 Pentathletes: jumpers flanking a diskos thrower. The jumper on the left holds a spherical halter, the jumper on the right a pair of long halteres. Red-figure column krater by Myson, ca. 480 B.C. Rome, Villa Giulia, inv. no. 1044.

Fig. 115 Front and rear view of a spherical stone halter dedicated by Akmatidas of Sparta, who won his victory akoniti at Olympia. The inscription running from the front to the back reads, "Akmatidas of Lakedaimonia having won the five without dust dedicated [this]." Weight: 4.629 kg, ca. 550 B.C. Olympia, Archaeological Museum, inv. no. Λ189.

More characteristic are simple, rounded halteres fitted to the hand, such as we see in figures 103, 104, 122, 123, and 127, while a more elaborate, articulated pair is stamped with signs, presumably of ownership (fig. 118). The two halteres of this pair differ in weight by 0.131 kilograms, or nearly 9 percent. Another pair, discovered in a tomb in Taranto, differ by 0.285 kilograms (2.050 kilograms to 1.765 kilograms), or about 16 percent. Another halter (fig. 119), unique among preserved examples for its squared shape at the front end (although we see this shape in vase paintings; see figs. 114, 126) and its material (bronze), is inscribed with a rooster on both sides and a dedication to Apollo. Finally, from the Roman period comes a new, cylindrical halter, which is known in a single example (fig. 120).

From these and other examples, it is clear that the halteres did not have a standard weight, even within a pair. Nonetheless, the weights usually range from 1.5 to 2.5 kilograms, although the halter dedicated by Akmatidas (fig. 115) is much heavier. Probably he did not actually use this jumping weight, but made it as a dedication, like the diskos of Asklepiades discussed above (fig. 106). On the other hand, such a pair of weights might have propelled him to a better jump. Clearly the halteres were the personal possessions of the individual athlete, designed specifically for him. This must be why the halter, the physical representative of only one event of the five, was so frequently dedicated as thanks for a victory in the pentathlon as a whole.

The jump itself was made from the *bater* (literally, "that which is trod upon"), the precise nature of which is not known. I suspect that it was a simple board embedded in the surface of the stadium track for the halma and then removed. The jumpers

Fig. 116 Pair of spherical stone halteres from Corinth. Weight: 2.018 kg each, 6th–early 5th century B.C. Athens, National Museum, inv. no. 1926 (photo: © Treasury of Archaeological Receipts).

Fig. 117 Lead halter from Eleusis. The inscription reads, "Epainetos won the jump because of this halter." Weight: 2.199 kg, late 6th century B.C. Athens, National Museum, inv. no. X 9075 (IG 1² 802; photo: © Treasury of Archaeological Receipts).

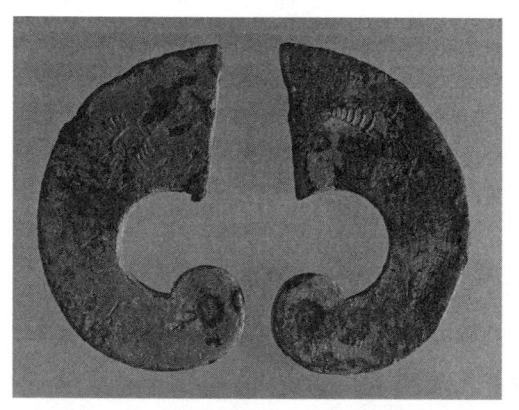

Fig. 118 Pair of long lead halteres stamped with stylized lobsters (perhaps a sign of ownership). Weight: 1.611 and 1.480 kg, 5th century B.C. Copenhagen, National Museum, Department of Classical and Near Eastern Antiquities, inv. no. Aba 364.

Fig. 119 Long bronze halter with an incised rooster and an inscription reading, "And Eumelos dedicated me to Good-Throwing Apollo." Weight: 1.847 kg, ca. 500 B.C. Courtesy George Ortiz (see *In Pursuit of the Absolute: Art of the Ancient World, the George Ortiz Collection* [rev. ed.; Bern, 1996], no. 128 bis).

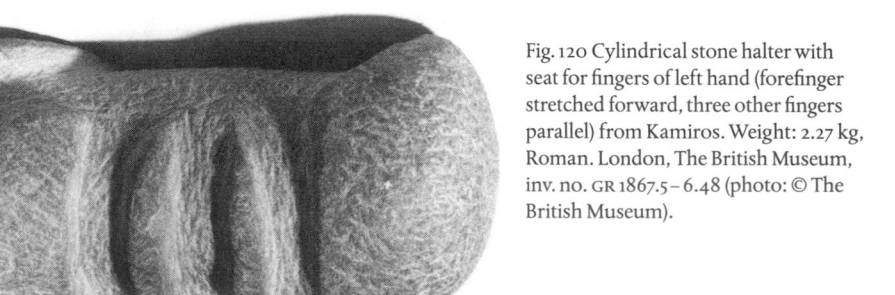

Fig. 120 Cylindrical stone halter with seat for fingers of left hand (forefinger stretched forward, three other fingers parallel) from Kamiros. Weight: 2.27 kg, Roman. London, The British Museum, inv. no. GR 1867.5–6.48 (photo: © The British Museum).

Fig. 121 Athletes digging the skamma in preparation for the jump. Red-figure stemless cup, side B, 430–420 B.C. Leiden, Rijksmuseum voor Oudheden, inv. no. GNV 71.

Fig. 122 Pentathlete (center) poised for the jump while the flute player (left) provides the rhythm. Another pentathlete (right) stands poised for the javelin throw. The athletes wear close-fitting caps indicating that they are simply practicing, not competing. Red-figure kylix by the Colmar Painter, ca. 500 B.C. Munich, Staatliche Antikensammlungen und Glyptothek, inv. no. 2667.

Fig. 123 Pentathlete with halteres running toward the jumping line. A pair of javelins leans against the wall behind him. The inscription reads, "Athenodotos is kalos." Red-figure tondo by the Proto-Panaitian Group, ca. 510–500 B.C. Boston, Museum of Fine Arts, inv. no. 98.876 (photo: © 2002 Museum of Fine Arts, Boston, reproduced with permission).

Fig. 124 Pentathlete leaping from the bater swinging his halteres forward. Black-figure tondo near the Painter of Vatican G 69, ca. 510 B.C. Paris, Musée du Louvre, inv. no. C 10376, Réunion des Musées Nationaux / Art Resource, New York.

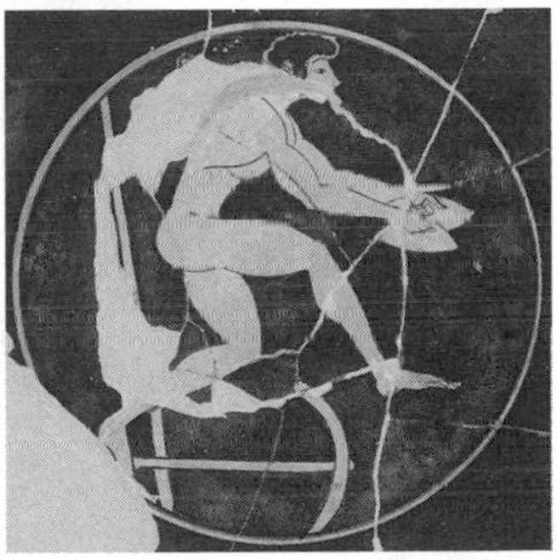

Fig. 125 Pentathlete leaping from the bater swinging his halteres forward. The pick used for digging the skamma lies below, and a javelin is behind him. Red-figure tondo by Pamphilos, ca. 510 B.C. Paris, Musée du Louvre, inv. no. CA 2526, Réunion des Musées Nationaux / Art Resource, New York (photo: Herve Lewandowski).

landed in a skamma, or "dug-up" area, which is sometimes misleadingly translated as "pit." Sand in the jumping pit is a modern invention, attested from the ancient world neither in written sources nor in the physical remains. Rather, the skamma was a simple, temporary space dug at the time of the competitions (fig. 121); the picks that are frequently seen in depictions of pentathletes are an allusion to the skamma and thereby the halma (for example, figs. 104, 108, 110, 125).

The nature of the jump can be deduced from the various phases portrayed by ancient vase painters. The athlete would lean back, bracing himself on his right leg, which was bent at the knee (fig. 122), and extending his left leg forward. Holding a

Fig. 126 Pentathlete in mid-jump flanked by two other pentathletes holding halteres, a flute player, and a judge (at left). Red-figure kylix by Douris, ca. 490 B.C. Antikenmuseum Basel und Sammlung Ludwig, inv. no. KÄ 425 (photo: Claire Niggli).

Fig. 127 Pentathlete descending from the apex of his leap while another pentathlete warms up at left and a judge watches from the right to see how his feet land. Red-figure kylix by Onesimos, 500–490 B.C. Boston, Museum of Fine Arts, inv. no. 01.8020 (photo: © 2002 Museum of Fine Arts, Boston, reproduced with permission).

Fig. 128 Pentathlete landing, having pulled the halteres back behind him, watched by a judge on right and a pentathlete with javelins on left. Beneath the jumper are the semeia marking earlier jumps. Black-figure amphora of the Tyrrhenian Group, ca. 540 B.C. The inscriptions seem intended to label athletes by name, but they are mostly nonsense. London, The British Museum, inv. no. B 48 (1847.8–6.26) (photo: © The British Museum).

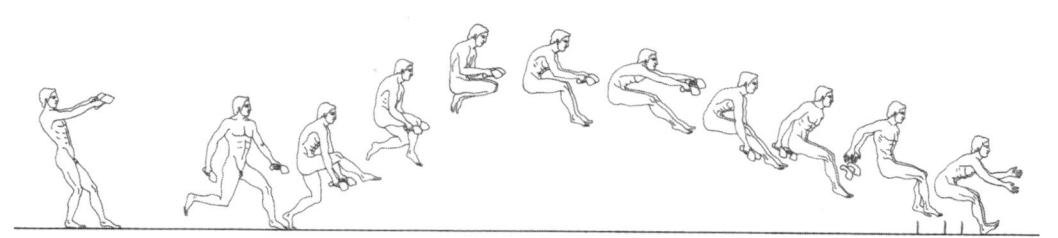

Fig. 129 Reconstruction of the halma sequence based on vase paintings. Drawing by Ruben Santos.

halma in each hand and extending his arms in front of him, he would stand poised, muscles tensed, listening to a flute player, an essential component of the halma. The music of the flute was supposed to help the athlete establish his rhythm and timing so as to coordinate the motion of his hands and feet with the correct use of the halteres. As Philostratos tells us: "The rules regard jumping as the most difficult of the competitions, and they allow the jumper to be given advantages in rhythm by the use of the flute, and in weight by the use of the halter" (*On Gymnastics* 35; A 47).

We should picture the athlete, then, rocking back and forth as he listens to the music and then breaking forward into his run (fig. 123). At the bater he springs into the

Fig. 130 The three events unique to the pentathlon (from left): halma, akon, diskos, akon again. Panathenaic amphora by the so-called Euphiletos Painter, ca. 520 B.C. London, The British Museum, inv. no. B 134 (1842.3–14.1) (photo: © The British Museum).

air swinging the halteres to pull him forward (figs. 124, 125; note that the images of the actual leap were particularly fitted to the circular tondo of the interior of a drinking cup—to the best of my knowledge they are never shown on the outside of a cup or on any other vessel). Once in the air the athlete pulls his legs up into an aerodynamic tuck while the halteres continue to pull him forward by inertia (fig. 126). To complete the jump, he stretches out his feet and his hands in front of him (fig. 127), then swings the halteres behind him for added thrust, and finally drops them as he lands (fig. 128). The whole sequence can be reconstructed based on these and other vase paintings (fig. 129). The longest jump won, but the footprints had to be clear for the jump to count. As in the diskos, each athlete marked his jump with a semeion.

Some modern scholars reconstruct the ancient jump as a triple jump. However, the only evidence for the halma are the images presented here, and they can be satisfactorily reconstructed as a jump that is similar to today's long jump, with the addition of the weights and flute. The attempts to reconstruct it as a triple jump derive from a source ascribing a jump of an extraordinary 55 ancient feet (about 16.5 meters) to Phaÿllos of Kroton (perhaps actually portrayed in figure 109). Phaÿllos was, indeed, a well-known, successful athlete who won at Delphi in 482 and 478, but he was fighting against the Persians at the time of the 480 Olympics, and never won at Olympia. The first mention of his fabulous leap comes about six hundred years after his death; earlier authors who mention him do not say anything about it. Further, the ditty that credits him with that incredibly long jump also states that he threw the diskos 95 ancient feet (about 28.5 meters), which is not particularly impressive. In fact, the anonymous author of the poem about Phaÿllos that mentions his long jump and his short throw is clearly engaging in creative writing. The 55–foot jump belongs to the same category of late mythologizing as the run from Marathon to Athens.

The third competition unique to the pentathlon was the javelin, or akon, throw (fig. 130). To judge from the vase paintings, the akon (or *akontion*, as it was sometimes

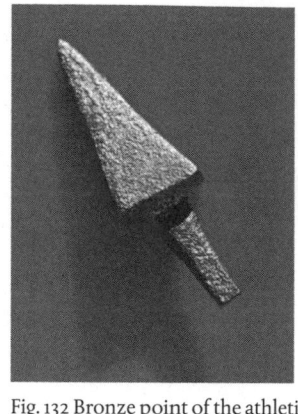

Fig. 131 Pentathlete preparing to throw the akon. His athletic kit of aryballos, stlengis, and sponge hangs to the left, while another javelin and a diskos with an owl emblem lie on the right. The black at the end of the javelin denotes a bronze tip on the wooden shaft. Red-figure amphora attributed to the Eucharides Painter, 490–470 B.C. Brussels, Musées Royaux d'Art et d'Histoire, inv. no. A 721, A (photo: museum).

Fig. 132 Bronze point of the athletic akon. Length of point: 2 cm. The tine is broken, but other examples show that it was typically about twice as long as the point itself, flattened to a sharp end to ease insertion in wood. Nemea, Archaeological Museum, inv. no. BR 1577 (photo: University of California, Nemea Excavations Archives).

called) was about 1.9 meters long and about the diameter of a human thumb or slightly thicker. We read in our sources that it was made of elder wood and tipped in bronze. Few vase painters even try to show the bronze point at the end of the akon; the images we have show that it was small and hardly differentiated in size from the shaft (fig. 131). Clearly the vase painters understood the difference between the athletic akon and the military and hunting *dory* with its broad-bladed head, frequently made of iron, and always intended for destructive purposes. Modern scholars have sometimes failed to make this distinction, calling both types "spears." I shall use the word "javelin" for the piece of equipment used in the pentathlon, and "spear" for the one used in hunting and battle. Pyramidal-shaped bronze points with tines at the back for insertion into the end of a wooden shaft are probably javelin tips (fig. 132).

The feature of the akon throw that differentiates it from the modern javelin competition was the use of the *ankyle,* a thin leather thong that was wrapped around the shaft to make a loop for the first two fingers of the throwing hand. This is seen repeatedly on ancient vase paintings (figs. 103, 122, 130, 135–39). The loop provided leverage and acted like a sling to propel the akon, and as it was released the ankyle unwound, producing a rifling effect on the shaft. Erroneous modern reconstructions notwithstanding, it is clear that the ankyle was not tied to the shaft of the akon: it would fall off after unwinding completely. Indeed, the vase paintings clearly show that no knot was used on the ankyle.

Wrapping the ankyle took care and skill, for it played an important role in the success of the throw. Thus, one vase painting shows the javelin being measured to determine the best place to attach the ankyle (fig. 133). Depictions of pentathletes bending down to the ground with their javelins show them actually wrapping the ankyle around the shaft (fig. 134). The athlete would loop the center of the ankyle around his

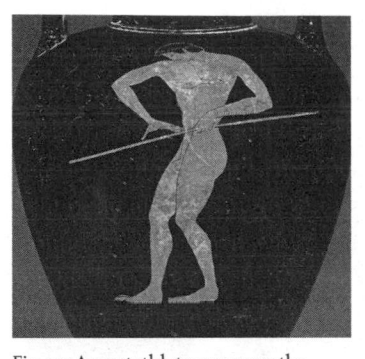

Fig. 133 A pentathlete measures the shaft of his akon with his hand to determine the best place to attach the ankyle. Red-figure amphora by Euthymides, 520–510 B.C. Malibu, Calif., The J. Paul Getty Museum, inv. no. 84.AE.63 (photo: Ellen Rosenbery).

Fig. 134 Pentathlete wrapping the ankyle around the shaft of his javelin. Note that the ankyle passes around the big toe of the left foot. Red-figure kylix by the Bowdoin Eye Painter, ca. 510 B.C. Martin von Wagner Museum, Universität Würzburg, inv. no. L 469 (photo: K. Oehrlein).

Fig. 135 Four pentathletes preparing their javelins under the supervision of a judge or trainer. Note that the second and fourth athletes from the left have inserted only their index fingers into the loop of the ankyle. Red-figure kylix by the Triptolemos Painter, ca. 490 B.C. Toledo, Ohio, Toledo Museum of Art, inv. no. 1961.26, gift of Edward Drummond Libbey.

big toe and place the loose ends on the javelin shaft, which he would then roll so as to wrap the ankyle over the loose ends. He would finish by removing his toe from the loop. To throw the javelin, he would insert his index and, usually, the second finger of his right hand (there are no instances of left-handed javelin throwers except where modern publications have reversed photographs) into this loop, while his two smallest fingers and thumb gripped the javelin shaft (figs. 135–137). At the same time, he would hold the tip of the javelin by the fingers of his left hand in order to force the javelin, and the loop of the ankyle, back, thereby maintaining the pressure necessary to keep the ankyle from unraveling prematurely. Pindar calls this the shaking-down of his javelin (Pythian 1.43–45; A 63). The vase painters sometimes show flute players

Fig. 136 Pentathlete preparing to throw a javelin. Note that he has inserted his index and second fingers into the loop of the ankyle. Red-figure kylix by Oltos, ca. 500 B.C. Paris, Musée du Louvre, inv. no. F 126, Réunion des Musées Nationaux / Art Resource, New York (photo: Herve Lewandowski).

Fig. 137 Pentathlete preparing to throw a javelin. Note that he has inserted his index and second fingers into the loop of the ankyle. Red-figure tondo by the Thalia Painter, ca. 500 B.C. Paris, Musée du Louvre, inv. no. G 37, Réunion des Musées Nationaux / Art Resource, New York (photo: M. Chuzeville).

accompanying the javelin throw as if difficulty in the use of the ankyle necessitated their help, but the written sources are silent on this practice. Perhaps the presence of flute players at one event of the pentathlon (the jump) caused vase painters to associate them with all the events.

Now came the actual throw. This began with a run up, during which the javelin was raised to shoulder level, although the athlete still held the tip with his left hand, maintaining pressure on the ankyle (fig. 138). As he released the tip (fig. 139) he would bring his right arm forward to throw the javelin. The final phase, after the javelin was released and the ankyle flew off, does not appear in any extant works of art. (Note, likewise, that the diskos is never shown in the air.)

But two vase paintings suggest that the sequence was not this straightforward (figs. 140, 141). In them we clearly see that the javelin thrower has also twisted his body, somewhat like a diskos thrower. The torsion of the body, along with the centrifugal force exerted on the javelin by the hand traveling in a half-circle, would add to the force of the throw. The slingshot effect of the ankyle was an extension and enhancement of the same effect from the untwisting of the body. It is not surprising that an ancient javelin might be thrown as far as a modern one; recent experiments with the twisting release and the ankyle have produced throws of as long as 94 meters; the best javelin throws at the Atlanta Olympics of 1996 were in the range of 88 meters.

The winner was determined by the length of the throw, as we see from images showing athletes using a marker (semeion), just as they did in the diskos throw (fig. 142), and as we read in Pindar: "I hope that I shall not throw the bronze-tipped akon

Fig. 138 Pentathlete running up in the javelin throw. He is still holding the javelin with his left hand and pushing it back against the ankyle. Detail from a black-figure krater by the Rycroft Painter, ca. 520–510 B.C. Toledo, Ohio, Toledo Museum of Art, inv. no. 1963.26, gift of Edward Drummond Libbey.

Fig. 139 A pentathlete running up in the javelin throw has released the tip and begun his throw. His fingers are still in the loop of the ankyle. Panathenaic amphora, 510–500 B.C. Vatican, Museo Gregoriano Etrusco, Sala XIX — emiciclo inferiore, inv. no. 17048 (photo: P. Zigrossi).

which I shake down with my hand outside the limits of the contest, but shall conquer my opponents with long throws" (*Pythian* 1.43–45; *A 63*). Claims by modern scholars that accuracy played a role in the victory have only the evidence of a father defending his son in a case involving an accidental death in the gymnasion:

> We would not be able to show that my son had not caused the boy's death had the akontion struck him outside the area marked for its flight. But the boy ran into the path of the akontion and thus put his body in its way. Hence my son was unable to hit what he aimed at, and the boy was hit because he ran under the akontion; the cause of the accident, which is attributed to us, was not of our own making. Running into the path was why the boy was hit, and my son is unjustly accused. He did not hit anyone who stayed away from his target. Moreover, since it is clear to you that the other boy was not struck while standing still, but only after moving of his own volition into the path of the akontion, it should be quite clear to you that he was killed because of his own error. He would not have been killed had he remained still and not run across. [Antiphon, *Second Tetralogy* 2.1–8: *A 64*]

Fig. 140 Four pentathletes performing the sequence of the javelin throw. From left: 1) fixing the ankyle and shaking down the akon; 2) bringing the akon to shoulder height and releasing the tip; 3) twisting the upper body to introduce torsion, with the javelin at shoulder height; 4) extending the throwing arm with the javelin and untwisting the body, shifting the weight to the left, forward, leg. A fifth pentathlete (right) holds a diskos with an owl device and stands next to an altar above which hang an aryballos and a sponge. Red-figure kylix by the Carpenter Painter, 515–510 B.C. Malibu, Calif., The J. Paul Getty Museum, inv. no. 85.AE.25 (photo: Ellen Rosenbery).

Fig. 141 Three pentathletes in the javelin-throwing sequence. From left: 1) fixing the ankyle and shaking down the akon; 2) twisting the upper body to introduce torsion, with the javelin at shoulder height; 3) extending the throwing arm with the javelin and untwisting the body, shifting the weight to the left, forward, leg. The caps, worn perhaps to protect against getting the hair caught by the ankyle, indicate that this was a practice, not a competition. Red-figure kylix by the Colmar Painter, ca. 500 B.C. Munich, Staatliche Antiken-sammlungen und Glyptothek, inv. no. 2667.

Fig. 142 Two pentathletes hold their javelins while a judge prepares to mark a distance with a semeion. In the background, from left, are a diskos, javelin, and diskos bag hanging on the wall, and two javelins and a pick. Red-figure kylix by Onesimos, 490–480 B.C. Paris, Musée du Petit Palais, inv. no. 325A, Réunion des Musées Nationaux / Art Resource, New York (photo: Bulloz).

This is hardly evidence that the javelin was thrown at a target in the pentathlon competition, especially in the face of the other evidence that distance alone was the criterion of victory. Thus, the longest of five throws would have been marked and counted for each athlete.

Although we know most of the details of what happened in the individual competitions, how the overall decision was reached in the pentathlon is not well documented. We can estimate that the order of the events was stadion, diskos, halma, akon, pale. The evidence for this order is consistent in the sources, but all are from the Roman period. Since the order of events is significant for the determination of the winner of the pentathlon, other sequences are sometimes suggested to support different theories. The simple truth is that we do not know how the victor in the pentathlon was determined.

It is clear from the written sources and from visual evidence that the winner of any three of the competitions was the overall winner of the pentathlon event (fig. 143).

Fig. 143 Statue base of a pentathlete showing the starting positions for the stadion, pale, and akon, suggesting that he had won these three competitions (see also fig. 255 for another side of this base). Marble with traces of paint, ca. 510 B.C. Athens, National Museum, inv. no. 3476 (photo: © Treasury of Archaeological Receipts).

If there were only two competitors, a victor was assured. But how could there be a clear winner if the field were larger? Many possible solutions have been offered: point systems, elimination tournaments, and variations of the two. None has the advantage of ancient evidence. For every suggestion, someone has pointed out fatal flaws. It is perhaps the most frustrating of the gaps in our knowledge. As one recent scholar lamented, "We will probably never know how the pentathlon victor was determined." In fact, we can't even answer the question a student once asked me: "Are we sure the same system was used at all the sites for more than a millennium?"

I have already noted that the Olympic Games exhibited a sensitivity in restricting the number and type of competitions for boys. This concern was one of the differences between the games at Olympia and those at the other sites, and it holds true for the pentathlon paidon. Pausanias (5.9.1 and 6.15.8) tells us that the competition for boys was added to the Olympic program in 628, when it was won by Eutelidas of Lakedaimonia, but it was suspended immediately thereafter. It never reappeared in the Olympic program, and probably was never part of the Nemean Games. A pentathlon for boys was certainly common in the other games by the sixth century B.C., however. It would be nice to think that the Olympic authorities were concerned about the overdevelopment of young men at too early an age, and it may even be true, but it cannot be proven. We should note, however, that Aristotle, who produced a new edition of the list of Olympic victors from his own research, mentioned that not many athletes who won as paides won again as andres. Those who peaked too soon were too soon washed up, and it may be that the restriction at Olympia of competitions for boys in the pentathlon and most of the footraces was an acknowledgement of that potential harm.

In the ancient crown games the gymnikoi agones consisted of competitions in which each winner would be clear and obvious to the whole crowd. The criteria for victory were simple: the fastest, the strongest, the farthest. The winners knew they had won because they were—at least at that place for that moment—the best. Every other Greek knew it too.

Fig. 144 Chariot races at the funeral games of Patroklos. The inscriptions running between the horses and spectators read, "Sophilos painted me" and "The games of Patroklos"; the label to the right of the spectators identifies "Achilles." Black-figure dinos by Sophilos, ca. 590 B.C. Athens, National Museum, inv. no. 15499 (photo: © Treasury of Archaeological Receipts).

Fig. 145 Tethrippon shown in three-quarter view, with the turning post at the right. Panathenaic amphora by the Painter of Munich 1519, ca. 500 B.C. Vatican, Museo Gregoriano Etrusco, Sala XIX — emiciclo inferiore, inv. no. 17059 (photo: P. Zigrossi).

The Hippikos Agon (Horse Races)

The horse races were a fundamental component of the ancient games, especially the four-horse chariot race. As we have seen, they enjoyed the preeminent position in the funeral games of Patroklos; and they appear early in artistic portrayals as well (fig. 144). Yet despite its apparent popularity, the four-horse chariot race, or *tethrippon* (plural, *tethrippa*), was not added to the Olympic program until 680, after most of the events of the gymnikos agon had been established. Horses were expensive and could not be trained as a team for chariot racing unless someone was willing to cover the expenses. The relative costs of the gymnikos and the hippikos agon largely determined how often they were contested and who could compete in them.

Our evidence for details of the equestrian events is not very good. Ancient authors were interested in the excitement of the race as a spectacle, but not in the nuts and bolts of running it. Modern scholars generally agree that the tethrippon consisted of twelve laps around the hippodrome (horse track), but the length of the hippodrome is not known. The evidence is late and fragmentary, and no Greek hippodrome has been completely excavated. If we assume, as some have argued, that the hippodrome was three stadia long, then twelve laps (that is, twelve times down the track and twelve times back) would be a distance of about 14 kilometers.

The chariots would turn around a post that was sometimes called a kampter, as in the stadion races, and sometimes a *nyssa*. It appears frequently in representations of horse races (fig. 145). There was no dividing wall down the center of the track (the Roman spina), and head-on crashes did happen, as described in literary sources (see, for example, Sophokles' *Elektra* 727–28; A 68).

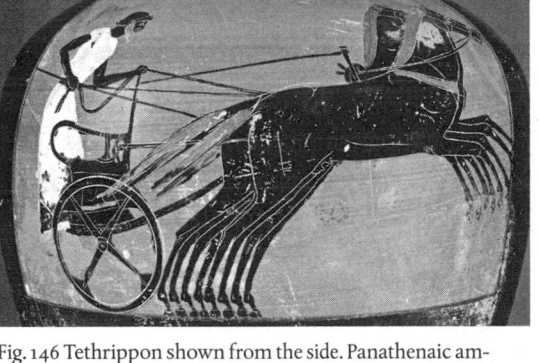

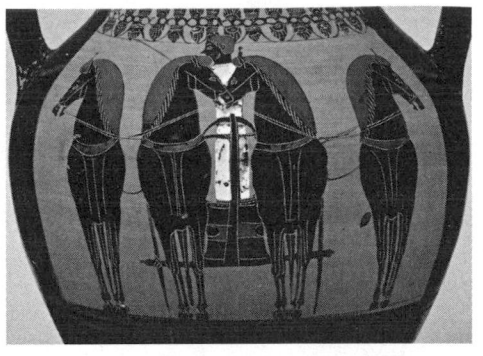

Fig. 146 Tethrippon shown from the side. Panathenaic amphora by the Kleophrades Painter, 490–480 B.C. Malibu, Calif., The J. Paul Getty Museum, inv. no. 77.AE.9, gift of Nicolas Koutoulakis in memory of J. Paul Getty (photo: Lou Meluso).

Fig. 147 Front view of tethrippon, showing how the horses were yoked to the chariot. Black-figure amphora by Exekias, ca. 540 B.C. Munich, Staatliche Antikensammlungen und Glyptothek, inv. no. 1396.

The chariot appears to have been a light vehicle with a metal or wicker cage around the floor where the charioteer stood (fig. 146). The wheel had four spokes with a central hole for the axle. It narrowed toward the rim, which was sheathed in metal. The horses were attached to the chariot in several ways (fig. 147). The yoke extended out and up, where it was attached to the collars of the two central horses, with a yoke pole that rose above the horses' backs tied to the top of the chariot frame, perhaps assisting in the stability of the chariot. The outside horses would be loosely connected by means of traces. The charioteer was usually a slave or a professional driver; he was rarely the owner of the tethrippon. He is always shown wearing a long *chiton* (tunic), holding a long lash and a number of reins, usually divided into two groups, one in the right hand and one in the left (see fig. 181). These were vital for negotiating the turn around the kampter, in which the two left (inside) horses had to be reined in, while the outside horses were encouraged to pull harder. Indeed, "right-trace horse" was used metaphorically to designate the fastest runner in a group regardless of the nature of the race or the number of legs on the runner. The charioteer also wore a broad waistband to which the ends of the reins were fastened. Something not always shown in artistic depictions, this device kept him from losing the reins completely.

Successful teams were cherished and sometimes had lengthy careers. Kimon, the father of Miltiades, the hero of Marathon, won three Olympic crowns with the same team of four horses. Obviously, speed was not the only prerequisite for victory; skill and teamwork in negotiating the turn played a decisive role. The horses were given names that ranged from the descriptive or hopeful to references to important men or mythic figures; some of these names appear on statues set up by victorious horse owners at Olympia. Pausanias (6.10.7; A 70) reports that Kleosthenes of Epidamnos set up statues of himself, his charioteer, and his horses, inscribed with their names: Phoinix and Korax (Raven) were the trace horses, and Knakias (Prickly) and Samos were the yoke horses. The names of horses were also given in painted scenes of tethrippon races; it is probable that some of these teams were famous and their names well known (fig. 148).

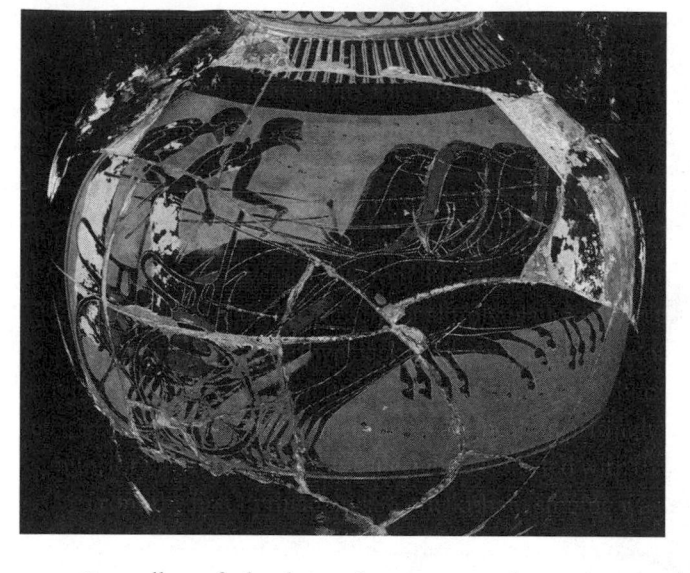

Fig. 148 Race between two tethrippa with labels giving the names of horses; only some are preserved. Legible at the top are "Minos," "Nikon" (Winner), and "Hipoto—" (Stud?); at the bottom one can read "Konon." Panathenaic amphora, 510–500 B.C. Paris, Musée du Louvre, inv. no. F 283, Réunion des Musées Nationaux / Art Resource, New York.

Regardless of who drove, the winner in a horse race was the owner of the horses, and his name entered the list of victors at Olympia and elsewhere. The prestige of an Olympic victory was enhanced in the equestrian events because of the wealth that such a victory implied. In 416, for example, Alkibiades of Athens entered seven tethrippa at Olympia. His son describes the reasons for his father's massive participation:

> During the years my father was married to my mother he saw that the festival at Olympia was beloved and admired by all men, and it was there that the Greeks made a display of wealth and strength of body and training, and the athletes were envied while the cities of the victors became renowned. In addition, he believed . . . that services at that festival offered credit to the city in the eyes of the whole of Greece. He thought these things through and, though in no way untalented nor weaker in his body, he held the gymnic games in contempt since he knew that some of the athletes were lowborn and from small city-states and poorly educated. Therefore he tried his hand at horse-breeding, work of the uppermost crust and not possible for a poor man, and he beat not only his competitors, but all previous winners. He entered a number of teams, something that not even the biggest city-states, as public entities, had ever done in the competitions, and their arete was such that he came in first, second, and third. [Isokrates, *Team of Horses* 32–33; A 67]

The reference to entries in the chariot race by city-states, rather than individuals, reveals another important difference between the gymnikos and the hippikos agon: the victor was not necessarily an individual. Indeed, we know from a fragment of papyrus with a partial list of Olympic victors (*POxy* 2.222; A 129) that the city-state of Argos

Fig. 150 Detail of figure 149. The second charioteer stoops to duck under handle of amphora.

Fig. 149 Tethrippon race. One kampter stands behind leading team, while another appears on the opposite side of the vase, giving the impression that one turn around the vase equaled a lap around the hippodrome. Black-figure amphora from the Circle of Leagros, 510–500 B.C. Cambridge, Mass., Arthur M. Sackler Museum, Harvard University Art Museums, William M. Prichard Fund, inv. no. 1933.54.

won the Olympic tethrippon victory in 472. Even more revealing is that a woman could win an equestrian victory at Olympia, even though women were prohibited from attending the games. The first female victor was Kyniska of Sparta, probably in 396. Her brother Agesilaos "noted that some of the citizens of Sparta thought that they were important because they were breeding horses, so he pressured his sister Kyniska to enter a chariot in the Olympic Games; he wanted to show the Greeks that an equestrian victory was the result of wealth and expenditure, not in any way the result of arete" (Plutarch, *Agesilaos* 20.1; A 151c).

Despite the snobbery of the chariot race, it was a popular spectacle, and some sense of that popularity appears in vase paintings of the sixth century where chariots race round and round the vase, accommodating the race to the vase (figs. 149, 150).

The horseback race, or *keles*, was added to the Olympic program in 648 and seems to have covered a distance of six stadia; that is, one run up and one down the hippodrome, approximately 1.2 kilometers. The jockeys were small boys, probably slaves, who rode without benefit of saddle or stirrups (which had not yet been invented), although they did have reins connected to a bit in the horse's mouth and a whip, similar to a riding crop (fig. 151). In early vases the jockeys are inexplicably portrayed in the

Fig. 151 Two entries in the keles race. Panathenaic amphora by the Eucharides Painter, ca. 490 B.C. New York, The Metropolitan Museum of Art, Fletcher Fund 1956, inv. no. 56.171.3. (Photo: © The Metropolitan Museum of Art).}

Fig. 152 The horses in a keles race are rounding the kampter while a judge raises his rhabdos as if to punish a foul. The vase was repaired in antiquity. Panathenaic amphora near the Painter of Berlin 1833, ca. 500 B.C. Leiden, Rijksmuseum voor Oudheden, inv. no. PC 7.

Fig. 153 Preparing for the keles race: a trainer or stable boy calms a fidgety horse as they head out to the track. Red-figure kylix by the Foundry Painter, ca. 480 B.C. St. Petersburg, The State Hermitage Museum, inv. no. B 1538.

Fig. 154 The synoris. Note the absence of details about the yoke and other equipment. Panathenaic amphora, ca. 200 B.C. Berlin, Staatliche Museen — Preussischer Kulturbesitz, Antikensammlung, inv. no. V.I. 4950.

nude. By the Hellenistic period they are usually shown wearing a chiton and frequently have negroid facial features. We also know that they, too, could be flogged for fouls (fig. 152). A sense of the nervous atmosphere of anticipation before the race occasionally comes through in some vase paintings (fig. 153), which also underline the extent of our ignorance about what went on behind the scenes in horse racing. For example, to the best of my knowledge no ancient stable has ever been identified.

Successful horses were as famous as they are today, both runners in the keles and the members of a tethrippon team. Hieron of Syracuse, for example, had a horse appropriately named Pherenikos (Victory Bringer) who won at Olympia in 476 and 472. Earlier (512) a mare named Breeze won for her owner, Pheidolas of Corinth, even though she had thrown her rider at the beginning of the race. She continued down the track, made the turn and, at the sound of the trumpet marking the home stretch, sprinted to the finish. Speed was important for a horse, but so was training.

The final equestrian event added to the Olympic program was the *synoris*, the

Fig. 155 The synoris. Gold coin of Philip II of Macedon (note his name on the coin) advertising his victory, probably at Olympia in 348 B.C. Note also the thunderbolt of Zeus beneath horses. Athens, Numismatic Museum, inv. no. 1395B (photo: © Treasury of Archaeological Receipts).

Fig. 156 The apene. Panathenaic amphora in the manner of the Kleophrades Painter, 500–480 B.C. London, The British Museum, inv. no. B 131 (1837.6 – 9.75) (photo: © The British Museum).

two-horse chariot race, in 408. The distance seems to have been eight laps of the hippodrome for a total of about 9.5 kilometers. Otherwise, it appears to have been basically the same as the tethrippon. It should be noted, however, that its relatively late addition to the program means that there are no representations of it in the art of the sixth and fifth centuries (figs. 154, 155).

The equestrian competitions were expanded with the addition of races for foals (about two years old), or *poloi* (singular, *polos*), the equestrian equivalent of the competitions for paides, although they appeared much later: the tethrippon polikon in 384, the synoris polikon in 264, and the keles polikon in 256. The distances were shorter than those for the races for full-grown horses, but otherwise the same rules apparently applied.

Two additions to the hippikos agon at Olympia in the fifth century were dropped relatively quickly. The first was the *apene*, or mule-cart race, added in 500. A pair of mules pulled a low cart carrying a seated driver (fig. 156). According to Pausanias (5.9.2; A 72) the race, or at least the animal, was thought to be undignified, so the apene was last competed at Olympia in 444. That was the same year another race, the *kalpe*, was also dropped. Pausanias tells us that the kalpe was added to the program in 496; apparently riders jumped off their mares and ran alongside them for the last lap. No certain depiction of the kalpe has come down to us. The limited period in which the apene and the kalpe were part of the Olympic program and the implicit lack of popularity of these events resulted in few representations made then or preserved now.

As mentioned before, no ancient Greek hippodrome has been discovered; therefore, we have no details about the size and shape of the track. Indeed, it is not even clear how many entrants may have participated in the various horse races.

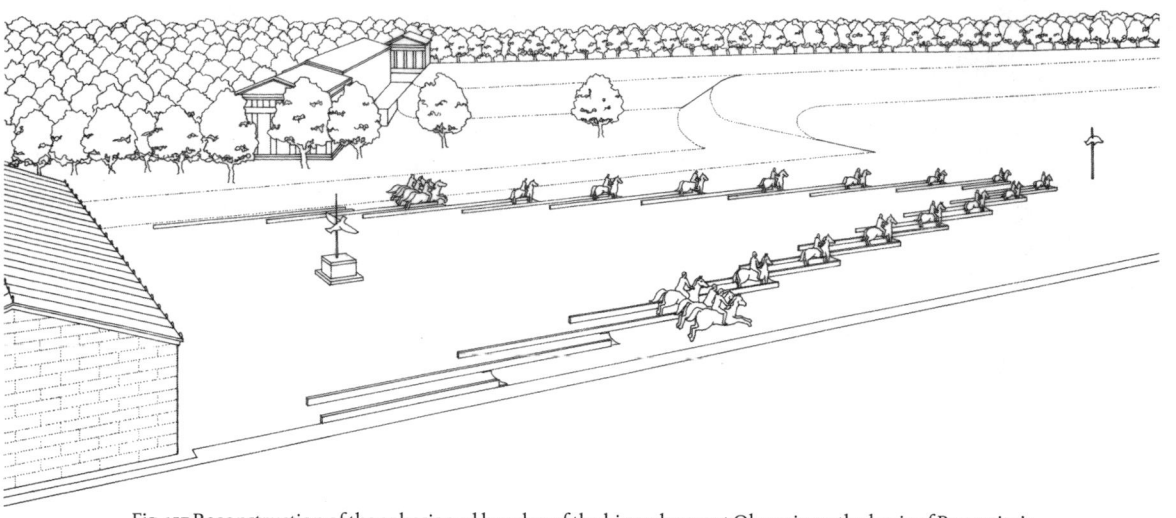

Fig. 157 Reconstruction of the aphesis and hysplex of the hippodrome at Olympia on the basis of Pausanias's description. Drawing by Ruben Santos.

Modern estimates have ranged from fifteen or twenty to fifty or sixty chariots. Despite this dismal lack of knowledge, we can still form a picture of features of the hippodrome at Olympia through Pausanias's description (6.20.10–19; A 69).

Pausanias writes that the starting area for all the horse races, the *aphesis,* was shaped like the prow of a ship pointed down the track, with a bronze dolphin on a rod at the tip of the prow (fig. 157). Each side of the aphesis was more than 400 ancient feet (about 120 meters) long and had stalls built into it, one for each entrant, who were assigned to their stalls by lot. Cords were stretched in front of the horses in their stalls. A mudbrick altar, plastered on the exterior, was constructed in the middle of the aphesis at the time of the games, and a bronze eagle with its wings outstretched was placed on top. When the race was ready to begin, the mechanism inside the altar was set in motion: the eagle would jump up and the dolphin fall, signals that the race had started. Then the cord across the stalls of the horses on each side of the aphesis farthest from the track would drop, and the horses in those stalls would take off. As they came up to the second stalls, the cords would drop for the second pair of horses; as they reached the third stall, the cords dropped for the third set, and so forth. And the race was on. The reason for this complicated staggered start is not clear.

Pausanias also tells us that on one side of the hippodrome stood an altar to Taraxippos, literally, "Horse Frightener." As they passed the circular altar, horses would suddenly, for no apparent reason, be seized with fear. There was a similar impediment at Isthmia in the form of an altar to Glaukos, son of Sisyphos, who had been killed by his horses at the funeral games of Akastos. Nemea had no hero like Taraxippos or Glaukos, but the glare from a red rock at the far turn scared the horses. In addition to speed, skill, and good training, then, the hippikos agon required a sure and

Fig. 159 An aulos player performs standing on a platform flanked by judges. Note the strap around his head and mouth. Panathenaic amphora by Eucharides, 500–470 B.C. St. Petersburg, The State Hermitage Museum, inv. no. Π 1911.12.

Fig. 158 A kithara singer performs on a platform in front of a young judge with a rhabdos who leans on a cane (left) and two older judges. Red-figure pelike by the Argos Painter, 500–475 B.C. St. Petersburg, The State Hermitage Museum, inv. no. B 1570.

steady hand from the charioteer or jockey, for his anxiety and fear of Taraxippos must have been transmitted to his horses.

The presence of such psychological hurdles emphasizes the basic difference between the hippikos agon and the gymnikos agon. They have little to do with competition, appealing more as spectacle. The need for wealth, the lack of direct participation by the people who received the victory crowns, and the possibility that owners could shift the odds in their favor by entering more than one horse or team set the horse races in a different category from the competitions between men. The horse races were a popular component of the games, but more for their entertainment value than as an expression of arete. The crowd might enjoy a chariot race, but it honored the individual who had developed his talents and used them to their limits.

The Mousikos Agon (Musical Competition)

There were many differences between the four stephanitic games, but none was so marked as inclusion of the mousikos agon, which was never part of the Olympic Games, nor originally of the Nemean Games, but integral to the Pythian and the Isthmian Games. This explains why there are theaters at Delphi and Isthmia (built specifically for the competitions) but none at Olympia or Nemea. In fact the mousikos agon was not added to the Nemean Games until after they transferred to Argos, where there is a theater.

We can best study these musical competitions through examining the program

Fig. 160 A singer and an aulos player perform on a platform before a judge (right). Nike approaches from the left. Red-figure pelike by the Cassel Painter, 450–440 B.C. Leiden, Rijksmuseum voor Oudheden, inv. no. RO II 60.

Fig. 161 A kithara player performs on a platform in front of a seated judge while Nike approaches with a victory ribbon. Note the plektron in the player's right hand. Red-figure pelike by the Cassel Painter, 440–430 B.C. Athens, National Museum, inv. no. 1469 (photo: © Treasury of Archaeological Receipts).

of the Pythian Games at Delphi. I must caution, however, that our information about the competition and the musicians who took part is much more limited than for either the gymnikos agon or the hippikos agon. Pausanias (10.9.2; A 60b) expresses the ancient prejudice that accounts for this relative dearth of information: "Most men take no account of the competitors in the musical contests, and I think that they are not worth much trouble."

The most venerated of the musical competitions at Delphi was the kithara (lyre) singing, in which a musician sang while accompanying himself on the kithara, although it is not always possible to tell from a vase painting whether a contestant is singing to kithara accompaniment or simply playing his instrument. Only when the head of the musician is thrown back in an obvious attitude of singing while he holds a kithara can we be sure what he is doing (fig. 158). We do know that the piece most often performed by the competitors was (not surprisingly) the Pythian Hymn to Apollo, for kithara singing was especially associated with that god.

From the first Pythiad, in 586, the kithara singing was joined by the playing of the *aulos*, or flute. This was a double pipe (hence the name of the diaulos race) with holes pierced along the sides. We have fragments of auloi made of bone. The performer would blow through reeds, however, so the instrument was clearly more like a modern oboe than a modern flute (fig. 159). The performer held a pipe in each hand, while a strap around his head helped keep the pipes properly positioned in his mouth.

The winner of the aulos competition at the Pythian Games received an extra reward; he would play the flute to accompany the pentathlon at the Olympic Games. Indeed, Pythokritos of Sikyon, who won the aulos at Delphi six times (574–554) not

only played at Olympia six times, he was honored there with a relief statue showing him holding his flutes. It was sufficiently strange to have a musician honored at Olympia that Pausanias (6.14.9; A 76) made specific mention of the monument to this *auletes*. Pythokritos is a rare example of a victor in the mousikos agon whose name is still known; Sakadas of Argos, the victor at the first Pythiad, is another.

The first Pythiad also included aulos singing, in which a singer was accompanied by a flute player. To judge from vase paintings, the singer typically was much younger than the aulos player (fig. 160). Although aulos singing became an important competition at the other games, portrayed in art and mentioned in literature, it was only contested once at Delphi. At the second Pythiad, in 582, "they then abolished the aulos singing, whose sound they considered inauspicious, for the notes of the aulos itself were most brooding and the words sung with the aulos were funereal" (Pausanias 10.7.5; A 75). The final event of the mousikos agon at the Pythian Games was kithara playing, which was added in 558 (fig. 161).

All these events took place in the theater at Delphi, and the contestants performed on a platform, as we see in the vase paintings. The platform must have been specially constructed; in the preparations for the Pythian Games of 246 B.C., we learn that a certain Melission was paid one of the larger contract prices for the construction of a pedestal in the Pythian theater (CID 2.139; A 81). The competitors seem to have performed the same piece in each event, and the winner was selected by a panel of judges, who might be susceptible to influence from the audience and, of course, their own prejudices. If there is a single reason for the long-term predominance of the Olympic Games, it is that the subjectivity inherent in the mousikos agon was not present at Olympia, as it was in the Pythian, the Isthmian, and, ultimately, the Nemean Games.

Other Events

The games at Olympia, Delphi, Isthmia, and Nemea included competitions that do not belong to the gymnikos, hippikos, or mousikos agon. Only two of these—the herald and the trumpet events—were formal components of the Olympic program, and both were added in 396. A special altar, or platform, stood at Olympia near the entrance to the stadium. Here the contestants in these events stood to compete, apparently to give everyone a clear view of them. We can guess that the judges were arranged down the length of the track to determine the distance each competitor was audible. As best we can tell, winners were chosen by their clarity of enunciation and the audibility of their voice or horn blast.

The winner of the *keryx*, or herald, competition was crowned like any other athlete and added to the Olympic victor list, but he also had work to do thereafter. His job was to make the announcements: the names of the competitors entering the stadium or hippodrome, the names of the winners making their victory lap after each event (fig. 162). The winner of the *salpinx*, or trumpet, competition also had work to do: the winning *salpinktes* worked with the keryx to create the ancient equivalent of the pub-

Fig. 162 A horse and rider in the keles make their victory lap, followed by a youth holding a victory crown and a tripod cauldron. A keryx leads the way, announcing, "the horse of Dy[s]neiketos won," in words that spill down from his mouth. Black-figure amphora by the Princeton Painter, 540–520 B.C. London, The British Museum, inv. no. B 144 (1849.11–22) (photo: © The British Museum).

Fig. 163 The keryx, wearing a long himation, announces the winner, who stands with tokens of victory (palm branch, crown, tainia) while an athlete runs off to left, perhaps a reference to a footrace. At the right stands the salpinktes with trumpet in hand wearing a chiton, chlamys, and military-style leggings. Panathenaic amphora of the Nikomachos Series, 340/39 B.C. Paris, Musée du Louvre, inv. no. MNC 706, Réunion des Musées Nationaux / Art Resource, New York (photo: Herve Lewandowski).

lic-address system (fig. 163). His job was to blow his horn to bring the crowd to attention so that it would quiet down and listen to the announcements of the keryx. The trumpeter would also blow a fanfare at the start of each event.

The keryx and salpinktes should probably be understood as the first professionals to compete in the Olympics, for they already had careers in their field of competition. The salpinktes, in particular, was used in military operations, in the same way buglers were employed in modern (pre-electronic) armies (fig. 164). Some became famous; one Herodoros of Megara is described as short, with powerful ribs and possessed of an extraordinarily loud trumpet blast, which inspired courage in soldiers. Herodoros is said to have won the circuit of four stephanitic games ten times, which, if true, would mean he competed at Olympia for four decades. He was also reputed to eat 6 kilograms of bread and 9 kilograms of meat at a sitting, while drinking 6 liters of wine, and to play two trumpets simultaneously (Athenaeus 10.414F–415A; A 74). Regardless of whether we accept this story, or the ten Olympic victories of Herodoros, it is evidence that the salpinx was contested at all four stephanitic sites. The keryx was equally important to the functioning of the games, and should also be recognized as a normal part of the competitive program at each of them.

Delphi and Isthmia also hosted competitions in poetry writing and prose composition. The details of these competitions are not known, and it is also unclear when they were added to the program. They were certainly well established by the first century A.D., as Plutarch documents (Moralia 674D–675B; A 77), and the entrants (and victors) included women. The winner was chosen by a panel of judges, and the reaction of the crowd played a large role in the choice. We even hear of cases of plagiarism:

Fig. 164 A salpinktes blows his horn. Note his crown and diazoma. Behind him is a shield seen in profile with the device of a tripod cauldron. Red-figure kylix by the Scheurleer Painter, 510–500 B.C. Paris, Musée du Louvre, inv. no. G 70; Réunion des Musées Nationaux / Art Resource, New York (photo: Herve Lewandowski).

Fig. 165 A rhapsode recites from a platform (inscribed *kalos*) while the opening words of the poem come from his mouth: "Oh sing of a time in Tiryns . . ." Red-figure amphora by the Kleophrades Painter, ca. 490 B.C. London, The British Museum, inv. no. E 270 (photo: © The British Museum).

competitors entered other poets' work as their own creations (Vitruvius 7 *praef.* 4–7; A 78). As we shall see, such competitions were well known at other, local festivals, but they were never a formal part of the Olympic program. Nonetheless, the Olympic Games did provide a venue where such artists could recite their works. Indeed, in 388 B.C. Dionysios, the tyrant of Syracuse, hired the best *rhapsodes* he could find to recite his own poems at Olympia. The crowd's reaction to the rhapsodes and the quality of their voices was positive, but they were still not impressed by Dionysios's poems (Diodorus Siculus 14.109; A 245). These rhapsodes were professional reciters, who appear to have been present at all the games (fig. 165).

Competitions in tragic acting were also a part of the Pythian Games, at least by the time poetry and prose joined the program. Once again the details of this competition are unclear. It may be simply that at a festival where plays were presented, the best actor was chosen from the leading roles, although it has also been suggested that actors competed by performing set pieces from popular dramas. A list of the victories by an actor (whose name is not preserved) suggests that both individual performances and acting within a full-scale dramatic production were contested. (SIG³ 1080; A79).

Finally, there were competitions in painting, which were established at Delphi and Isthmia in the middle of the fifth century B.C. (Pliny, *NH* 35.58; A 80). No more details are known, and it is clear that these competitions were not contested at Olympia (and probably not at Nemea), even though painters did display their works at Olympia. The painter Aëtion displayed his *Marriage of Roxane and Alexander* at Olympia and won not only fame but also the hand of the daughter of a Hellanodikes (Lucian, *Herodotus* 4; A 143).

5

THE SITES OF
THE CROWN COMPETITIONS

Olympia

THE GRANDDADDY OF THE GAMES was situated on the western side of the Peloponnesos, about 16 kilometers from the Ionian Sea (although the coast was closer in antiquity). The Alpheios River flows westward down from the Arkadian Mountains
through rolling hills to the coastal plain at the sea. Where the land flattens out from
hills to plain and the Alpheios is joined by the Kladeos River lies the prominent Hill of
Kronos, the father of the gods. These three natural features defined the limits of the
Altis, the Sanctuary of Zeus, and of appendages to the sanctuary such as the gymnasion, stadium, and hippodrome (fig. 166). It is important to remember that Olympia
was not a city-state; it passed no laws, issued no coins, pursued no independent foreign policy. It was administered by the city-state of Elis, with which it had extremely
close ties, even though it was almost 60 kilometers distant by road.

In the earliest times of the Olympic Games, the sanctuary was clustered at the
southwest corner of the Hill of Kronos (fig. 167). Excavations have revealed an extensive layer of sacrificial debris including hundreds of bronze and terra-cotta figurines,
largely of horses or chariots (fig. 168), that date to the eighth and seventh centuries B.C.
This Black Layer (as the excavators call it) lies beneath the later Heraion (Temple of
Hera) and Pelopion (Shrine of Pelops), and near the Altar of Zeus and the Prytaneion.
This is the core of Olympia. The Prytaneion was the home of Hestia, the goddess of
the hearth, whose eternal flame attested to the health and welfare of Elis. Every city-
state had a prytaneion with a hearth and an eternal flame, but that the Eleans placed
theirs at Olympia shows how closely Elis was tied to Olympia. Indeed, given the sacro-
sanct character accorded Elis because of the Olympic Games (according to Polybius
4.73.6–10; A 85), the Prytaneion at Olympia was in some sense a hearth common to
all Greeks. Here the victors at the games were given a banquet, and it was from this
point that the sacrificial processions around the Altis began and ended.

Fig. 166 Model of the Sanctuary of Zeus at Olympia seen from the south. The Hill of Kronos is at the center rear (K) and the white-roofed Temple of Zeus in the center (TZ). The gymnasion lies to the upper left (G), with the stadium on the upper right (S), and the start of the hippodrome at the lower right (H) (photo: © The British Museum, neg. inv. no. PS254092).

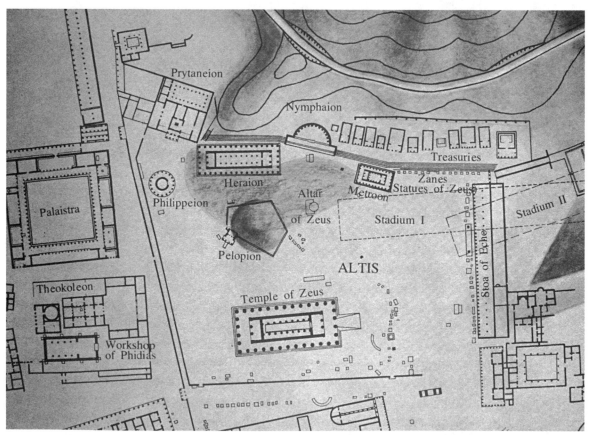

Fig. 167 Plan of the Sanctuary of Zeus at Olympia. The Black Layer marks the core of the sanctuary: the Heraion, the Pelopion, and the Altar of Zeus. Note the outline of Stadium I near the altar and that of Stadium II farther to the east, beneath the Echo Stoa but still within the Altis. After N. Yalouris, ed., *The Olympic Games* (Athens, 1976), 100–101.

Fig. 168 Figurine of a chariot and charioteer. Bronze, 8th century B.C. Olympia, Archaeological Museum, inv. no. B 1670 (photo: author).

Fig. 169 The Temple of Hera, ca. 600 B.C. The stone columns replaced wooden versions, accounting for the subtle differences in shape and proportion between the columns and their capitals. In the recessed areas on the columns bronze plaques were attached, inscribed with such public documents as regulations for the games, treaties between city-states, and other public announcements (photo: author).

Adjacent to the Prytaneion was the Heraion, the temple of the goddess Hera, wife of Zeus and queen of the gods. Its remains are among the earliest extant of a stone temple in ancient Greece. Actually, the columns were originally made of wood; the stone columns were replacements for those early wooden versions that were erected at later dates throughout antiquity (fig. 169). Pausanias (5.16.1) tells us that there was still one wooden column in his day. It is one of the greatest ironies from antiquity that the oldest large-scale monument at Olympia, a bastion of male domination, was dedicated to Hera. The Temple of Zeus, lying to the south and outside the earliest sacred area, was constructed about 150 years later. Both topographically and chronologically (so far as the remains tell us), Zeus was a later addition to Olympia.

On the other hand, the Altar of Zeus (which was the center of his worship) occupied a prominent position somewhere in or near this early core of the sanctuary. Made of the ashes of previous sacrifices, the altar does not survive, but Pausanias makes its general location clear (see fig. 167); in fact, it has been suggested that the Black Layer represents an early version of the Altar of Zeus. Furthermore, there are no figurines of females mixed in with the hundreds of male examples from the eighth and seventh centuries.

At the core of the early sanctuary lies the Pelopion, the shrine of the hero Pelops, whose story was told by a group of statues on the eastern end of the Temple of Zeus. This simple shrine consisted in prehistoric times of a mound that in the fourth century was enclosed by a wall in the shape of a lopsided pentagon. Here Pelops, who gave his name to the Peloponnesos, was worshiped with libations and sacrifices of black rams, appropriate for a figure associated with the underworld. More than that, Pelops is the key divinity at Olympia; the Eleans made sacrifices to him before they offered them to Zeus (schol. Pindar, Olympian 1.149a). It is important to note that the central role played at Olympia by a hero, a mortal who had become more than mortal, was repeated at the other sites. These heroes and their cults represent the enduring goal of the athlete to achieve immortality through superhuman effort, and they offer encouragement to him by celebrating the actual achievement of that status by his predecessors.

The Temple of Zeus, constructed around 460 B.C., may have been a relatively late addition to the sanctuary, but it was the major monument of Olympia and soon became the center of the Altis. As impressive as it was in size, its sculptural decoration was even more compelling. The eastern pediment told the story of the first Olympic Games, when the local king, Oinomaos, offered his daughter Hippodameia (mistress of horses) and his kingdom as the prize for anyone who could beat him in a chariot race. (If the challenger lost he forfeited his life.) Pelops won by bribing Oinomaos's stable boy, Myrtilos, to replace the linchpin of the king's chariot with a peg made of wax. In the heat of the race the wax melted, and the chariot wheels came off, throwing Oinomaos to his death in the ensuing crash. The ancients seem not to have been bothered by this bit of Olympic cheating.

The western pediment of the Temple of Zeus depicted the battle of the centaurs and the Lapiths presided over by Apollo, the god of music and culture. It is an allegory of the struggle between the centaurs' bestiality and the Lapiths' civilization, between barbarianism and Hellenism, and it served to unify and edify all the Greeks who came to Olympia.

The sculptural decoration of the Temple of Zeus included, inside the colonnade of the exterior, six metopes over the front porch and six over the back. These portrayed the twelve Labors of Herakles, beginning with his defeat of the Nemean lion (see fig. 99) and ending with his retrieval of the Apples of the Hesperides. But the labor that resonated the most powerfully in the region of Olympia was the cleaning of the stables of the local king, Augeas (fig. 170). To accomplish this feat Herakles actually had to divert the Kladeos River to wash away the filth. In some ancient versions Herakles himself was credited with founding the Olympics; at the least he was viewed as a particularly Dorian and Peloponnesian hero, hence the prominent placement of his exploits on the Temple of Zeus.

The most splendid of the sculptural decorations of the Temple of Zeus, however, was the chryselephantine (gold and ivory) cult statue of Zeus inside the building

Fig. 170 Herakles cleaning the stables of Augeas, king of Elis, with the help of Athena. Metope from the frieze over the inner porch of the Temple of Zeus. Olympia, Archaeological Museum (photo: © Treasury of Archaeological Receipts).

(fig. 171). This magnificent statue was the work of Pheidias, who also created the enormous cult statue of Athena for the Parthenon in Athens. The statue of Zeus was completed by about 430, and it was regarded as one of the Seven Wonders of the Ancient World. Although it has long since disappeared, the many verbal descriptions of it, and its portrayals in many media (especially the coins of Elis), allow us to reconstruct the image. Zeus was seated on a throne holding a scepter topped by his eagle in his left hand. On his extended right hand stood Nike, the personification of victory. The Nike was 6 ancient feet (1.8 meters) high, and Zeus himself more than 40 ancient feet (12 meters). One ancient critic claimed that Pheidias had made the statue too large; if Zeus tried to get up and leave, he would hit his head on the ceiling of the temple. The exposed flesh of Zeus (face, arms, feet) and of Nike were wrought in ivory, and the remainder of the composition in gold embossed and worked with various designs. When the front (east) doors of the temple were thrown open at daybreak on the god's festival day, the first rays of the sun striking this image must have been overwhelming.

Behind the Temple of Zeus to the west was the sacred olive tree from which the Olympic victory crowns were cut, and scattered throughout the Altis were dozens of altars to various gods. The dominant element within the Altis, however, was the hundreds and hundreds of dedications. Many of these were statues set up by athletes and horse owners after a triumph at the games, but many were spoils of war. In both cases, the common element was victory, and Olympia should be understood, most of all, as

Fig. 171 Reconstruction of the gold-and-ivory cult statue of Zeus at Olympia by Pheidias, ca. 430 B.C. Drawing by Ruben Santos.

a place where victory was celebrated. That is the message personified by the Nike on the outstretched hand of the cult statue of Olympian Zeus.

The open area of the Altis was framed by a number of buildings. To the north, a row of small structures known as treasuries lined the foot of the Hill of Kronos (see fig. 166). Each was constructed by a different Dorian city-state in the late sixth or early fifth century and intended, at least in part, to advertise the importance of that city-state. To the west of these treasuries, still on the north side, a Nymphaion (fountain house) was added in the second century A.D. by the wealthy Herodes Atticus. This new source of water was an important if late addition to Olympia, extremely popular with the spectators at the games. On the west, across the road from the Prytaneion, was the large practice track of the gymnasion and the associated wrestling school (*palaistra*), which were added in the third century B.C. Immediately south of the palaistra, and directly west of the Temple of Zeus and aligned with it, was the workshop of Pheidias where the cult statue of Zeus was created (fig. 172). The importance of the statue was recognized from the beginning, and the workshop was preserved as a kind of museum commemorating Pheidias's craft. Farther to the south was a large square building with a central courtyard known as the Leonidaion, after the donor, Leonidas of Elis. Built in the early Hellenistic period, this was a kind of hotel.

The most important building along the south side of the sanctuary was the Bouleuterion, or council house, which was actually two apsidal buildings joined by a smaller central building. The Olympic Council met here, and the athletes came to its Altar of Zeus

Fig. 172 Aerial view of the stadium and the Sanctuary of Zeus from the east, showing the Bouleuterion (B), the area of the Hippodrome (Hipp), the Leonidaion (L), the Prytaneion (P), the Temple of Hera (TH), the Temple of Zeus (TZ), and the workshop of Pheidias (W) (photo: © H. R. Goette, Berlin).

Horkios (Zeus of the Oath) to take the Olympic oath. The entire east side of the Altis was framed by the long, narrow continuous exterior colonnade of the Echo Stoa, which faced out onto the open area and provided shelter for the crowd from sun and rain.

East of the southeast corner of the Altis and parallel to the stadium was the hippodrome (see figs. 166 and 172, center right). Although modern scholars believe that the hippodrome was washed away by the Alpheios River, the region has never been excavated. Indeed, new evidence from Nemea suggests that hippodromes may have been located in floodplains; layers of river gravel might thus represent the successive surfaces of the horse track.

The entrance to the stadium was along the north short end of the Echo Stoa next to the Treasury Terrace wall (fig. 173). A series of bases here mark the location of bronze statues of Zeus, called Zanes, that were paid for by the fines levied against athletes caught giving or taking bribes; they were intended "to make clear that an Olympic victory is to be won not by money but by swiftness of foot or strength of body" (Pausanias 5.21.2–4; A 103). It is no coincidence that these statues were placed directly on the path of the athletes entering the stadium.

The competitors passed through a gate made of Corinthian-style columns between the Echo Stoa and the Treasury Terrace (fig. 174). From this point on, access was

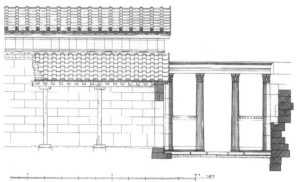

Fig. 173 Entrance to Olympic stadium seen from the west. It lies north of the Echo Stoa (stone blocks in right foreground), with bases for the Zanes (left) in front of the terrace wall of the treasuries and the tunnel to stadium behind to the right (photo: author).

Fig. 174 Entrance to Olympic stadium seen from the inside (east). From right: a cross-section through wall of the Treasury Terrace, the Corinthian gate, and the back wall of the Echo Stoa. The shed roof against wall of the Echo Stoa was supported by wooden columns; this was the roof of the locker room. From W. Koenigs, *Die Echohalle*, Olympische Forschungen XIV (Berlin, 1984), pl. 76, courtesy Deutsches Archaeologisches Institut.

restricted to athletes and judges. The area between the back wall of the Echo Stoa and the retaining wall for the stadium embankment was the location of the *apodyterion* (undressing room). This ancient equivalent of the modern locker room was partly open to the sky; the rest was covered by a shed roof built against the back wall of the stoa.

From the apodyterion the athlete passed through the *krypte esodos* (hidden entrance; fig. 175). This was a vaulted tunnel originally more than 30 meters long, covered by the earth embankment on which the spectators sat. This embankment took advantage of the natural slope along the north side, but the remainder was artificial. The track was surrounded by a water channel with basins at intervals and a *balbis* (line of starting blocks) across each end (see fig. 37). Along the north side was the marble altar of Demeter Chamyne (Demeter on the Ground), whose priestess was the only woman of marriageable age allowed at the games. Opposite that altar was the area marked off for the judges (*Hellanodikai*), the *Hellanodikaion*. (Apparently the judge of the Olympic Games was originally called a *diaitater* [arbitrator]; the rather more grandiose title *Hellanodikes*, "judge of the Hellenes," was adopted afterward, perhaps as a result of the Greek successes in the Persian Wars.) This was an enclosed platform where judges who were not directly involved in a specific event could oversee the competitions (fig. 176; see also fig. 34). But some of the Hellanodikai would always be on the track.

The stadium we can see today at Olympia came into existence around 340 B.C. or a little earlier, undergoing only minor changes during the remainder of its active history. But there were at least two earlier versions of the stadium (see fig. 167). The immediate predecessor followed the same orientation as the extant stadium, but it lay farther to the west, closer to the core of the sanctuary. The earliest stadium is poorly documented, and its precise location and size are not really known, but it lay closer to the Altar of Zeus and the Pelopion. Indeed, we hear from a late author that the original

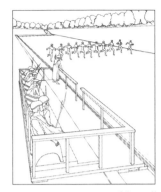

Fig. 175 The tunnel entrance (krypte esodos) to the stadium at Olympia. Originally constructed, with a narrower passage, in the 4th century B.C., the modern reconstruction of a small part of the vault is based on an ancient reconstruction of Roman times. The end of the Treasury Terrace wall appears at the extreme left (photo: author).

Fig. 176 Reconstruction of the Hellanodikaion at Olympia, seen from the southeast. Note the krypte esodos at the back, in the northwest corner of the stadium. Drawing by Ruben Santos.

stadion race was connected directly to the altar (Philostratos, *On Gymnastics* 5). According to this account, the athletes stood one stadion distant from the altar, on which were placed the sacrificial offerings to Zeus. A priest standing next to the altar signaled the start of the race by waving a lighted torch. The runner who finished first lit the fire, burned the sacrificial offerings, and was proclaimed Olympic victor. If this account is accurate, and if we have located the Altar of Zeus correctly, then the race would have begun more or less where the later Hellanodikaion stood and passed beneath the Echo Stoa. But precision and confidence in these details are impossible. Nonetheless, despite the fragmentary state of our knowledge, two basic evolutionary trends are clear and will be examined in more detail later: the stadium moved progressively farther from the religious center of Olympia, and increasingly more room was created for spectators.

Delphi

It is hard to imagine a physical setting for our next stephanitic site that could be more different from that of Olympia. The bucolic rolling hills and broad river plains are exchanged for the rocky precipitous crags and bubbling springs of Mount Parnassos, to whose slopes Delphi clings (fig. 177). This difference in setting is matched by a difference in character, immediately identifiable by the existence of a theater (fig. 178), where the *mousikos agon,* never a part of the Olympic Games, was contested. The difference between the two appears equally in Delphi's choice of central deity, Apollo, the patron of music and culture, as dedicatee of the site and the games.

Some sources claimed that the original name of the site was Pytho, from the verb *pythein,* "to rot," a reference to Apollo's killing of either a dragon/serpent or a human robber, leaving the body to rot. Whatever the true etymology, Pythian Apollo

Fig. 177 Aerial view of the southern face of Mount Parnassos with the site of Delphi set on a diagonal natural ledge. From the left center to the lower right: the stadium (S), Peribolos of Apollo, gymnasion (G), and Sanctuary of Athena Pronoia (AP), all identifiable by gaps in the trees (photo: courtesy of the Ecole Française d'Athènes, inv. no. E 2218 [Philippe Colett]).

was more closely associated with the northerly areas of Greece than with the Peloponnesos. Among other myths is the story of Apollo's pursuit of a mortal named Daphne (laurel) who fled before his advances. He pursued her northward to the Vale of Tempe, where the Peneus River cuts through a gorge at the southern foot of Mount Olympos. There Daphne prayed for deliverance and was turned into the tree that bears her name. Thereafter, victors in the Pythian Games received a laurel crown, which had to be cut from the tree in Tempe by a boy who had ceremonially reenacted the slaying of the Pytho at Delphi and then went to Tempe for purification.

These mythical connections with Thessaly were reflected in the Amphiktyonic Council, which controlled Delphi and the Pythian Games. The council consisted of a board of representatives from twelve Greek tribes, most of whom came from Thessaly and central Greece. The council met twice a year and, in the earlier period, was an important force in Panhellenic unity. Gradually and perhaps inevitably the town of Delphi, which conducted most of the day-to-day business of the Sanctuary of Apollo, took more of the decisions on itself.

The Pythian Games were organized as a quadrennial celebration in 586 B.C., which was reckoned the first Pythiad, even though the games became stephanitic only four years later. From the beginning it hosted a full program of competitions in the *gymnikos agon* and the *hippikos agon,* as well as the *mousikos agon* that set it apart from the Olympic Games. But though the Pythian Games rank second among the four stephanitic games in chronology and importance, there is a vast difference between

Fig. 178 The theater at Delphi from above with the Temple of Apollo visible below and, in the distance above the columns of the temple, the gymnasion and, a little to the right and above, the Sanctuary of Athena Pronoia (photo: author).

Fig. 179 The columns at the southeast corner of the Temple of Apollo at Delphi from the northwest, 4th century B.C. (photo: author).

them and the Olympics because they were not essential to the town of Delphi. Olympia would have been a place of little outside interest without its games, but Delphi would have flourished regardless: ancient Greeks called it the *omphalos* (navel) of the earth — the center of the world — and it boasted the most famous of the ancient oracles, the Pythia.

The Pythia was a woman (originally a young virgin but later a woman over the age of fifty, although she would dress in the clothes of a virgin) who sat in the depths of the Temple of Apollo and became "inspired," apparently by the fumes that issued from a chasm in the ground. Supplicants would ask her about the future, putting their questions to a priest, who forwarded them to the Pythia. She would respond with inarticulate cries that were translated by the priest for the suppliant; usually the answers took a form that could be interpreted in different ways. When King Kroisos of Sardis asked whether he should invade the Persian Empire, for example, he was told, "If you cross the border you will destroy a great empire." The confident Kroisos thus attacked the Persians and was soundly defeated, thereby destroying his own great empire.

The Sanctuary of Apollo was called the Peribolos after the wall that surrounded and defined it. At the center was the Temple of Apollo, which had a long history (fig. 179). The remains today date from the fourth century B.C., but there are physical remains from an earlier structure, and literary sources mention several that were even earlier. The first of these was said to have been made of laurel. The Pythia sat in a sunken area toward the rear of the temple, and inscribed on the porch of the temple were the famous maxims given by the Seven Wise Men of ancient Greece: "Know thyself" and "Nothing to excess."

Everything within the Peribolos was dedicated to Apollo, and the numerous dedications took various forms, including small buildings; the treasuries dedicated by the Ionian city-states of Siphnos and Athens were especially elaborate. Delphi was enormously rich, especially in sculpture, and even though "borrowings" by the Ro-

Fig. 180 Kleobis and Biton of Argos, stone statues from about 590 B.C. Delphi, Archaeological Museum (photo: © Treasury of Archaeological Receipts).

Fig. 181 The Charioteer of Delphi. Bronze statue from a group dedicated by Polyzalos of Gela, 478 or 474 B.C. Delphi, Archaeological Museum (photo: © Treasury of Archaeological Receipts).

mans Sulla and Nero had depleted that wealth, there was still much left for Pausanias to see and describe. Excavations have shown that more athletic sculpture has been preserved at Delphi than at Olympia, even though the original quantity of athletic sculpture at Olympia was much greater than at Delphi, as is attested by Pausanias and other written sources, including the inscribed statue bases discovered within the Altis.

The earliest extant athletic statues depict two brothers, Kleobis and Biton of Argos (fig. 180), famous for their strength. When their oxen were late returning from the fields, they pulled the cart carrying their mother to the Sanctuary of Hera located several miles outside the city. Their mother was proud of them, especially when her neighbors congratulated her on her good sons, and she asked the goddess to grant Kleobis and Biton the most perfect gift possible. A little later the youths entered the Temple of Hera, where they went gently to sleep and never awoke. They had died at the peak of glory, loved and admired by all—the perfect gift. The city of Argos voted to put up statues of them at Delphi, and the miracle of the survival of these statues matches the story of the young men themselves.

Another athletic statue is one of the best known preserved from antiquity. The Charioteer of Delphi has lost his chariot, his horses, and his left arm, but he stands as a triumph of athletic art (fig. 181). The statue was part of a victory monument in the *tethrippon* at Delphi, probably in 474, and its artistry shows us how much has been lost from antiquity, especially among athletic victory dedications. But athletics were only part of the business of Delphi. We see this vividly in the Daochos dedication, named

Fig. 182 The base of the Daochos dedication at Delphi (lower right) with the Temple of Apollo at upper left (photo: author).

Fig. 183 Agias of Pharsalos, pankratiast, victor at Olympia in 484 B.C., three-time victor at Delphi, and five-time victor at Nemea and Isthmia. Delphi, Archaeological Museum (photo: author).

for a Thessalian from Pharsalos who was a leader at Delphi in the 330s. Around 335 Daochos dedicated a group of statues that amounted to a family hall of fame. The base of these statues overlooked the Temple of Apollo, and inscriptions beneath each statue socket help us identify the surviving statues (fig. 182).

These statues include three nude brothers, Agias, Agelaos, and Telemachos, who were athletes and ancestors of Daochos. Agias (fig. 183) was a multiple victor at all four stephanitic games in the *pankration,* and Telemachos won in the *pale* at Olympia on the same day Agias won the pankration. Yet there is no record that statues were ever dedicated to them at Olympia. They had to wait 150 years for Daochos to erect statues to them at Delphi. Their younger brother, Agelaos, is recorded only as a victor in the *stadion paidon* at Delphi. Clearly, these three athletic brothers were celebrated at Delphi not because of their athletic accomplishments per se but because their feats enhanced the reputation of their descendant Daochos. An athletic victory dedication at Olympia and one at Delphi did not necessarily have the same value. Indeed, so much more than athletics went on at Delphi that the Peribolos bears only the most basic similarities with the Altis.

As travelers approached Delphi in antiquity, coming along the same road we take today from the direction of Athens, the first monuments encountered were those in the Sanctuary of Athena Pronoia (forethought). Shortly thereafter, and still at some distance from the Peribolos of Apollo, came the gymnasion-palaistra cluster of buildings (fig. 184). The gymnasion is immediately recognizable by its stadion-long covered

Fig. 184 The gymnasion at Delphi with its xystos (X) and paradromis (P) and the palaistra with its circular pool in the loutron (L) seen from the north. The Sanctuary of Athena Pronoia lies hidden around the side of the hill to the left beyond the gymnasion (photo: author).

Fig. 185 Southern end of the gymnasion, with the balbis extending out from the third (missing) column of the facade of the xystos (photo: author).

Fig. 186 Model of the gymnasion and palaistra with its loutron. To the left of the circular pool of the loutron are the remains of baths added in the Roman period (photo: courtesy of the Ecole Française d'Athènes, inv. no. E 963 [Philippe Colett]).

Fig. 187 Regulation forbidding wine in the stadium inscribed on a block of the retaining wall of the stadium track (see fig. 35 for the location): "Wine is prohibited in the vicinity of the track. If anyone breaks this rule, he shall make amends to Apollo by pouring a libation, making a sacrifice, and paying a fine of $110, half to Apollo and half to the informer." 450–420 B.C.(?) (photo: author).

and open tracks (the *xystos* and *paradromis*, respectively), including a balbis for the open track (fig. 185). The smaller palaistra is recognizable by its open central courtyard and the *loutron* (bath) next to it by its open-air circular pool (fig. 186). As at Olympia, these buildings were added to the topography of Delphi only in about 300, and they represent the new structures that set athletes apart from the rest of the crowd.

The stadium and the hippodrome are some distance from the Peribolos of Apollo. We know that the hippodrome was situated far down in the plain, as was demanded by the terrain of Delphi, and no trace of it has ever been identified. The stadium is closer, but still at some distance beyond and above the Peribolos (see figs. 35 and 177). The stone seats were added by the same Herodes Atticus who built the Nymphaion at Olympia. However, the track seems to have existed here much earlier. A date in the fifth century B.C. is suggested not only by the fine polygonal masonry of the retaining wall on the downhill side of the track but also by an unusual inscription (fig. 187). This early, difficult Greek has been variously translated, but the real meaning is clear:

> Wine is prohibited in the vicinity of the track. If anyone breaks this rule, he shall make amends to Apollo by pouring a libation, making a sacrifice, and paying a fine of $110, half to Apollo and half to the informer. [*CID* 1.3; A *100*]

As we leave Delphi we should note that although the stadium and the hippodrome are located at a distance from the Peribolos of Apollo, the theater is right next to the sacred area and should be understood as an extension of it (see fig. 178). This expresses very clearly the relative importance of the mousikos agon to the other competitions at Delphi.

Isthmia

The site of Isthmia takes us to yet another of the geological faces of Greece. Situated on the eastern side of the 6-kilometer-wide neck of land that connects the Peloponnesos to the rest of the Balkan peninsula, the Sanctuary of Poseidon, where the Isthmian Games took place, lay along the lines of the most important crossroads of ancient

Fig. 188 View of the Isthmos of Corinth from Acrocorinth; "X" marks the site of the Sanctuary of Poseidon at Isthmia (photo: author).

Greece (fig. 188; see also fig. 2). The coastline has expanded since antiquity, and Isthmia was closer to the sea than it is today, occupying a proportionately larger part of the Isthmos. Hence, north-south traffic by land necessarily ran through Isthmia, as did the east-west sea traffic that consisted of boats dragged across the Isthmos in order to avoid the long and dangerous voyage around the southern end of the Peloponnesos (fig. 189). Controlled by the city-state of Corinth, the leader in Greek maritime commerce and overseas colonization in the seventh century, the Sanctuary of Poseidon was a natural extension of Corinthian interests and would have been a significant site even if stephanitic competitions had never taken place there.

Mythology reflects the importance of the Isthmos to commerce and lines of communication in the story of Sinis. A robber who preyed on travelers, Sinis would bend down pine trees and tie the traveler's arms and legs to them. When he released the trees, the traveler would be torn apart. The Athenian hero Theseus relieved the road of this ancient toll-taker by giving Sinis a dose of his own medicine. Poseidon's sacred grove of pine trees and Isthmia as a whole are revealed by the myth of Theseus to be of special importance to Athens, another way this site differed from the festival centers at Olympia and Nemea, where Herakles—a more Doric hero—played a similar patron's role.

As at the other sites, a death was key to the story of the founding of the games. A woman named Ino (subsequently identified with Leukothea) was pursued by her husband, Athamas, enraged by her scheming, to the Molourian cliff (a few kilometers northeast of Isthmia). She threw herself into the sea together with her younger son, Melikertes. They both perished, but the body of the boy was taken ashore at Isthmia

Fig. 189 Aerial view of the Sanctuary of Poseidon at Isthmia with the Corinth Canal (built 1892) in the background and the Temple of Poseidon in the foreground (T), the theater above to left (Th), and the Hellenistic stadium above to right (S) (photo: Raymond V. Scoder, S.J., © 1987 Bolchazy-Carducci Publishers, Inc.).

by a dolphin and ended up alongside the sea in the pine grove of Poseidon. Sisyphos, the long-suffering Corinthian hero, found the corpse and buried it. The boy was renamed Palaimon, and the Isthmian Games were founded in his honor, with a wreath of pine as the symbol of victory. At some point, probably in the fifth century, the victory wreath at Isthmia was changed to dry celery "out of jealous rivalry with the Nemean Games" (Plutarch, *Moralia* 676F; *A* 235).

The Isthmian Games became a part of the stephanitic cycle in 580 but were held biennially rather than quadrennially and celebrated in late spring, April–May in our calendar. We do not know the specifics of the competitive program, but we can assume that it encompassed a full set of competitions like those at Delphi. Indeed, the existence of a theater at Isthmia shows that its program was more closely related to that of Delphi, with its mousikos agon; it also shared with the Pythian program competitions in creative writing and painting.

The strategic location that made Isthmia important was also decisive in its destruction. This was due in part to the ravages of passing invaders but even more to the efforts to ward off those invaders. Sometime around A.D. 410–420 a massive defensive wall was constructed across the Isthmos, and it was extensively repaired about 150 years later. In both phases this Hexamilion Wall made use of architectural blocks from the Sanctuary of Poseidon. The result is that the Temple of Poseidon exists only in the negative impressions left when its walls were pillaged. So, too, the theater survives only in its substructures (see fig. 189). The Palaimonion, or Sanctuary of Palaimon, survives in its concrete and rubble core, but the large blocks that once covered it are gone.

This destruction in the name of defense, however, obliterated a site that had only come into existence during the Roman period. The Roman Mummius had already destroyed Corinth in 146 B.C., and it was only refounded, as a Roman colony, a century later by Julius Caesar. Pausanias (2.2.2) tells us that the Isthmian Games continued during that period, though now under the supervision of the Sikyonians. But excavations at Isthmia have shown that the games were not held at Isthmia during this time: they seem to have been moved to Sikyon after the Sikyonians took over. The revival of Corinth and of the Isthmian Games in 44 B.C. did not lead to the immediate refurbishing of the site; it was a century and more before the damaged monuments were replaced. Pausanias saw this reconstructed Isthmia, and thanks to his description (2.1.7–2.2), we can form some image of Roman Isthmia.

> Worth seeing at Isthmia are a theater and a stadium of white marble. As you enter the sanctuary of the god, there are statues of Isthmian victors on one side, and pine trees in a row on the other, most of them growing upright. On the temple, which is not very large, stand bronze Tritons. In the porch of the temple are statues: two of Poseidon, one of Amphitrite, and a Sea which is also of bronze. Inside are dedications of our own time by Herodes Atticus: four horses gilded except for their hooves, which are of ivory, and two golden Tritons alongside the horses. They are of ivory below the waist. In the chariot stand Amphitrite and Poseidon, and the boy Palaimon is upright on a dolphin. These are also chryselephantine. In the middle of the base upon which rests the chariot a figure of Sea has been wrought, holding the young Aphrodite with the so-called Nereids on either side. . . . Within the Peribolos of Poseidon on the left is the Temple of Palaimon, and inside it are statues of Poseidon, Leukothea, and Palaimon himself. There is also his *adyton* (inner sanctum), and the descent into it is subterranean; they say that Palaimon is hidden here. No one, either a Corinthian or a foreigner, has any means of escaping his oath sworn here.

Several things emerge from this description that tie Isthmia to other stephanitic sites. First, the sacred area of Poseidon at Isthmia, like that of Apollo at Delphi, was called the peribolos, although excavations show that the Isthmian shrine, which is Roman in date, is much smaller and simpler than the one at Delphi. Secondly, we see the hand of Herodes Atticus once again, endowing yet another stephanitic site. Finally, it is clear that the Temple of Palaimon was a roofed construction with its own entrance to the netherworld, appropriate to a hero cult but very different from the Shrine of Pelops at Olympia. Again, however, excavations at Isthmia have revealed that all physical remains of the Palaimonion are of Roman date; nothing has been identified from the earlier periods that could tell us about the cult then.

We can nonetheless learn much about ancient athletics from Isthmia, despite

Fig. 190 Crown of wild celery with
inscription, "NEMEIA." Bronze coin
of Argos, Antoninus Pius, A.D. 138–161.
Athens, Numismatic Museum,
inv. no. 4405 (photo: © Treasury of
Archaeological Receipts).

the fragmentary condition of the remains. Especially important are its successive stadiums. The last of these was built into a natural ravine southeast of the Sanctuary of Poseidon (see fig. 189). Although it still lies buried, test trenches have established its location and put its original date in the late fourth century B.C. It appears, although only full excavation can prove this, that the stadium matches the stadiums at Olympia, Nemea, Epidauros, and elsewhere in date and form. Especially tantalizing are Pausanias's reference to the use of white marble for a building material and the discovery of fragmentary wall frescoes in a fountain at the closed end of the track.

The single most important discovery at Isthmia for our understanding of ancient Greek athletics is the early *hysplex* (starting gate) that we examined in Chapter 4 (see figs. 47–50). This was the unsuccessful, multi cord system that was quickly replaced by the grooved balbis. The early stadium, with the new balbis, served until the time of Alexander the Great; then the new stadium was built, farther away from the Temple of Poseidon. Thus the trend toward distancing athletics from their religious center, seen already at Olympia, was followed at Isthmia. This tendency probably resulted from the need to provide larger and more elaborate spectator space as athletics developed into more of an entertainment industry.

The Isthmian Games also included the hippikos agon; so Isthmia must have had a hippodrome. It has been suggested that a large ancient foundation about 2 kilometers southwest of the Temple of Poseidon might have been related to the hippodrome. We cannot confirm this, however, without extensive further excavation.

Nemea

If Isthmia, in some sense, was a junior Delphi, Nemea was certainly a junior Olympia, for its program did not include the mousikos agon, and it was dedicated to Zeus. Although biennial, its games, like the Olympics, were held at the second full moon after the summer solstice. Located in a small valley in the foothills of the Arkadian Mountains at an elevation of 333 meters above sea level, Nemea lies slightly off the main

Fig. 191 Aerial view of Nemea from the west with the Temple of Zeus (T), early Hellenistic stadium (S), bath with modern roof (B), and pentagonal Shrine of Opheltes (O). University of California at Berkeley, Nemea Excavations Archives, no. Aerial 01.2.

route into the eastern and central Peloponnesos from the Isthmos. Excavations have revealed that this valley is naturally swampy with poor drainage; it is therefore unarable and was uninhabitable before a drainage system was created. This was done in the Bronze Age, in the fifth and twelfth centuries A.D., and in 1884. Despite its swampy condition, sheep and goats were able to graze (as is documented in the pre-1884 valley); the name Nemea may thus derive from the verb *nemein*, "to graze" (one's flocks). This is how Diogenes the Cynic understood it when he saw an Olympic victor grazing sheep and called out, "Hey, Mr. Winner, it didn't take you long to get from Olympia to Nemea!" (Diogenes Laertius, *Diogenes* 6.49). Nemean Zeus is not, then, the philandering, thunderbolt-throwing Olympian Zeus but a shepherd Zeus. This explains one of the major differences between Olympia and Nemea revealed by excavation. At Olympia there are hundreds of dedications of weapons and armor, and many monuments were erected to commemorate military victories; none have been discovered at Nemea.

The struggle between Herakles and the Nemean lion was the first of the hero's twelve labors. A venerable myth, it was depicted frequently in art of all periods (see, for example, fig. 99), but it is not given in our sources as the reason the Nemean Games were founded until the Roman period. Rather, the early founding myth concerned Opheltes, the infant son of the local king. An oracle had declared that Opheltes should not be allowed to touch the ground until he had learned how to walk. But one day his nurse set him down on a bed of wild celery in order to fetch water for the Seven Against

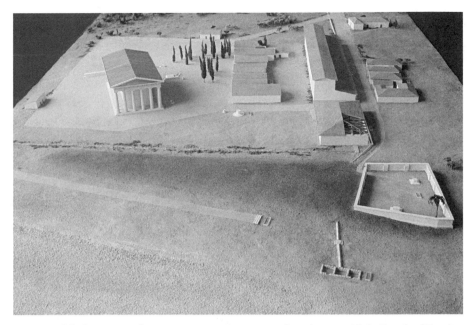

Fig. 192 Model of Sanctuary of Zeus at Nemea, ca. 300 B.C., seen from the west with the Temple of Zeus (at top left) and its long altar on the far (east) side of it. The sacred grove of cypress trees lies in the Epipola south (right) of the temple. Next toward the south a row of oikoi (embassies) and then the long, narrow xenon (hotel) with the bath in the same line to the west. At the lower right is the pentagonal enclosure of the Shrine of Opheltes with reservoirs in the foreground and a practice running track to the left. The gravel in the left foreground represents the area of the hippodrome. University of California at Berkeley, Nemea Excavations Archives, no. Mus. 03.5.

Thebes, heroes who were passing through on their way from Argos to Thebes. A serpent killed the baby while he lay in the wild celery, and the Seven, recognizing this as a bad omen for their expedition, held funeral games for the baby, whom they renamed Archemoros (beginner of doom), in an attempt to propitiate the gods. Hence the victory crown of the Nemean Games was made of wild celery (fig. 190; see also fig. 212), and the judges wore black robes as a sign of mourning for Opheltes/ Archemoros.

The Nemean Games entered the stephanitic cycle in 573 and were held under the supervision of the small neighboring town of Kleonai, which functioned as a surrogate for the larger, more important city-state of Argos. Indeed, it is clear that the officials of Nemea were a part of the general administrative structure of Argos.

The name of the sacred area at Nemea was the Epipola, an Argive term used officially for a flat open space. At Nemea the Epipola is the equivalent of the Altis at Olympia or the Peribolos at Delphi and Isthmia. It contained altars, monuments, and a sacred grove of cypress trees, representing the funereal aspect of the games. Many of the planting pits of those trees have been discovered, and cypress trees have been replanted in them (figs. 191, 192). The eastern and northern sections of the Epipola have not been excavated, but the southern side was defined by a row of buildings, many with kitchens and dining rooms attached, that were erected by different city-states.

Fig. 193 The Temple of Nemean Zeus, ca. 330 B.C., from the southeast as it appeared in 2002 (photo: author).

Farther away, outside the sacred area, are secular buildings like a hotel and a bathhouse. The core of the Epipola was the Temple of Nemean Zeus (fig. 193). The extant structure was built over the top of an earlier temple that was destroyed around 415 B.C. In front of the temple was a long, narrow altar, paralleled only by the altar of Poseidon at Isthmia. This correspondence demonstrates the conscious similarities — and the rivalries — between Nemea and Isthmia.

The history of the Nemean Games was a troubled one. After Nemea was destroyed in about 415, the games were moved to Argos until about 335. They returned to Nemea at that time, launching a major building program, of which the Temple of Zeus was the centerpiece. By 271 the games had been moved back to Argos, where they were held for the remainder of antiquity. But two structures built during the times the games were at Nemea offer significant information concerning ancient Greek athletics. The first of these is the bath, the first at a festival site. It included an elaborate hydraulic system that fed water to a pair of tub rooms flanking a central pool (fig. 194). This is the physical setting we see portrayed on a vase in which water is scooped from a tub to be poured over a young athlete (fig. 195).

The second building constructed in around 330–300 that has much to tell about ancient athletics is the early Hellenistic stadium that lies about 450 meters southeast of the Temple of Zeus (fig. 196; see also figs. 63, 191). This was created by hollowing out a natural ravine between two ridges at the south and building up an artificial terrace for the track at the north. The latter has eroded badly since antiquity; and the first 400 ancient feet (118 meters) are preserved today.

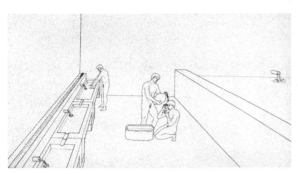

Fig. 194 Reconstruction of the bath at Nemea showing one of the tub rooms at the left and the central pool at the right. Drawing by Ruben Santos.

Fig. 195 A youth pours water over a young athlete in a bath; at the left we see a tub, with two more youths standing behind it. Red-figure kylix by the Codrus Painter, 430–420 B.C. London, The British Museum, inv. no. E 83 (photo: © The British Museum).

West of the stadium, also built between two ridges is the apodyterion (locker room) where the athletes prepared for their competitions (fig. 197). This was a simple structure with a three-sided colonnaded court open to the air and surrounded by roofed areas. The tiles of this roof bear the name of its architect, Sosikles, who was the "director of public works" of Argos. This is where the athletes disrobed, rubbed their bodies down with oil, and prepared themselves psychologically for the games (see fig. 273).

From the apodyterion the athlete passed through a vaulted entrance tunnel 36 meters long: the krypte esodos, to use the name given it at Olympia (fig. 198). The effect on those who pass through today is transforming and we can believe that it helped bring the athlete's full attention to the job at hand. At the far end of the tunnel the athlete would wait for the herald to call his name and then run out onto the track (fig. 199). Apparently competitors had to wait in the tunnel for their names to be called, and some passed the time defacing public property. At least that seems to be the explanation for the ancient graffiti scratched all over the tunnel walls. One of these, the name Telestas (fig. 200), could refer to a victor in the boxing at Olympia in around 340. Another offers a difference of opinion about the physical beauty of a man named Akrotatos.

The balbis, hysplex, and kampter of the Nemea stadium have already been discussed (see figs. 51, 54–57, 63, 66–67), but another discovery should be mentioned. About four hundred coins were found during the excavation of the stadium, but few of them were at the closed southern end. We were able to figure out why after our revivals of the Nemean Games in 1996 and 2000. The view from the end of the track (fig. 63) shows the stadium and its surroundings clearly. But spectators cannot really follow the races from there. Hence the coins were found where the spectators would have sat, along the sides of the track where they could more easily see the competi-

Fig. 196 Aerial view of the early Hellenistic stadium at Nemea from the north. The apodyterion (undressing room, A) lies about halfway between the stadium track and the asphalt road at the right. University of California at Berkeley, Nemea Excavations Archives, no. Aerial 90.16.

Fig. 197 Cut-away of a reconstruction of the apodyterion at Nemea from the northwest. University of California at Berkeley, Nemea Excavations Archives, no. PD 93.8. Drawing by Ruben Santos.

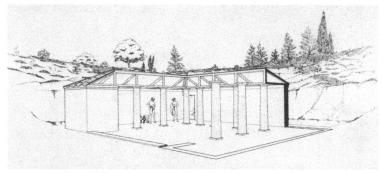

tions. In addition, the area around the judges' stand yielded the largest concentrations of coins from Argos, while the coins of Corinth were concentrated on the opposite side of the track, and the coins of Sikyon a little farther along. We thus have evidence that groups of fans gathered in cheering sections, just as they do today, and as is suggested by Lucian's description of an experience at the Olympic Games: "Recently I sat to the left of the Hellanodikai at Olympia thanks to Euandrides of Elis, who kept a seat for me among his fellow citizens. I wanted to see close at hand everything that happened among the Hellanodikai" (*Hermotimos* 39; A 106).

Finally, we have recently uncovered clear evidence about the earlier stadium at Nemea, used in the sixth and fifth centuries. Excavations have shown that the original Shrine of Opheltes, in the late fourth century a pentagonal enclosure, was a tumulus. This mound was artificially created in the first half of the sixth century—a date close to 573 would not be far wrong. Rounded at the south end, the mound continues as a long, gradually narrowing dike to the north (fig. 201). Along the eastern side of this elongated tumulus ran the track of the early stadium, consisting of a fine layer of white clay, which was equipped with the single-foot starting blocks noted above (see fig. 45).

To the west of the mound dozens, perhaps hundreds, of layers of alluvial silt and

Fig. 198 The underground entrance to the stadium at Nemea from the west, ca. 320 B.C. This 36-meter-long tunnel was discovered with its ends silted up but the central part still standing empty. University of California at Berkeley, Nemea Excavations Archives, no. STAD 95.95.

Fig. 199 One athlete waits as another comes through the passageway from the tunnel to the track at Nemea. The keryx announces the next competitor while the crowd shows its partisanship. University of California at Berkeley, Nemea Excavations Archives, no. PD 93.4. Drawing by Ruben Santos.

gravel have accumulated over the centuries. The clay silt always contains a few grooves left behind by chariot wheels, although the gravel shows no traces of them. This must be the early hippodrome, a conclusion supported by the absence of any other possible space in the Nemean valley for it. Not enough has been exposed to discern its overall dimensions, but future excavations can accomplish that. Apparently the single mound served as the viewing stand for both the gymnikos agon and the hippikos agon, as we perhaps see in a fragment of a sixth-century vase (see fig. 144).

Perhaps the most important result of these discoveries is the inevitable conclusion that Argos created an athletic festival center at Nemea out of nothing in the first half of the sixth century B.C. Although there is evidence of activity in the valley in the twelfth and thirteenth centuries B.C., there is no bridge over the intervening 600–700 years, and no evidence that Nemea had any venerable tradition of ongoing activity. Rather, it seems clear that Nemea was created on the basis of the preexisting model of Olympia: the mound of Pelops and the location of the early stadium nearby at Olympia served as prototypes for Nemea. We may also note that, as at Olympia and Isthmia, the early stadium was close to, and tied with, religious cult centers but later moved away from the sanctuary because of the need to provide new, larger, and more permanent facilities for the athletes and spectators.

Together the games at Olympia, Delphi, Isthmia, and Nemea formed the athletic cycle, or *periodos,* and the best athletes of antiquity were those who had won at

Fig. 200 Graffiti on the wall of the entrance tunnel to the Nemean stadium. The graffito above brags, "I win!" Below, Telestas has scratched his name. University of California at Berkeley, Nemea Excavations Archives, no. I 59.

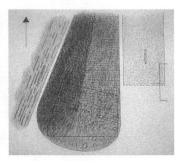

Fig. 201 Schematic reconstruction of the Archaic festival center at Nemea with the Shrine of Opheltes (center) flanked by the hippodrome and the early stadium. Drawing by author.

least once at each site and were entitled be called *periodonikai* (circuit winners). Although the full cycle would be completed within an Olympiad of four years, and there were four festivals, the cycle was not straightforward since the Isthmian and Nemean Games were biennial. One cycle included six festivals. Using 480 B.C. as the starting point, a typical cycle would have looked like this:

480	(July–August)	Olympia
479	(July–August)	Nemea
478	(April–May)	Isthmia
478	(July–August)	Delphi
477	(July–August)	Nemea
476	(April–May)	Isthmia
476	(July–August)	Olympia

Since the ancient year began at the summer solstice, the Isthmian and Nemean Games took place in the same year while the quadrennial Olympics and Pythian Games were each in separate solar years. The doubling of the Isthmian and Nemean Games also meant that it was easier to win in one of them than at the single festivals of Olympia or Delphi, so a victory there counted for a bit less. We can read, for example, about each of the victories of Milo of Kroton at Olympia and Delphi, but not at Isthmia and Nemea (Pausanias 6.14.5; *A 163a*). When all the victories are listed, as for Theagenes of Thasos (Pausanias 6.11.3; *A 167a*), we see that the victories at the two junior sites far outnumbered those at the senior: Theagenes had two Olympic victories, three Pythian, nine Nemean, and ten Isthmian. But if an Isthmian or Nemean victory was less important than one at Olympia or Delphi, it was still more valued than a victory at any other games.

6

THE OLYMPIC GAMES,
300 B.C.:
A RECONSTRUCTION
OF A FESTIVAL

ANY ATTEMPT TO RECONSTRUCT an ancient Olympic festival is doomed to inaccuracies, for we must take our evidence from widely different times and from different sites. We don't even know exactly how Olympia was laid out in 500 or 400 B.C. In one of the ironies of archaeology, hardly anything is left to help us reconstruct the physical setting of the most important competition in Greek athletics during its heyday in the sixth and fifth centuries. I shall therefore look at the 120th Olympiad, which took place in 300 B.C. — not because anything special happened at these games but because we can thus set the ancient Olympics in a recognizable framework of time and place (see figs. 166, 167).

What happened at that long-ago Olympic festival? Let us examine the evidence and try a reconstruction. We can start with the date. The Olympic Games always took place at the second full moon after the summer solstice. In 300 B.C. that fell on August 9.

Preparation

We must begin our reconstruction with the months leading up to the festival, however, and we must start at the city-state of Elis, not at Olympia itself. Elis is located about 36 kilometers northwest of Olympia, although the distance by road was some 57–58 kilometers. This sleepy and conservative rural town controlled Olympia and supervised its games. Some excavations have taken place at the site, where a small museum is located, but they tell us little about the ancient town as a whole. Pausanias offers a revealing description, though it is difficult to reconcile with the reconstruction in figure 202, a drawing based on the excavated remains.

The first monument Pausanias (6.23–24; A 83) mentions at Elis is "an old *gymnasion*," in which "the athletes go through all the customary training before they repair to Olympia." This gymnasion held a racetrack, as well as a separate practice track for runners and pentathletes. There was also an area called the *plethrion* (the 100–footer),

Fig. 202 Reconstruction of ancient Elis based upon the partially excavated remains. After N. Papahatzis, Παυσανίου Ελλάδος Περιήγησις vol. 3 (Athens, 1979), p. 397, fig. 360.

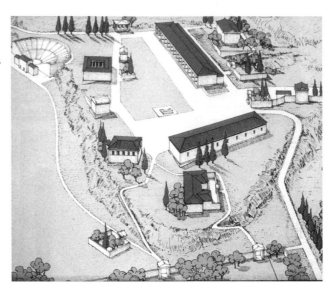

"where the *Hellanodikai* [judges] match the wrestlers by age and ability." Pausanias continues, "There is another gymnasion, smaller in size, that adjoins the older. It is called Square because of its shape. Here the athletes practice wrestling and, when they are done, the boxers practice with soft gloves as protection from the blows. . . . A third gymnasion . . . is reserved for the young men of the city [*epheboi*] for the whole time of the Olympic festival. . . . In this gymnasion is also the council house [Bouleuterion] of the Eleans."

We next learn that one road from this second gymnasion led to baths, and another "leads to the agora and to the so-called *Hellanodikaion* [judges' building]. . . . The Hellanodikai are accustomed to take this road to the [old] gymnasion. They enter before sunrise to match the runners, and at midday to watch those in the pentathlon and in the competitions that are called heavy."

Note that from his entrance into Elis until he reaches the *agora* (marketplace), Pausanias mentions only buildings connected with athletics in general, and training for the Olympic Games in particular. But the athletic orientation of the public spaces of Elis does not end there. Even the marketplace has an athletic bias: "The agora is now called the hippodrome, and the natives train their horses there. . . . In the portico on the southern side of the agora the Hellanodikai generally spend their days. . . . Parallel to the end of this portico is the Hellanodikaion." Elis, then, was an athletic training town, the ancient predecessor of the Olympic Village.

For three of the four years of each Olympiad nothing much connected with the festival would have occurred at Elis, but about a year before the games the Olympic preparations would begin. Ten months before the actual games the ten Hellanodikai, elected by the Eleans to supervise the Olympics, would move into the Hellanodikaion.

So for the games of 300, the judges would have taken up residence in this building in October 301. After they were installed officials known as "guardians of the law" (*nomophylakes*) would begin to instruct them on their duties at the Olympic Games. We know nothing else about these guardians of the law, but we should probably imagine them as successful, long-term veterans of the games who had frequently served as Hellanodikai themselves. We don't know whether they were also associated with the Olympic council (*Olympiake boule*), a fifty-member panel that exercised some sort of general supervision over the games, although we do know that the council was the group to whom athletes would appeal if they wished to dispute a judgment by the Hellanodikai.

The number of Hellanodikai varied in the early years of the games, but it was stabilized in 348 at ten and remained at that number throughout the remainder of antiquity. All ten were responsible for the smooth functioning of the competitions, but they split into subcommittees for the various events—one group was in charge of the horse races, another the footraces, and the third the heavy events of boxing, wrestling, and the *pankration*. These last two subcommittees may also have worked together in the pentathlon, which included both footracing and wrestling along with the specialized events of javelin, *diskos,* and jumping.

As the training of the judges progressed, preparations also had to be made to announce the sacred truce, the *ekecheiria,* which covered the month before the games or, in 300 B.C., the period from July 10 to August 9. This allowed the participants, both athletes and spectators, to travel in safety to the games. The announcement was broadcast by groups of heralds, sometimes called *spondophoroi* (truce-bearers) and sometimes *theoroi* ("envoys," especially to religious festivals). We can get some notion of the highly developed system that must have existed at Olympia by what has been documented at Nemea. A fragment of an inscription discovered at Nemea reports that groups of six theoroi are to travel to specific regions of Greece. Another inscription at Nemea gives the name of a region followed by the names of cities within it, listing one, two, or three key people in each city (fig. 203). The listing for Cyprus, for example, includes prominent local men in the cities of Salamis, Kourion, and Soloi. These were the *theorodokoi,* or envoy-receivers, whose job was to facilitate the task of the heralds when they arrived in their cities. The theorodokoi served as the local representatives of the games, and they demonstrate that a highly organized support system for the games existed throughout the Greek world. Attested at Nemea and Delphi, theorodokoi surely must have been involved in the Olympic and Isthmian Games as well.

After the sacred Olympic truce month had been announced throughout the Greek world, it was time for the athletes to gather at Elis. There they would undergo a month of training under the watch of the Hellanodikai. An athlete who got there late and could not prove that he had been delayed by illness, pirates, or shipwreck was assessed a fine. If he didn't pay it, he was flogged (*IvO 56; A 199*).

At the start of the competition the athletes took an oath stating that they had

Fig. 203 Marble stele listing the names of theorodokoi (envoy-receivers) of the Nemean games, organized by geographical region, 323 B.C. Nemea, Archaeological Museum, inv. no. 185 (photo: University of California, Nemea Excavations Archive).

adhered strictly to their training for the past ten months. In fact, the judges could be sure of at least the last month because the athletes spent it under their supervision. During this month, athletes trained with and against one another, and there must have been attrition as the best athletes in different events became clear. Only some such process would explain the occasions when an Olympic athlete was awarded the victory prize without having to compete against anyone.

Meanwhile, the spectators would begin to trickle in. Each athlete had arrived with his entourage of friends, relatives, and trainer, but we also hear of fans and casual tourists coming to Elis days and even weeks before the games to watch the athletes practice. Although the final pairing of athletes, done by drawing lots from a vessel, may have occurred at this time, it is more likely that it took place at Olympia itself.

Throughout the Olympic month preparations were also under way at Olympia. The festival site was probably never abandoned—pilgrims and tourists might visit at any time during the four-year Olympiad, and a permanent staff of officials was needed to take care of them. An inscription dating from the 189th Olympiad (28 B.C.) probably reflects the situation in 300: the marble slab lists a number of on-call officials who could help visitors make a sacrifice to Zeus. Such was the "on-call sacrificing priest," whose efforts were aided by a flutist, a libation-pourer, a three-man group of libation-dancers, a woodman who provided the special fuel for the sacrifice, and a "butcher-cook," whose job can be guessed from his name. There were also five bailiffs to keep order, and even an official guide to satisfy visitors' curiosity. Each of these officials was paid with a portion of the sacrificial animal; the payment of an

Fig. 204 The stadium at Olympia at harvest time, viewed from the northeast (photo: author).

animal skin as well as the monopoly on firewood for sacrifices provided a significant source of income for the Eleans (*IvO 64; A 133*).

As the games drew near, expert craftsmen came in to perform specialized tasks. The stadium, which might be rented out for grazing or even for growing wheat into the early summer as still happens at Olympia today (fig. 204)—had to be cleared and prepared for action. Many other buildings at the site also needed repairs, and the workers would apply fresh whitewash and paint. They also fixed any problems that might have cropped up in the water channel surrounding the racetrack in the stadium. There had to be some sort of sanitary facilities, but we have no ancient evidence about what form they took.

The next step would be to dig up the surface of the track with handpicks and sprinkle it with water. We can reconstruct this process from inscriptions discovered at Delphi and Delos (*CID* 2.139; *A 81*) and from vase paintings (fig. 205). After this the surface must have been compacted with rollers to create a smooth running surface. The pits (*skammata*) for the jumpers also had to be dug, but this took place during the competition. No trace of these pits has ever been discovered, and their precise location within the stadium is unknown. Finally, inscriptions tell us that white earth was applied to the stadium floor. This must be the same as the white lime used in the modern revival of the games at Nemea to mark out the lanes on the running surface (see figs. 63 and 64).

Now it was time to install the starting mechanism for the races. Since we have selected 300 B.C. for our reconstruction, we must envision a *hysplex* II (see figs. 54–58).

Fig. 205 Digging up the track and sprinkling it with water. On the other side of the vase an athlete draws water from a well. Red-figure skyphos by the Lewis Painter, ca. 460–450 B.C. Archaeologisches Institut der Universität Zürich, ex-collection Hirschmann (photo: Silvia Hertig).

This work may have been done by a specialist. At least we know from Epidauros that one Philon of Corinth was fined for his failure to install the hysplex in a timely fashion (IG IV² 1.98; A 82). The hippodrome also had to be cleaned up and its starting mechanism installed (see fig. 157).

The day is August 6, 300 B.C. At Olympia the stadium and the hippodrome are cleaned, cleared, equipped, and ready for action. And so is the crowd at Elis. They are ready to set off for Olympia, the games are about to begin, the winners and the losers will soon be decided. But before departing Elis, the Hellanodikai gather the athletes together and deliver this charge: "If you have worked to be worthy of going to Olympia, if you have done nothing indolent or ignoble, then take heart and march on; but those who have not so trained may leave and go wherever they like" (Philostratos, Vita Apoll. 5.43; A 84).

With these words the procession to Olympia begins. It is impossible to know precisely how many were in this march, although the participants surely included the ten Hellanodikai, probably the fifty-member Olympic council, perhaps two hundred athletes (sometimes the total was less), and about a hundred equestrian units (both single horses and four- and two-horse chariot teams). Throw in the entourages — trainers, family members, and fans, as well as at least a few slaves or assistants to the Hellanodikai — and dozens (if not hundreds) of curious tourists, and you have a procession that probably exceeded one thousand, and may have numbered several.

The day and the night of August 6 would be spent on the road. We have no details of what, if any, accommodations were provided for the marchers, but on the morning of August 7 they would nearly have arrived at Olympia. But first they will halt at a spring called Pieria, and the Hellanodikai will undergo a ritual purification: they will be sprinkled with the blood of a pig and then washed in the spring water. Now cleansed, they can enter the Sanctuary of Zeus. The games are, at their core, a religious festival.

The Festival

A huge crowd is awaiting the procession, and the sacred grove of Olympia is surrounded by a tent city, housing thousands of spectators. Strangers crowd together—even celebrities:

> Plato the son of Ariston shared a tent at Olympia with some men he did not know, nor did they know him. He so gained their affection with his comradery, eating with them simply and passing the days with all of them that the strangers felt fortunate to have met this man. He made no mention of the Akademy, nor of Sokrates. He only told them that his name was Plato. Later, when they visited Athens, he received them graciously, and the strangers said, "Plato, please take us to see your namesake, the student of Sokrates, take us to his Akademy, and introduce us to that man so that we can enjoy him."
>
> He responded, quietly and with a smile as was his custom, "I am that man." [Aelian, VH 4.9; A 144]

As the crowd settles in, smoke from fires and sacrifices is thick overhead and the air fills with the cries of people from all walks of life. One ancient author describes the scene at the Isthmian Games of about fifty years before our Olympics (probably of 359 B.C.): "That was the time to hear crowds of wretched sophists around the Temple of Poseidon as they shouted and heaped abuse on each other, and their so-called students as they fought with one another, and many historians reading out their stupid writings, and many poets reciting their poetry to the applause of other poets, and many magicians showing their tricks, many fortune-tellers telling fortunes, countless lawyers perverting justice, and not a few peddlers peddling whatever came to hand" (Dio Chrysostom 8.9–12; A 145).

Other sources relate that poets, painters, and sculptors attended the games to display their works and seek commissions from victorious athletes or pious pilgrims. Indeed, Herodotus publicized his *History of the Persian Wars* by going to the back porch of the Temple of Zeus and reading to the crowds from the manuscript he had just completed. Dio Chrysostom's reference to peddlers is hardly surprising, but the excavations at Olympia show that all the official weights, used in commercial activities to weigh produce and other goods, belong exclusively to the fifth and early fourth centuries. This suggests that in later times commercial activities were removed from close proximity to the religious center. Further, all the weights of the earlier period found within the Altis (Sanctuary of Zeus) were located in the northwestern corner, at the entrance; none were in the central area around the Altar of Zeus.

All this hustle and bustle went on against a backdrop of discomfort that served to show just what visitors were willing to put up with in order to be a part of the festival: "There are unpleasant, difficult things in life. But don't they happen at Olympia? Don't you suffer from the heat? Aren't you cramped for space? Don't you bathe badly? Don't you get soaked whenever it rains? Don't you get your fill of noise and shouting and other annoyances? But I suspect that you compare all this to the value of the show and endure it" (Epictetus, *Disc.* 1.6.26–28; A 146).

Returning to the morning of August 7: now the Hellanodikai must go to the council house (Bouleuterion) with the athletes to make their final determination of the athletes' age and administer the oath. This determination will be based at least in part on an examination of the athletes, as well as of their fathers, brothers, and trainers, and even after an athlete's age is established the Hellanodikai must decide whether an eighteen- or nineteen-year-old is so well-developed physically that he has to compete in the *andres* (men's) category. We hear of athletes having nightmares because they feared that even though they had marched from Elis to Olympia with the boys (*paides*), on this day they would be assigned to compete against men (Artemidoros, *Oneir.* 5.13; A 93). The age certification for the horses will also be made, apparently at the same time and place as for the athletes.

The classification by age clearly had a lot to do with an athlete's chances, and the Hellanodikai had to swear that they would not accept bribes in making their decisions. The whole scene would have been chaotic, with pushing and shoving all round, and arguments undoubtedly breaking out about the age classification of various boys and horses. Adding to the confusion would be the horses, who were apparently excited by the statue of a horse that was considered by the Eleans to be magical:

> It is much inferior in size and beauty to all the horses standing within the Altis. Moreover, its tail has been cut off, which makes the figure uglier still. But stallions, not only in springtime but on any day, are in heat towards it. In fact, they rush into the Altis, breaking their tethers or escaping from their grooms, and they leap upon it much more madly than upon a living brood mare, even the most beautiful of them. Their hoofs slip off, but nevertheless they keep on neighing more and more, and leap with a yet more violent passion, until they are driven away by whips and sheer force. In no other way can they be separated from the bronze horse.
> [Pausanias 5.27.3–4]

Yet it is here in the Bouleuterion that the formal oath is now administered in front of the statue of Zeus Horkios (Zeus of the Oath). Pausanias describes the scene: "Of all the images of Zeus, the Zeus in the Bouleuterion is the one most likely to strike terror into the hearts of sinners. This Zeus . . . holds a thunderbolt in each hand. Beside this statue it is established for the athletes, their fathers and brothers, and their trainers to swear an oath on slices of the flesh of wild boars that they will do nothing evil against the Olympic Games" (5.24.9; A 90; fig. 206).

Fig. 206 Zeus Horkios holding a thunderbolt in each hand, flanked by his altar and a sacrificial pig. Bezel of a gold finger ring. London, The British Museum, inv. no. GR 1988.10–20.2 (photo: © The British Museum).

Now come the first competitions, but these are not for the athletes. The contests take place on an altar near the entrance to the stadium, and they are for the trumpeter (*salpinktes;* see fig. 164) and the herald (*keryx;* see fig. 163). The winners of these two events will function as the ancient equivalent of the public-address system, announcing events, competitors, and winners. On this August 7 in 300 B.C., the winner of the trumpet contest is Herodoros of Megara.

The remainder of the day will be taken up with sightseeing, watching the crowd, and making sacrifices. The horse owners, in particular, will attend to these duties for their competitions will take place the next day, and they want to appease the evil spirits (embodied in the Taraxippos) that might operate against them in the hippodrome.

At dawn on August 8 a procession sets out from the Prytaneion, at the northwest corner of the Altis, where the sacred flame burns (see figs. 166, 167). Leading this procession are the priests of Zeus and the Hellanodikai, clad in purple and carrying switches with which to punish athletes committing a foul. The marchers visit sixty-three altars to various gods located within the Altis. (There were actually more altars, but some were used for special purposes and did not belong to the standard processional sacrifices.) Perhaps the most interesting altar they stop at is the Altar of Zeus Apomyios (Fly Averter). Given the crowds at the Olympics and the number of sacrifices, involving huge quantities of blood and meat, fly control was clearly a concern.

Now the scene shifts to the hippodrome. The trumpeter blows a blast to summon the crowd, and the competitors and their horses pass in review. As each competitor goes by, the herald announces his name, his father's name, and his native city-state. This information is given so that challenges can be voiced about the competitor's eligi-

Fig. 207 The Nike at left holds a palm branch for the winner of the pankration, while another hovers with the ribbon. Another athlete watches from the right. Panathenaic amphora by the Painter of Athens 12592, 360/59 B.C. Athens, National Museum, inv. no. 20046 (photo: © Treasury of Archaeological Receipts).

bility: is he under any charges of homicide or sacrilege? Is he a citizen in good standing of his city-state or an exile? Is he Greek? Every competitor in every event has to pass through this review.

The first competition is the one most geared to the aristocracy: the *tethrippon* (four-horse chariot) race (see figs. 145–150). Here the wealthy will display their economic power. Alkibiades, for instance, entered seven different tethrippa in 416 B.C. (Isokrates 16.32–35; *A 67*, and Thucydides 6.16.2; *A 219*), and the unpopular Dionysios of Syracuse entered several in 388 (Diodorus Siculus 14.109; *A 245*). The crowd was pleased when they all crashed. Today the victor is a repeater, Theochristos of Cyrene.

Next comes the horseback race (*keles;* see figs. 151–153), followed by the two-horse chariot race (*synoris;* see figs. 154, 155), which was a more recent addition to the program but was well-established by the end of the fourth century. Finally, a few years before our games a four-foal chariot race (the *tethrippon polikon*) was added to the program, and this would be the final event in the *hippikos agon*. Once more the Hellanodikai would have examined the horses to determine who belonged in this age category (the *polos*). Just as with the athletes, a horse might be declared too old (or too well developed) to belong to the polos category (Pausanias 6.2.2). Unfortunately, we don't know who won any of these races in 300.

With the completion of the equestrian competitions, the scene would shift to the stadium, immediately north of the hippodrome, and to the competition in the pentathlon. This will be the first of the *gymnikoi agones* (nude competitions). As already discussed, we don't know how the victor in the pentathlon was chosen, but once someone won, his name would be announced, and he would receive a ribbon (*tainia*) to tie around his head and a palm branch (*klados phoinikos*). (The winners of all the events got these; fig. 207). The herald would announce his name (fig. 208), and he

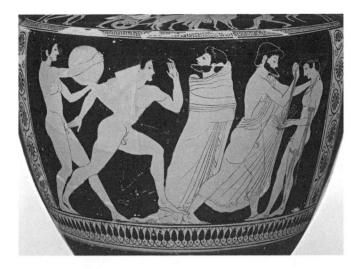

Fig. 208 A diskos thrower and a runner approach the herald, who is announcing the victor. Meanwhile, a judge ties another ribbon around the head of the victor, who already has ribbons on his arm and leg and holds the branches and flowers showered on him by the crowd. Red-figure hydria of the Pezzino Group, ca. 500 B.C. Munich, Staatliche Antikensammlungen und Glyptothek, inv. no. 2420.

would make his victory lap (*periageirmos*) while the crowd cheered and showered flowers and ribbons on him in a tradition known as *phyllobolia*.

As in today's Olympics, some athletes were more popular than others and received more ribbons and flowers: the victor in figure 208 has three ribbons, and other paintings show even more. In the Olympics of 448 B.C., two brothers from Rhodes, Akousilaos and Damagetos, each won a victory — one in boxing, the other in the pankration (Pausanias 6.7.2 – 3; A 170; Pindar, *Pythian* 10.22; Plutarch, *Pelopidas* 34.4; Cicero, *Tuscul. Disp.* 1.46.111). They took a joint victory lap and then ran into the crowd to pick up their father — who had himself been an Olympic victor (see fig. 289). As the two sons paraded their father around the track, the crowd went wild and showered them with flowers. At that point a Spartan shouted out to the father, "Die now Diagoras! You will never be happier."

We should not forget, however, that most of the competitors lost and returned empty-handed to the locker room. These are the defeated ones who, as Pindar says, run home to their mothers by slinking through the back alleys (*Pythian* 8.77 – 78; A 249).

The pentathlon would conclude the first day's competition. In the evening the victors would celebrate and stage parties for their friends. One of the most famous such celebrations took place in 416 when Alkibiades, after his victory in the tethrippon, borrowed the official golden ritual vessels of the Athenians to serve his guests. But he allowed them to believe that he owned the vessels, much to the chagrin of the Athenians ([Andokides] 4.29; A 116). On the evening of August 8, then, the tent city surrounding the Altis would be pricked with isolated spots of light, where the winners rejoiced with their friends. Meanwhile, in the silent darkness, the losers would bemoan their luck, and athletes still to compete would hope that they would be having their own victory parties in the nights to come.

Fig. 209 The central part of the Altis at Olympia with the Temple of Zeus and the conical Altar of Zeus, formed from the ashes of previous sacrfices. Reconstructed drawing from F. Adler et al., *Die Baudenkmäler von Olympia* (Berlin, 1896), pl. 132.

There is evidence to suggest that the day of August 8, 300, ended with sacrifices to Pelops at his shrine, located between the temples of Zeus and Hera. This was the earliest cult center at Olympia, and the sacrifices performed late in the day on August 8 served as a preliminary to the great sacrifice to Zeus that would occur on the next day, even as Pelops probably represents an early cult figure who was supplanted by the great Olympian god.

The night of August 8–9 marked the full moon, the *panselinos,* that ushered in the religious high point of the games: the great sacrifice at the Altar of Zeus. In the second century A.D. we know that the altar was conical, roughly 7 meters high and about 10 meters in diameter (fig. 209). But because it was created entirely from the ashes of previous sacrifices, it has disappeared without a trace, and we must rely upon Pausanias (5.13.8–11) for this description and dimensions. Its bulk was created in part by individual sacrifices performed at various times during the year, but most of it came from the sacrifice held on the day of the full moon every four years. This was August 9 in 300, although in ancient times the new day actually began at sunset on the 8th.

The morning of August 9 would begin with the great procession through the Altis led by the priests and the Hellanodikai followed by the athletes and the official ambassadors of the various city-states, all eager to make a good impression for their home towns. Ambassadors would bring the finest table service from their city-states in order to entertain guests at Olympia, and these gold vessels and incense burners would be set on display, especially during the procession of the panselinos. (We can thus understand why the Athenians were outraged when Alkibiades implied in 416 that their vessels were his.) But the central element in the procession were the hundred oxen for the *hekatomb*, the sacrifice the Eleans would offer to Zeus. The animals would be taken to the great altar and slaughtered. Then their thighs would be placed on the top of the altar and burned for the gratification of Zeus, while the rest of the meat was roasted and distributed to the crowd. This was the great banquet put on by the local hosts for their guests (who probably supplemented the feast with food of their own). Anyone who has been in a Greek village on Easter will have a feeling for this scene.

Now we come to a problem that has yet to be solved. Many scholars have placed the competitions for the boys, the paides, on the afternoon of the day following the panselinos. If they are right, and if we are correct in assuming that the competitions for the boys were completely separate from those for the men, then in 300 the boys' competitions in the stadion, wrestling, and boxing would have been held on the afternoon of August 9. But would anyone pay much attention to the competition after all the feasting? Given the brevity of the program for the boys, it is possible that they competed late in this day, but I suspect that they actually competed on the morning of the next day and that the remainder of August 9 was spent in recovering from the feast.

On August 10, however, the program is as clear as our sources can make it, for this was the day of the gymnikoi agones for the individual athletes. Here the path of the athletes can be traced, following the same route the pentathletes and the boy competitors marched on the previous days.

The Hellanodikai and the competitors approach the stadium from the Altis. Before arriving at the stadium, they pass twelve bronze statues of Zeus, set in two groups of six (see fig. 173). These are the Zanes — statues paid for out of the fines levied against athletes who were caught giving and taking bribes to throw a match. The first group was erected in 388, the second in 332; both stand as warnings to our athletes in 300 that an Olympic victory is not to be bought or sold; if they cheat, the shame of their corruption will live long past their lifetime.

After they pass the Zanes, the Hellanodikai and the athletes come to the locker room (*apodyterion*) behind the Echo Stoa, where the athletes will undress, oil their bodies, and begin to focus on the competitions. Leaving them there the Hellanodikai now enter the stadium through the tunnel (*krypte esodos*), cross the track, and and take their places on the Hellanodikaion — the only permanent seating in the stadium, and the base from which they will run the games. While the committee responsible for the running events is supervising on the track, the other Hellanodikai remain in their seats watching over the whole competition. They are surrounded by spectators, the closest of whom are from Elis.

This home-field advantage had sometimes been exploited, but not this year. In the early sixth century the Eleans had been advised not to participate in the games if they wanted to convince people of the absolute fairness of their games, essential to

maintaining the Olympics' preeminence (Herodotus 2.160; A 105). They decided to ig-
nore this advice, but later, after charges of favoritism following the double victory by
the Hellanodikes Troilos of Elis in the synoris and the tethrippon polikon in 372 (Pausanias 6.1.5; A 107), the Eleans decided that a judge could not enter the hippikos agon.

Once the judges have settled in the stadium, the athletes enter the tunnel, where
they wait for their names to be called. They pass from the sunlight into the dark tunnel, back into the sunlit track. The alternation of light and dark, heat and cold, will increase their tension, which heightens further as the noise of the crowd hits them. As
each athlete's name is announced, and he runs out onto the stadium track, we can
imagine his friends and fans cheering and applauding, while those of his opponents
jeer (see fig. 199). The moment is dramatic — and magical. Athlete and spectator tran-
scend their usual selves. For a few moments everyday life is left behind.

The first race is the *dolichos* (long-distance) race (see fig. 65). The competitors approach the *balbis* (starting blocks), position their toes in the cool stone grooves, and
wait for the signal as the hysplcx falls (see fig. 37). Because it takes much longer to run
than the other races the dolichos serves as a warm up for the crowd, who probably
now drag themselves in, recovering from the parties and feasting of the day before.
But everyone is surely in the stadium on this morning of August 10 for the original and
still the premier event of the Olympics: the stadion race.

We have some evidence that there were so many competitors in the stadion
that it was run in two heats, followed by a runoff between the victors of each (Pausanias 6.13.4; A 99). If so, there may regularly have been up to forty-four competitors
in the stadion since the balbis at Olympia had twenty-two lanes. Indeed, we know of
one occasion where seven competitors in the stadion came from a single city-state
(Strabo 6.1.12).

The winner of the stadion race can expect to gain even more than the ribbons
and palm branch, the victory lap and the phyllobolia. His name will be added to this
Olympiad; the 120th will forever be known as the Olympiad when Pythagoras of
Magnesia (in Asia Minor) won the stadion. Ancient historians referring to events that
occurred in, say, 297 (by our reckoning), wrote that they took place in the fourth year
of the Olympiad when Pythagoras won, events in 293 were dated to the fourth year of
the Olympiad when Pythagoras won for the second time (this athletic star repeated
his victory four years later). Because of this custom of naming the Olympiad after the
victor in the stadion we know the names of more than 250 ancient sprinters, that is,
more than a millennium's worth of stadion victors.

Back at our games, runners once again take their places at the balbis, but now
they form in alternate lanes for the *diaulos,* the double-stadion race (see figs. 63–64).
Today's winner is a local Elean named Nikandros, and the absence of protest suggests
that he has won without any help from his fellow citizens, the judges. After the diaulos there may have been an intermission while the skamma was prepared for the
heavy events. Pairs of athletes have to be selected for these events, and they may

already have been chosen, either at Elis or in the Bouleuterion here at Olympia. Or they could be chosen now, at the stadium. This seems the most likely, for it would make it harder to "fix" the pairs.

Whenever it was done, we know that the procedure called for the athletes to be arranged in a circle around the Hellanodikai, who had a silver vessel that held the small lots, marked in pairs with letters of the alphabet (Lucian, *Hermotimos* 40; A 97). Next to each athlete stood a slave known as a *mastigophoros*, a whip-bearer for punishing fouls. It was the job of the mastigophoros to prevent his athlete from looking at the letter on his lot until everyone had drawn from the vase. Then one of the Hellanodikai would go around the circle inspecting the lots and announce who was paired with whom. If there was an uneven number of competitors, one would get a bye for the first round of competition.

The first of the heavy events was usually the wrestling (*pale*). But the sequence could be changed if an athlete was entered in two events, for example, and did not want to be hurt in the riskier boxing before continuing in the second event (Pausanias 6.15.4; A 95). Such changes usually involved putting the boxing at the end of the program. Once, however, the favorite for the wrestling was so unpopular with the Eleans that they actually canceled the event rather than allow him the chance to win an Olympic victory (Dio Cassius 80.10; A 96). The practice, though it appears contrary to the ancient Greeks' commitment to impartiality, is continued in the modern Olympics, where schedules are often juggled to accommodate particular athletes. On this day of our Olympics the victory goes to a famous strongman: Keras of Argos, who, it is said, has such a tremendous grip that he once tore the hoof from a bull struggling to get away from him (Africanus, *Olympiad* 120).

Next comes the boxing (the *pyx* or *pygmachia*), won by Archippos of Mytilene. The final event of the heavy competitions is the pankration. A Boiotian from Anthedon, Nikon, takes the prize; he will win his second victory at the next Olympiad in 296. The final event of the day, and of the Olympic Games — at least according to modern scholars — would be the *hoplitodromos* (race in armor).

As the evening of August 10 draws in, the last athletes clean up and leave the apodyterion. Many have already departed Olympia, hoping for a fast getaway ahead of the crowds. These are probably the losers and their friends, for there are still the final ceremonies to come, and the victors are sure to remain for them.

On the last day of the festival, August 11, in front of the Temple of Zeus, the final prize of victory is awarded to each winner, a crown of wild olive leaves that has been cut from the trees behind the temple. These branches must be cut with a golden sickle by a boy whose parents are both still living (*Schol.* Pindar, *Olympian* 3.60). The crowns have been sitting on display on a special gold-and-ivory table stored in the Temple of Hera (fig. 210). The table was made by Kolotes, a pupil of Pheidias, who also helped the master create the gold-and-ivory statue of Zeus inside the temple (Pliny, *NH* 34.87 and 35.54).

Fig. 210 The table of Kolotes with a crown. Bronze coin of Elis, A.D. 117–138. Olympia, Archaeological Museum, inv. no. M 876 (photo: author).

Fig. 211 A victorious athlete bearing his preliminary tokens of ribbon and branches prepares to receive the olive crown from Nike while another athlete, holding a stlengis, looks on. Red-figure pelike by the Painter of Louvre G 539, ca. 410 B.C. Vienna, Kunsthistorisches Museum, inv. no. IV.769.

Now the victors, wearing their ribbons and clutching their palms of victory, pass before the Hellanodikai to receive their crowns—the ultimate proof of victory, which they will take home to share with their countrymen (fig. 211). They will be welcomed with an *eiselasis,* a triumphal entry into the city (Aelian, *VH* 12.58, and Pliny the Younger, *Letters* 10.118; *A 172b* and *211*) and awarded a free meal every day for the rest of their lives (*IG* I³ 131 and Plato, *Apology* 36d–e; *A 221* and *231*). They or their families may have already commissioned a statue or an ode to commemorate the victory. And their names will be entered into the official register of victors. But the leafy crown of olive will quickly wilt, dry up, and finally disintegrate. It is ephemeral. The real prize lies in the victory itself.

The Olympic festival ends with a victory dinner given by the Eleans to the newly crowned winners in the Prytaneion, where the ceremonies had begun three days earlier. These victors now join the select few who enter the chapters of Olympic history. Meanwhile, the spectators look for carriages, and the roads from Olympia are filled with pedestrians and horses, satiated by their experience and resolved to come again, but determined next time to find a way to beat the traffic. As one spectator groused in A.D. 165, "The end of the Olympic Games soon came—the best Olympics which I have seen, incidentally, of the four which I have attended. It was not easy to get a carriage since so many were leaving at the same time, and therefore I stayed on for another day against my will" (Lucian *Peregrinus* 35; *A 147*).

7

THE MONEY GAMES AT
EPIDAUROS, ATHENS, LARISSA,
AND SPARTA

ALTHOUGH THE STEPHANITIC FESTIVALS were the big athletic competitions of Greek antiquity, they were only the most prestigious of a host of other athletic festivals. The lesser games fell into two basic categories depending on whether they were sponsored by a sanctuary or a city-state. Both, however, were *chrematitic*. This adjective derives from *chremata*, the word for money, and it denotes a fundamental difference in the prizes of victory between this type of athletic festival and the stephanitic (crown) games. In the chrematitic festival, the winner's prize was either cash or something that could be converted into cash. Athletes might be most proud of their stephanitic victories, but they boasted of their chrematitic victories as well. This point is made graphically in a dedication by a Greek athlete of the early Roman period that displays the victory tokens from stephanitic and chrematitic festivals mixed together (fig. 212).

There were literally hundreds of chrematitic festivals scattered throughout the Greek world. Some were famous, others obscure; relative fame usually depended on the value of the prizes or the amount of prize money. The games sponsored by a religious sanctuary most resembled the stephanitic games, at least in their environment, but they offered prizes of material value, and participants were not protected by a sacred truce, even though these games were theoretically international. One of the most famous such festivals was sponsored by the Sanctuary of Asklepios at Epidauros.

The Asklepeia

The small city-state of Epidauros was located in the Peloponnesos on the northern side of the Argive peninsula, facing the island of Aigina across the sea. Inland about 8 kilometers as the crow flies (but nearly double that by road) stood the secluded Sanctuary of Asklepios. Although closely connected with his father, Apollo, who had sired him by a mortal woman, the hero-god of healing rose to greater and greater prominence until he came to dominate at Epidauros.

The Sanctuary of Asklepios at Epidauros was largely constructed during the fourth century B.C., and its best-known monument today is the excellently preserved

Fig. 212 Images of the victory prizes of an Athenian athlete, whose name is not preserved: Panathenaic amphora from Athens, pine crown from Isthmia, gilt shield from the Aspis games of Argos, and wild-celery crown from the Nemean Games. Marble relief, 1st century A.D. New York, The Metropolitan Museum of Art, inv. no. 59.11.19, Rogers Fund, 1959. (photo: © The Metropolitan Museum of Art).

theater southeast of the sanctuary (fig. 213). On the opposite side of the sanctuary stood the Temple of Asklepios, with the circular tholos and the *abaton* where the sick went to spend the night while being cured, sometimes by the licking of the wound or infected area by either the sacred snakes of Asklepios or sacred dogs; sometimes by visions. Whatever the treatment, the sanctuary operated on a private basis, responding to the specific needs of individuals as they arose. Women were certainly allowed in the sanctuary, and almost half the recorded cures that survive were for females.

We do not know, however, whether women were allowed to take part in the festival or the procession from the city-state to the sanctuary before the Asklepeian Games. The procession did include the sacrificial animals (bulls, cocks, and the like, though not goats), which were then roasted at the sanctuary, providing the basis for the ritual banquet. The meat had to be consumed within the sanctuary, presumably at the time of the feast (Pausanias 2.27.1). The festival took place nine days after the Isthmian Games (in late April or early May), and it was highly organized with a system of *theoroi* and *theorodokoi* (envoys and envoy-receivers; see fig. 203).

For our purposes, the important competitions of the festival were the *gymnikos agon* (nude competition) and the *mousikos agon* (musical competition). There is no evidence that a *hippikos agon* (horse-racing competition) was part of the Asklepeian program. The mousikos agon must have included events in playing the kithara, *aulos* (flute), and other instruments, and we also hear of competitions for rhapsodes and actors. These competitions took place in the theater.

The program in the gymnikos agon is not fully known, either, although we hear specifically of the *stadion* race, the *pankration,* and the pentathlon. The existence of a stadium typical of its day suggests that the program was equally characteristic (fig. 214). We

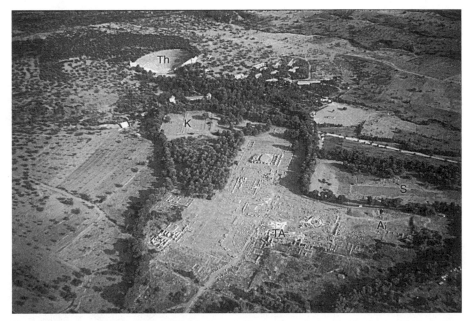

Fig. 213 Aerial view of the Sanctuary of Asklepios at Epidauros, from the north. The theater (Th) is at the upper left with the hotel (katagogeion, K) marked by the large square open space below and to the right of the theater. The Temple of Asklepios is the white rectangle below center at the right (TA), with the circular tholos just to the right of it. The stadium (S) lies above and to the right of the tholos and continues out of the picture to the right. The locker room (apodyterion, A) is on the near side of the stadium and connected to it by a tunnel just above the tip of the A (photo: Raymond V. Scoder, S.J., © 1987 Bolchazy-Carducci Publishers, Inc.).

Fig. 214 The stadium at Epidauros from the east during reexcavation in August 2001 (photo: author).

Fig. 215 The vaulted entrance tunnel to the stadium at Epidauros from the south (photo: author).

have already seen that the *hysplex* (starting mechanism) at Epidauros developed along standard lines (see figs. 58–59). And as at Olympia and Nemea, also built in the second half of the fourth century, spectators sat on earth embankments, but stone seats were soon added near the starting blocks of the *balbis* at the closed end of the stadium. This emphasizes what we have already seen in the location of the judges' stand at Olympia and Nemea: the best seats were near one end of the track. Probably the *skamma* (dug-up area) for the wrestlers, boxers, and pankratiasts was located in front of those seats.

The stadium at Epidauros shares another feature with Olympia and Nemea: athletes entered it through a vaulted tunnel, which also dates to the second half of the fourth century (fig. 215). At the far end of the tunnel, again like Olympia and Nemea, stood a locker room (*apodyterion*; fig. 216). We should thus understand that by 300, if not earlier, a standard type of competitive athletic facility had developed for religious festival centers. Its features included seating for spectators on earth embankments, an entrance tunnel for the athletes and judges, and a locker room for competitors where spectators were not welcome.

The Panathenaia

In addition to games at religious festival centers, games with money prizes were held in every city-state in Greece. Many of these were basically local and did not attract the best athletes, but others fell only a step below the stephanitic games in importance. Preeminent among these were the games of the Athenian Panathenaia, held to honor

Fig. 216 The apodyterion at Epidauros from the east. At the left is the tunnel entrance, whose walls are bonded into the massive wall that helped retain the earth embankment of the stadium to the left and also served as the back wall of a colonnaded roofed area to the right of center. The individual stone blocks are the bases for columns that supported a shed roof like that at Olympia (see fig. 174) (photo: author).

the city-state's patron goddess. We have seen the ubiquity of the Panathenaic amphoras, which supply so much of our primary evidence concerning those competitions, but many written sources also deal with the Panathenaic Games, especially a section of Aristotle's *Constitution of the Athenians* (60; A 119). Particularly important is a large fragment of a fourth-century B.C. marble stele listing the individual competitions together with the prizes awarded in each (*IG* II² 2311; A 120). From all this evidence we can offer a fairly close reconstruction of the Panathenaia.

Originally the Panathenaic Games were held annually and were open only to citizens of Athens. Beginning in 566/5, however, the annual games were augmented every four years by competitions open to all Greeks. These quadrennial games were called the Greater Panathenaia to distinguish them from the annual Lesser Panathenaia, and they included the gymnikos agon, the hippikos agon, and the mousikos agon, similar to the program at Delphi. The last of these consisted of four competitions, for kithara singers, aulos singers, kithara players, and aulos players. The inscription on the fourth-century marble stele refers to the competitions for the aulos singers and the kithara players as belonging to the *andres* (men's) category; probably the part of the text that has broken off listed competitions for these events in another age category, presumably the *paides* (boys).

The prizes, however, set these musical competitions apart from those of the stephanitic games. Not only did they take the form of cash, they included prizes for second, third, fourth, and even fifth place. For example, the winner of the kithara-singing competition for men received a gold crown worth 1,000 drachmas plus 500 silver drachmas in cash. The value of this prize in modern terms is impossible to establish with any degree of accuracy, but the lowest value assigned to the drachma in recent times is $22, so the total prize might have been worth $33,000. More helpful, perhaps, we know that one drachma was about the daily wage of a skilled workman at the time of this inscription; by that standard the drachma must have been worth at least $100 in today's terms, and probably much more. In other words, the first-place prize for the kithara singers at the Panathenaic Games could have been worth in the neighborhood of $150,000.

It is also striking that the prizes for the runners-up were of considerable value:

1st prize	a gold crown worth 1,000 drachmas and 500 silver drachmas;
2d prize	1,200 drachmas;
3d prize	600 drachmas;
4th prize	400 drachmas;
5th prize	300 drachmas.

The fifth-place finisher, then, still took home several thousand dollars. Although the other competitions offered fewer prizes, of lesser value (winners in the kithara playing received just over half the amount awarded the kithara singers), the total value of the prizes in the mousikos agon at the Greater Panathenaic Games was certainly more than a million and probably several million dollars.

The only running event in the gymnikos agon seems to have been the stadion (as preserved on the stele), but there was a full schedule of pentathlon, *pale* (wrestling), *pyx* (boxing), and pankration for all three age categories (*paides, ageneioi,* and *andres*). Each victor received a number of amphoras filled with oil. The winner in the boys' stadion, for example, got fifty amphoras, and the boy who took second place ten. The analogous prizes for the ageneioi (youths) were sixty and twelve amphoras, respectively. The prizes in the men's category are not preserved on the stele, but the winner in the stadion probably took a hundred amphoras.

The amphoras were always decorated with an image of Athena on one side. In our surviving examples, she bears a shield with the snake-edged aegis over her shoulders as she strides confidently forward with her spear ready to be thrown or plunged into the enemy (fig. 217). The other side depicts the competition for which the amphora was the prize (see, for example, fig. 3). The amphora itself had some intrinsic value, probably about $50, and it was the real trophy, to be displayed and cherished. We see this in the care taken to repair them in antiquity (see, for example, figs. 84, 152), even though they could no longer hold liquids. The economic value of the prize, however, came from the olive oil. Although the Panathenaic amphora gradually evolved into a taller, more slender shape, its capacity seems to have remained stable at the

Fig. 217 The standard image of Athena on Panathenaic amphoras: she is flanked by two columns, here topped by cocks, with the painted notation "the prize at Athens." Panathenaic amphora, ca. 490 B.C. Toledo, Ohio, Toledo Museum of Art, inv. no. 1961.24, gift of Edward Drummond Libbey.

ancient standard known as the *metretes*: about 38.9 liters. Hence the winner of the boys' stadion received about 1,944 liters of olive oil. If olive oil can be valued at $5 a liter, the prize (including the amphora) was worth at least $10,000, and the total value for all the prizes in the gymnikos agon approached, and probably exceeded (perhaps substantially), half a million dollars.

Only the last two events of the hippikos agon are preserved on the stele's inscription: the two-horse chariot race for full-grown horses and the same race for foals. We can be sure, however, that a full program of equestrian events took place because they appear on Panathenaic amphoras (see figs. 145, 146, 148, 151, 152, 154). There was probably no difference between these events and their counterparts at the Panhellenic games except, once again, for the prize of olive oil. We can estimate the relatively high value of horses in Greek society from the 140 amphoras awarded to the winner of the two-horse chariot in the full-grown category. This prize was significantly greater than any in the gymnikos agon yet less than the prize for the four-horse chariot, which (although not preserved on the stele) was always the premier event in the hippikos agon. Here we see another difference between the stephanitic and the chrematitic games: the practice of giving equal prizes (a simple crown) to every winner in every event is replaced by a system that awards prizes on a scale of evaluated victories. The winner of the men's stadion at Olympia had the whole Olympiad named for him, but the owner of victorious horses at the Panathenaia walked away with the most loot.

Fig. 218 Aerial view of Athens from the southeast. The Panathenaic stadium is in the foreground with the locker room for the first modern Olympics (S). The Akropolis (A), the area of the Archaic Agora, today's Plaka (P), and the Classical Agora (CA) are toward the center top. The three great gymnasia of Athens are the Akademy (Ak, top right), the Lykeion (Lyk, at right—continuing off the photo), and Kynosarges (Kyn, at left) (photo: © H. R. Goette, Berlin).

We learn from Aristotle, writing not long after the stele's list of prizes was inscribed, that a group of ten *athlothetai* (prize producers) were selected by lot, one from each of the tribes of Athens. These men held office for four years and were responsible for a variety of tasks associated with the Greater Panathenaia, including organization of the games, making the vases, gathering the oil, and presenting the prizes. In recognition of the importance of their duties, the Athenians fed them at public expense in the *prytaneion* (home of the sacred flame) for the month before the competitions.

The oil itself was collected during the four-year period between festivals and apparently stored directly in the prize amphoras. This can be surmised from the names of the annual *archons* (chief magistrates) painted on these vases during the period from at least 392/1 to at least 312/1 that allow us to date the amphoras. We do not know why this custom, which had neither antecedent nor descendant in the long history of Panathenaic amphoras, was introduced, but we can see that many archons whose names appear were not in office during the year of the actual festival. For example, the amphora that depicts the *hoplitodromos* (race in arms; see fig. 33) bears the name of the

Fig. 219 Aerial view of the Panathenaic stadium from the northwest. The 1896 locker room (and perhaps the ancient apodyterion) is marked by an A (photo: Raymond V. Scoder, S.J., © 1987 Bolchazy-Carducci Publishers, Inc.).

Fig. 220 The Panathenaic stadium with the track set up for a modern meet, seen from the southeast. The tunnel to the locker room is at the right (photo: © H. R. Goette, Berlin).

archon of the year 323/2, but the Greater Panathenaia took place in 326/5 and 322/1. Thus, the date on the amphora must refer to the year the oil was gathered, not to the year of the games themselves.

The sites of competitions would have stretched from the center of the city (the Theater of Dionysos where the mousikos agon was held) to the plain near the Bay of Phaleron, where the hippikos agon was contested. The gymnikos agon was originally held in the Archaic Agora north of the Akropolis (the area of today's Plaka; fig. 218), not in the Classical Agora as is sometimes said (though the civic events of the Panathenaia were competed in the Classical Agora). The construction in about 330 of the Panathenaic stadium east of the Akropolis provided a new venue for the gymnikos agon. This stadium was tucked into a natural ravine between two hills, reminiscent of the locations of the stadiums at Nemea and Epidauros of about the same period (fig. 219). Nearly half a millennium later, between A.D. 140 and 144, the Panathenaic stadium was sheathed in marble (including the seats) by the wealthy Athenian Herodes Atticus. We have already noted his gifts to Olympia, Delphi, and Isthimia.

The marble all but completely disappeared during medieval times, but it was replaced for the celebration of the first modern Olympics in 1896 (fig. 220). The modern reconstruction and the continued use of the Panathenaic stadium for a variety of events make the details of the structure in 330 B.C. virtually impossible to recover. Nonetheless, it is clear that a tunnel existed, partly carved into the bedrock of the hill behind and partly constructed in stone. At the far end of the tunnel entrance a locker room was built in 1896 over remains of what was almost certainly the ancient apodyterion (fig. 221). It seems that the Athenian stadium, like contemporary stadiums at Olympia, Nemea, and Epidauros, consisted of a track surrounded by earthen embankments for the spectators, a vaulted underground entrance for the athletes, and a locker room near the tunnel.

Fig. 221 The locker room for the first modern Olympics in 1896, constructed at the end of the tunnel entrance to the stadium, seen from the southeast (photo: author).

Fig. 222 Spear throwers on horseback flank the target. The chlamys (heavy cloak) and petasos (hat) worn by the contestants are the standard apparel issued to young men in training to become citizens. Panathenaic amphora of the Kuban Group, ca. 400 B.C. London, The British Museum, inv. no. GR 1903.2–17.1 (photo: © The British Museum).

In addition to the open quadrennial events Athens hosted an annual athletic festival exclusively for citizens or citizens-to-be. The program of this Lesser Panathenaia has aptly been called one of "civic" competitions. The marble stele lists its events and prizes:

PRIZES FOR THE WARRIORS
For the victor in the *keles* [horseback] race: 16 amphoras of olive oil.
Second place: 4 amphoras of olive oil.
For the victor in the two-horse chariot race: 30 amphoras of olive oil.
Second place: 6 amphoras of olive oil.
For the victor in the processional two-horse chariot race: 4 amphoras of olive oil.
Second place: 1 amphora of olive oil.
For the *akon* [spear] thrower from horseback: 5 amphoras of olive oil.
Second place: 1 amphora of olive oil.
For the pyrrhic dancers in the paides category: a bull and 100 drachmas.
For the pyrrhic dancers in the ageneios category: a bull and 100 drachmas.
For the pyrrhic dancers in the andres category: a bull and 100 drachmas.
For the winning tribe in *euandria:* a bull and 100 drachmas.
For the winning tribe in the *lampadephoros:* a bull and 100 drachmas.
For the individual victor in the *lampadephoros:* a water jar and 30 drachmas.

PRIZES FOR THE BOAT RACE
For the winning tribe: 3 bulls, 300 drachmas, and 200 free meals.
Second place: 2 bulls and 200 drachmas.
[The rest of the stone has broken off.]

Fig. 223 Dancers in the pyrrhiche. Marble relief dedicated by the victorious choregos, named Atarbos, 330–320 B.C. Athens, Akropolis Museum, inv. no. 1338 (photo: © Treasury of Archaeological Receipts).

Before turning to the individual events listed here, some general observations should be made. First, the prizes are significantly smaller than those in the corresponding events of the Greater Panathenaia. Contrast the 30 amphoras of oil for the two-horse chariot race with the 140 for the open version of the same event. Second, several of the victors are not individuals but groups of dancers or a tribal team. Finally, as is clear from the event labeled "akon thrower from horseback" as well as other events discussed below, these competitions all had a decidedly military slant.

Apparently the horseback and two-horse chariot races "for the warriors" were the same as those events in the Greater Panathenaia. At least the terse listing on the stele shows no distinction between the two categories. The "processional two-horse chariot" may be related to the procession to the Akropolis and Athena's sanctuary that opened the festival. We can imagine, although we do not know, that this was a competition for the most orderly, best-trained, most neatly presented team of horses in the goddess's parade.

The competition for the akon thrower from horseback is depicted on a Panathenaic amphora (fig. 222) showing a target suspended from a post. The winner must have been determined on the basis of accuracy. Note that the javelins are not equipped with an *ankyle* (throwing loop) as are the javelins in the pentathlon, and that the competitors wear a broad-rimmed *petasos* (hat) and a *chlamys* (cloak), symbols of young men who have begun their ephebic training in preparation for Athenian citizenship.

The competitions in all age categories for the *pyrrhiche* (pyrrhic dances) can be understood as a kind of military ballet, described by Plato as "movements that evade blows and missiles by dodging, yielding, leaping, [and] crouching, and the opposite, offensive postures of striking with missiles, arrows, and spears, and all sorts of blows" (*Laws* 7.815a). Surviving victory monuments of pyrrhic dancers show young men with

Fig. 224 Two young athletes, perhaps competitors in the euandria, with a judge to the right. Panathenaic amphora of the Kuban Group, 410–400 B.C. London, The British Museum, inv. no. B 605 (photo: © The British Museum).

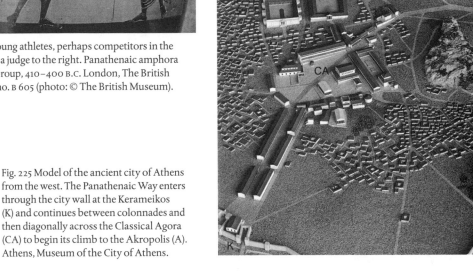

Fig. 225 Model of the ancient city of Athens from the west. The Panathenaic Way enters through the city wall at the Kerameikos (K) and continues between colonnades and then diagonally across the Classical Agora (CA) to begin its climb to the Akropolis (A). Athens, Museum of the City of Athens.

helmets and/or shields performing coordinated movements or acrobatics (fig. 223). Group choreography with military overtones was basic to this competition; the groups each represented a tribe. We also know that the cost of the production was borne by a citizen-sponsor, or *choregos,* from the tribe. In 409/8 one such sponsor paid 800 drachmas to produce the pyrrhiche competition at the Greater Panathenaia (Lysias 21.1; *A 121*).

The competition in euandria was another event of the Panathenaia not present in the stephanitic competitions. Although we don't fully understand what the competition in "beautiful manliness" or "manly beauty" (as the word implies) consisted of, it sounds like a beauty pageant organized by tribes and involving strength as well as physical fitness. It has been suggested that the competition represented on one Panathenaic amphora is the euandria (fig. 224), but the identification rests more on an absence of clear correspondence to some other competition than on any positive association of the euandria with the depiction. The fact that an amphora was not part of the prize for the euandria ("a bull and 100 drachmas") suggests that another competition is being portrayed here. Since the prize went to the team and not the individual,

Fig. 226 Passing the torch in the lampadedromia. The competitors wear headdresses that identify their tribe. Red-figure bell krater by the Kekrops Painter, 410–400 B.C. New York, The Metropolitan Museum of Art, inv. no. 56.171.49, Fletcher Fund, 1956 (photo: © 1983 The Metropolitan Museum of Art).

Fig. 227 Racing to the finish in the lampadedromia with the king archon waiting by the Altar of Athena, and the victory prize hydria on the ground next to the altar. Red-figure krater in the Manner of the Pelias Painter, 430–420 B.C. Cambridge, Mass., Arthur M. Sackler Museum, Harvard University Art Museums, inv. no. 1960.344, bequest of David M. Robinson.

perhaps we should imagine all the young citizens-to-be passing in review, tribe by tribe, with the most pleasing awarded the prize. According to one ancient source (Athenaeus 13.565F; A 122), the winners in the euandria were the most handsome and were allowed to bear the sacred objects in the Panathenaic procession. The frieze of the Parthenon may show euandria victors.

Much better understood is the competition listed in the inscription as the *lampadephoros,* "torch bearer," and known elsewhere as the *lampadedromia,* "torch race." Ten teams, each drawn from a tribe and each consisting of perhaps forty members, raced in a relay from the Akademy northwest of Athens to the Akropolis. According to one source, the race began at the Altar of Prometheus in the Akademy (Pausanias 1.30.1; A 123). Another source puts the start at the Altar of Eros (Plutarch, *Solon* 1.4). We do know that the route brought the runners past the memorial cemetery of Athens and into the city through the walls in the Kerameikos. From that point (fig. 225), they followed the Panathenaic Way into and diagonally across the Classical Agora up the ever steeper incline (fig. 218) to the Akropolis. The total distance was more than 2.5 kilometers, and each member of the team must have run about 60 meters.

The crucial element in the race was that the torches had to be kept burning; teams whose torch went out were disqualified (Pausanias 1.30.2; A 123). Although it was not portrayed on Panathenaic amphoras, since they did not constitute part of the prize, the torch race was a favorite of Attic vase painters (and probably of the crowd that lined the streets as it passed). It appears on many different vases, sometimes at the moment the torch is passed from one runner to the next (fig. 226), and sometimes at the finish (fig. 227). The notation in the stele inscription that a prize was also given to the individual victor is puzzling. Were there two races — one for individuals and one for teams? Or did the last member of the team, the anchor runner, receive the individ-

Fig. 228 Competition in armed combat, the hoplomachia. Pseudo(?)-Panathenaic amphora, ca. 530
B.C. Madrid, Archivo Fotográfico, Museo Arque-
ológico Nacional, inv. no. 10.901.

Fig. 229 The apobates competition. Panathenaic
amphora by the Marsyas Painter, 340/39 B.C.
Malibu, Calif., The J. Paul Getty Museum, inv. no.
77.AE.147 (photo: Ellen Rosenbery).

ual honor? Critical to our understanding is a vase that portrays an altar at whose base
stands a *hydria* (water jar) that was, according to the inscription, part of the prize for
the individual (fig. 227). The altar is stacked with wood awaiting the flame, and behind
it stands the *archon basileus* (king archon) dressed in his finery. The king archon over-
saw the religious activities of the Athenians, and his location in this picture can be
identified by the olive tree to the right of him and the altar. This is clearly the sacred
olive of Athena, and it identifies the altar as that of Athena Polias, the goddess of the
city. The runners wear headgear that marks their tribal teams, and the runner closest
to the altar is bringing the flame to Athena—and the victory to his tribe. But the appearance of the hydria suggests that it awaits him, personally, as the prize awarded to
the anchor runner on the team.

Bringing the fire from the *gymnasion* of the Akademy to light the fire on Athena's
altar for the principal sacrifice of her festival was a symbolic act celebrating Athens
as a civic entity, and it depended upon the zealous participation of the city's citizens.
The torch relay was inspirational in antiquity, and these images are one of the reasons
that today the Olympic flame is carried by runners from Olympia to the site of the
current games. The flame symbolized life, and the torch brought—and brings—that
symbol to all.

Uncertainty surrounds another possible Panathenaic event: the *hoplomachia*
(armed combat or fencing). We see it portrayed on an amphora of Panathenaic shape
and decoration (fig. 228). On the side depicting Athena, the standard painted legend pro-
claims the vase to be a prize at Athens. Since the amphora is shorter than usual, however,
scholars question whether it is a real prize; the hoplomachia portrayed on it would
therefore not be an event in the Panathenaic Games. Nonetheless, its military character
fits the emphasis of many other events in the civic side of the Panathenaic Games.

No such uncertainty surrounds the apobates event, which is mentioned frequently (though not on the preserved portion of the prize-list inscription) and

Fig. 230 The anthippasia competition. The tribal commander is on the left, overseeing the line of young cavalrymen. The reverse of the slab preserves the hindquarters of a lion, and the inscribed notation that "the tribe of Leontis won." Marble relief, early 4th century B.C. Athens, American School of Classical Studies at Athens, Agora Excavations, inv. no. I 7167 (photo: Craig Mauzy).

appears in sculpture and on Panathenaic amphoras (fig. 229). Participants consisted of chariot teams of four horses driven by a charioteer and accompanied by an armed warrior. Each of the ten tribes apparently entered one team, and the course of the race repeated a portion of the course of the torch race from the city walls in the Kerameikos, along the Panathenaic Way, and through the Classical Agora to end at the Eleusinion, where the slope becomes too steep for chariots and the road is paved with stone slabs. The total length of the course was, then, about 700 meters, and it seems that the warrior dismounted at specified places, ran alongside the chariot, and then remounted. This may have occurred at several intervals, and at the end the warrior would dismount one last time and run to the line, apparently at the steepest part of the course. A reference to a head-on crash during the apobates leads some scholars to suggest that there were several laps up and down the course, but the width of the Panathenaic Way does not really accommodate two-way traffic for ten chariots. More details are not known, but it is clear that teamwork between horses, charioteer, and warrior were critical in an event that recalls a time when chariot warfare was a normal part of military practice.

Another equestrian civic event was known as the *anthippasia*. Xenophon (*Hipparchikos* 3.10–13) describes this event as taking place in the hippodrome in the plain of Phaleron, mentioning that there two sides, who were observed by the citizen body. Each side consisted of five tribal contingents, and the two sides faced each other and charged through the other's lines three times. This must represent cavalry combat, again a training for military exercises, in which the team that operated best was adjudged victorious — a kind of four-legged pyrrhiche. A fragment from a marble relief set up by a victorious tribe gives us some idea of this event (fig. 230). A row of four prancing horses awaits the signal to charge. The older bearded rider at left must be the tribal commander, while the fresh-faced youths astride the other horses are the young Athenians-to-be who are using this competition to display their newly developed

Fig. 231 The taurotheria: on one side the competitor tries to throw the bull while on the other the competitor's riderless horse gallops off. The inscription above and below the horse gives the name of the city. Silver coin from Larissa, 440–400 B.C. St. Petersburg, The State Hermitage Museum, inv. no. 7778.

skills. They are, one imagines, hopeful of approbation from the older Athenians.

The final event in the Panathenaic Games was competed at sea: a boat race, which appears in the list of prizes inscribed on the stele. Details of this race are not known but can be inferred. Some suggest the race course ran from the tip of Cape Sounion to Phaleron, a distance of nearly 50 kilometers. Others argue that this distance is too great and suggest a race from the Kantharos harbor of Peiraeus around the promontory where the Tomb of Themistokles was located, and into the military harbor of Zea or the smaller Mounychia harbor. Given the close associations between Themistokles and the rise of Athenian naval power, this suggestion is attractive.

We also don't know what kind of boat was used, but again the stele offers some circumstantial evidence that allows us to make a guess. The warship that was crucial to Athens was the trireme, a long, narrow ship propelled by oarsmen seated in three banks on each side of the ship. Modern estimates of the number of oarsmen have ranged from 170 to 198. In addition to the oarsmen, each trireme had a captain (*trierarchos*) and a boatswain (*keleustes*), who gave the beat to the oarsmen. All of these, and perhaps others, must be included among the victors, so the two hundred free meals awarded the winning boat suggests the number of contestants. The size of the crew is implicit in the 200–drachma prize for second place.

This competition also tells us something important about the civil Panathenaic Games. First, the trireme was a military ship, and it was used to ram the enemy's ships with a bronze beak that jutted out at the bow just below the waterline. It therefore required precise coordination among a large group of men. So in this event as in others, young citizens are displaying their preparation for military service.

Second, the prizes awarded the tribal team victors include meat from the sacrificial oxen. The winners thus take their reward in the form of a communal meal in a civic and ritual context. The bonding that occurred at such meals, especially in celebration of victory, played an important role in generating esprit de corps among the next generation of citizens. The nature of these rewards underlines the fundamental role of civic athletics in regenerating the community.

The Eleutheria

Athens was not the only city to host games that put an emphasis on the good citizen as soldier and man of letters. Larissa in Thessaly provides us with another example with its Eleutheria (Freedom) Games in honor of Zeus. These games were apparently not open to other Greeks; only citizens of Larissa participated. An inscription from about the time of Christ lists the events and the names of their winners (*IG* IX 2, 531; *A* 124). Many of these are standard competitions of the gymnikos agon: stadion and diaulos races, the pyx, and the pankration, for both men and boys. There were also competitions for trumpeters and heralds. Competitions in literary composition and rhetoric were held, but none in music — a significant difference with the Panathenaia. The program also contained competitions that we recognize from the civic games of the Panathenaia: a torch race for boys, the apobates, and cavalry marksmanship, as well as a cavalry charge, an infantry charge, and infantry marksmanship and archery. All these competitions had individual rather than team winners.

There are also two competitions that emphasize the special interests of Larissa, just as the trireme race emphasized the naval concentration of the Athenians. Larissa, like Thessaly as a whole, was famous for its horses. It is therefore curious that the Eleutheria did not seem to have any of the standard horse races, but it did have a torch race on horseback. Even more characteristic was the *taurotheria* (bull hunt), which is vividly described by various ancient authors (*A* 125–126) and appears on the coins of Larissa (fig. 231). A rider would chase a bull around an enclosure until the animal became tired; then the rider would guide his horse alongside the bull "so that horse and bull mixed breath and sweat together. . . . People at a distance could believe that the heads of the two animals grew from a single body, and they cheered . . . this strange hippotauric *synoris*" (Heliodoros 10.29; *A* 126). Then the rider would jump from his horse onto the neck of the bull and use his weight to force the bull's head down until the knees buckled and the bull rolled over with its horns stuck in the ground and its hooves flailing at the air.

This sounds a lot like a rodeo competition, and it surely reflects the values of the local society in promoting the talents of their "cowboys." But the competition appears in a context which is otherwise similar in its essentials to the games of other cities. In other words, civic athletics are more concerned with the particular needs of a particular polis than are the international competitions of the Panhellenic sites.

The Karneia

This tendency to link an athletic festival to the needs of the host city can be found in the Karneia at Sparta, a city-state well known for its educational system, in which children were removed from their homes and placed in communal training centers. (The Spartan system also applied more inclusively to girls and women than is attested elsewhere.) The Spartans controlled both the valley of the Eurotas River (Lakonia) and the neighboring plain of Messenia on the other side of Mount Taigetos to the west, but these lands were tilled by the indigenous peoples. The Spartans thus had both the leisure and the need to develop a strong military force from their own citizen body: the homeland required protection against forces both without and within. As a result of this situation, a Spartan fighting force developed that was legendary for its invincibility. Even the slaughter of Leonidas and his three hundred heroic Spartans at Thermopylai against overwhelming numbers of Persians only fed the stories of Spartan military prowess, while the successes of the Spartans in the sixth and fifth centuries further burnished their legend.

This mythology created, or re-created, a similar system of education in the Roman period that was itself the source of even more stories. Later sources, together with an actual rejuvenation of Sparta in the Roman period, make it difficult to assess the true state of affairs in the earlier period of Spartan glory, but there is enough contemporary evidence from the Classical period to suggest that the later stories are not as exaggerated as they might appear.

Ancient sources offer an image of civic athletics that is similar in many ways to the correlation of games and civic needs in Athens and Larissa that we have examined, although we have no comprehensive program of the various games. Certainly, there were many games festivals throughout Lakonia, but the most important were the Hyakinthia and the Karneia, both sacred to Apollo and both having roots that went back to very early times. The Karneia were sufficiently important that a list of victors was compiled in the fifth century, and a foundation date sometime in the twenty-sixth Olympiad (676 – 673) was established. The festival included various events in the hippikos and mousikos agones, at least in the earliest period, while musical competitions are also attested in the Hyakinthia in many periods. They were always appropriate, of course, in festivals dedicated to Apollo.

More details are known about the program of events in the gymnikos agon of the Karneia. These included a stadion and diaulos race, as well as the long-distance *dolichos,* all of which must have been similar to the standard events at other sites. Another footrace called the *makros* (long-distance) was presumably longer than the dolichos; unfortunately, no details are known. The *pente dolichos* must have been five times the length of the dolichos, and it is clear that the Spartan games emphasized long-distance running more than games in other cities did. The hoplitodromos is attested only once, in a village outside of Sparta proper. It may be noted that no Spartan ever won — so far as we know — the hoplitodromos at Olympia. It seems not to have

Fig. 232 The temple of Artemis Orthia at Sparta (left), with the foundations of the Altar of Artemis at right (photo: author).

been a favorite. Much more popular was the pentathlon (including wrestling); the many dedications of *diskoi* and *halteres* (jumping weights) by successful Spartan athletes suggest that the pentathlon held a special place of honor.

A later Roman-period source (Philostratos, *On Gymnastics* 9; A 37) claims that the Spartans invented boxing because they had no helmets and wanted to toughen their faces, but they later "quit boxing and the pankration as well, because these contests are decided by one opponent acknowledging defeat, and this might give an excuse for her detractors to accuse Sparta of cowardice." While the mythic Lakedaimonian Polydeukes was described as an excellent boxer (Theokritos, *Idylls* 22.27–135; A 39), the Spartans' refusal to box in later times sounds like part of the mythology of historic Sparta. The same conclusion could be reached from Plato's assertion that Athenians who were fans of the Spartans emulated them by binding their hands with *himantes* and boxing so that they would acquire deformed ears like their heroes (*Protagoras* 342B–C). But there is no certain evidence that a Spartan won any victories in boxing or the pankration at any of the Panhellenic sites, nor were these events apparently held locally, though we have abundant evidence for the other events. From the year boxing was added to the Olympic program (688), until the end of the fourth century B.C., for example, Spartans won forty-four times in other events of the gymnikos agon but never in boxing or the pankration. It appears that the "myth" of the Spartan refusal to compete in these events had a basis in historic fact.

The Spartans certainly practiced a kind of boxing and, implicitly, the pankration, but only as part of two peculiar competitions. In one, *sphaireis* (ball players) competed in a game identified with the *episkyros,* a team sport in which tribal teams competed in a tournament. Although it was a ball game it involved, at least at Sparta, a lot of pushing and shoving and punches. Rugby is perhaps the closest modern analogy. Even rougher was the competition at the Platanistas (plane-tree grove). This was also organized by tribes into teams of ephebes who competed in a tournament format, two teams at a time. It took place on some sort of island, and the objective was to push the opposing team off the island. There was no ball; contestants would "fight with their hands and by jumping up to kick. They bite and gouge out eyes. They fight man to man in this way, but they also attack as a group violently and push one another into the water" (Pausanias 3.14.10). This is not boxing nor the pankration of Olympia, but it surely toughened faces.

Perhaps the most curious competition of ancient Sparta was the one contested at the Sanctuary of Artemis Orthia (Upright; fig. 232). In the Classical period, the rites here involved attempts by youths of Sparta to steal cheese from the altar while others whipped them. By the Roman period, this had been transformed into an endurance contest where the winner was the youth who held out the longest while the whips drew blood and "their fathers and mothers. . . . threaten[ed] them if they [did] not endure the lashes. . . . Many have died in this agon because they place no value in giving up under the eyes of their relatives while life was still in them. Their statues are set up at public expense" (Lucian, *Anacharsis* 38; A 127). Bases of such statues have survived, and they confirm the title bestowed on the victorious young man: *bomonikes,* the altar winner.

The violent games of the Spartans differ only in type and degree from the local civic games of the other Greek city-states. In each festival the ultimate aim was to train the youth of the city to become citizens, and the variations in this training from place to place reflect the particular concerns of each society. But all these competitions had a military aspect; the citizens-to-be were being prepared for service to their country. In this way they differed from the gymnikos agon of the stephanitic festivals, which were not, as some modern scholars have maintained, a training for war. This was recognized early in antiquity. The aggressively militaristic Spartan poet Tyrtaios (650–600, fragment 12) states clearly that the skills of the athlete and the skills of the warrior differ; the former are not admirable in a man who lacks the latter. The same sentiment was expressed a century later by Xenophanes (fragment 2; A 229) and again another century later by Euripides (*Autolykos,* fragment 282; A 230). This distinction between the war games of the local civic athletics, and the nonwar games of Olympia, Delphi, Isthmia, and Nemea must be kept clearly in mind, especially when we consider the relationship of the Panhellenic games to politics (see Chapter 15).

Some modern scholars cite the hoplitodromos as proof that the stephanitic games had their own military aspect, but the late addition of this competition to the

Olympic program suggests that the games were not focused on military training. Furthermore, athletes competed in the hoplitodromos event without fundamental military equipment: offensive weapons like spear and sword. And infantry maneuvers were predicated on team coordination not individual actions. If the Olympic event replicated anything common to military practice, it was running away from the battlefield.

Other differences must also be kept in mind. As already noted, civic athletics were chrematitic, and prizes were awarded for second-place (and sometimes third-, fourth-, and fifth-place) finishers. Further, many of the events were decided by subjective judgments. Who was the most handsome in the euandria? Which tribe had performed the best in the pyrrhic dancing? In the anthippasia? Who decided? At Athens a panel of ten judges, one from each tribe, voted, after which five of the ten votes were selected by lot as the "valid" votes. This was an attempt to reduce the subjectivity of the panel and the prejudices of its individual members. But embedded in such a system was a source of tension and confrontation. Favoritism could easily be charged, and such charges were probably valid in many cases. The stephanitic games, or at least the gymnikos and hippikos agones, avoided such tensions by the objective criteria they set in the competitions for individuals. They were truly an athletics for their own sake, unconnected with military training and conflict.

8

WOMEN AND ATHLETICS

IT IS A LONGSTANDING TRUISM that a woman's place in the ancient Greek world was in the home, tending the hearth and supervising domestic activities, while men concentrated on the more important affairs of politics, theater, athletics, and the like. A character presented by Xenophon explains how he trained his wife to "be the kind of woman a wife should be" (*Oik*, 7.10): when he caught the fifteen-year-old using cosmetics he advised her to become more active around the house. Stirring flour, kneading dough, and airing out clothes and bed linens would provide the kind of exercise that would give her a healthier, more natural complexion.

Implicit in the speaker's advice is the contrast between a wife, who represented one kind of woman in Greek society, and a *hetaira* (companion), who represented another. Hetairai were generally more sophisticated and cultured than housewives; but although their learning made them appropriate companions at the symposion, they were not considered fit for the home. However, neither of these stereotypes has any place in the world of athletics, and if we judge solely from the evidence of vase paintings, the stereotypes appear valid. If, for example, we use nudity as the criterion for identifying athletic competitions — as we have seen, it offers a good iconographic check for distinguishing male athletes — we do find images of nude women, but not in athletic contexts. A krater on which three naked women stand at a washbasin holding mirrors and shoes depicts a beauty shop, not a locker room (fig. 233). More athletic, at least in the sense of physical exertion, is a depiction of women swimming (fig. 234). But this is clearly a holiday group out to enjoy a day at the beach rather than participate in an athletic competition.

The female stereotype is further reinforced by the prohibition against women of marriageable age attending the Olympic Games, with the exception of the priestess of Demeter Chamyne. Pausanias (5.6.7–8; A *149*) emphasizes this point:

Fig. 233 Three women stand at a basin inscribed with the feminine adjective *kale* (beautiful). The clothed woman holds a shoe, the woman on the left a mirror, and the central figure an alabastron. Red-figure krater by the Painter of the Louvre Centauromachy, 450–430 B.C. Bologna, Museo Civico Archeologico, inv. no. 17948.

Fig. 234 Women at the seashore. The woman on the right is probably undressing behind the Doric column; a sponge and an aryballos hang next to her. The woman at the center is preparing to dive in next to a swimmer surrounded by fish, while the woman on the left anoints herself with oil. Behind her another kit hangs on the wall. Red-figure amphora by the Andokides Painter, ca. 520 B.C. Paris, Musée du Louvre, inv. no. F 203, Réunion des Musées Nationaux / Art Resource, New York (photo: Herve Lewandowski).

As one goes from Skillos down the road to Olympia, but before one crosses the Alpheios River, there is a mountain with high, very steep cliffs. The name of the mountain is Typaion. The Eleans have a law requiring them to throw off these cliffs any women discovered at the Olympic festival, or even on the Olympia side of the Alpheios, on the days that are forbidden to them. They say that no woman has ever been caught except Kallipateira. . . . She had been widowed, and, disguised as a male trainer, she took her son to Olympia to compete. When her son, Peisirodos, won, Kallipateira jumped over the fence that held back the trainers, and uncovered herself. She was thus discovered to be a woman, but the Eleans released her unpunished out of respect for her father, [Diagoras of Rhodes], her [three] brothers, [her nephew], and her son, all of whom had been victors at Olympia. They passed a law, however, that in the future trainers would have to attend the competition in the nude.

Clearly, women and athletics were not supposed to mix.

There is, of course, always an exception. In Greek myth that exception was Atalanta. Her father, who had wanted a son, trained her from a baby in hunting, wrestling, and running. She grew up skilled in masculine activities and participated in the hunt of the notorious Kalydonian boar; in fact, she was the first to hit the beast with her spear. Vase painters were particularly fond of showing her at the funeral games of Pelias, king of Iolkos who was murdered by Medea. There Atalanta wrestled Peleus, Achilles' father and a member of Jason's Argonauts. She is distinguished from the other athletes by the white paint used for her skin and by the fact that she wears a loincloth (fig. 235). In other images, she appears in scenes typical of athletic genre paint-

Fig. 235 Atalanta wrestling Peleus watched by two athletes waiting their turn and a Hellanodikes at the left. Black-figure amphora by an unidentified artist, ca. 500 B.C. Munich, Staatliche Antikensammlungen und Glyptothek, inv. no. 1541.

Fig. 236 Atalanta wrestling Peleus. Red-figure kylix by Oltos, ca. 500 B.C. Bologna, Museo Civico Archeologico, inv. no. 16558.

ings, showing judges and tripod cauldrons as victory prizes. It is noteworthy that as time passes Atalanta picks up more and more of a costume. Thus, by about 500 B.C. she has acquired a cap and her loincloth has become a pair of shorts embroidered with the figure of a feline (probably a lion in reference to her ultimate metamorphosis into that animal; fig. 236). Finally, by about 430 vase painters have added a bra to her ensemble and set her in a thoroughly athletic environment (fig. 237), prompting the question of what they were using for models if women did not participate in athletics.

The most popular myth about this female athlete brings her back, however, to her "proper" place in a man's world. Atalanta had no interest in marrying, but many men were interested in marrying her. She therefore announced that she would wed the man who could beat her in a footrace — and kill anyone who couldn't. Many made the attempt, and the victims piled up, until a young man (called Hippomanes in some sources, Melanion in others) took up the challenge. Before the race he prayed to Aphrodite, the goddess of love, for assistance, and she gave him three golden apples, which he threw one by one alongside the track whenever Atalanta seemed to be beating him. Distracted, Atalanta ran off the track in pursuit of the apples, enabling him to win the race — and the woman. In other words, no matter how good Atalanta was at the male pursuit of athletics, she remained at heart a frivolous female who could be distracted by baubles. (Of course, as far as we know, all the writers and vase painters who portrayed Atalanta were men.)

But these stereotypes of women and their place — or lack of it — in athletics are not as straightforward as they might seem. The evidence is fragmentary and slight in comparison to the material available about men's athletics; yet as more evidence has appeared in recent decades, it seems clear that women did participate in athletics and

Fig. 237 Atalanta (labeled by the inscription over her head), holds a pick for digging the jumpers' pit and stands next to a kampter, with the typical athletic kit hanging above. Red-figure tondo by the Euaion Painter, 450–440 B.C. Formerly Paris, Musée du Louvre, inv. no. CA 2259, stolen. Giraudon / Art Resource, New York.

were an important part of the athletic picture even if their competitions never approached an equal footing with men's. In fact, women could and did win Olympic victories. We recall Kyniska of Sparta, the first female Olympic victor, who won the *tethrippon,* although she didn't participate directly—the owners of the horses only rarely, if ever, actually drove the chariots. This was left to specialists, often slaves, and the owners did not even have to be present at the races.

The importance of wealth, rather than talent or training, in the equestrian competitions was recognized in antiquity and accounts in part for Kyniska's victory. In 396 B.C., the king of Sparta, Agesilaos, tired of hearing people brag about their victories in the horse races, encouraged his sister Kyniska to enter a four-horse chariot at the Olympics. Although she could not be present at the games, her horses won, making her the victor. As such, she was entitled to erect a statue, the base of which survives, with Kyniska's proud claim to be the first female victor: "Kings of Sparta were my fathers and brothers. Kyniska, victorious at the chariot race with her swift-footed horses, erected this statue. I assert that I am the only woman in all Greece who won this crown" (*IvO* 160; *A 151b*).

Other women followed Kyniska's lead and won victories in the *hippikos agon* (horse races) at Olympia, but those triumphs only reinforced the idea that women were not involved with the real athletics of a man's world, the *gymnikos agon* (nude competition). Further support for this stereotype comes from records of women's beauty contests and competitions in sobriety and housekeeping (Athenaeus 13.609E; *A 161*). There are, to be sure, records of victories by women in men's events. The best known is a dedication of A.D. 47 by one Hermesianax at Delphi on behalf of his daughters:

For Tryphosa, who won the Pythian Games . . . and the following Isthmian Games in the *stadion* [footrace], first of the virgins.

For Hedea, who won the chariot race in armor at the Isthmian Games . . . and the stadion at the Nemean Games and at Sikyon. . . . She also won the kithara-singing in the boys' category at the Sebasteia in Athens. . . .

For Dionysia, who won the Isthmian Games . . . and the games of Asklepios at sacred Epidauros . . . in the stadion. [*SIG*³ 802; A 162]

Scholars have debated whether the victories of Hedea and Dionysia were in the male competitions or whether they competed in special girls' categories. But all have taken such records, at least in part because of their dates, as aberrations of the Roman period. There is evidence, however, albeit slight and fragmentary, that women's athletics were widespread in earlier Greek antiquity.

Our attention must first focus on Sparta, where physical training was an important part of the education of both women and men. Xenophon describes part of the constitution established by the legendary Spartan lawgiver: "Lykourgos, thinking that the first and foremost function of the freeborn woman was to bear children, ordered that the female should do no less bodybuilding than the male. He thus established contests for the women in footraces and strength just like those for the men, believing that stronger children come from parents who are both strong" (*Constitution of the Lakedaimonians* 1.4; A 152).

Plutarch expands upon this theme:

Lykourgos exercised the bodies of the virgins with footraces and wrestling and throwing the *diskos* and the *akon* [javelin] so that their offspring might spring from strong roots in strong bodies, and so that they might be patient and strong in childbirth and struggle well and easily with its pains. He removed all softness, daintiness, and effeminacy from them and accustomed the girls no less than the boys to parade in the nude and to dance and sing at certain religious festivals in the presence of the young men as spectators. . . .

The nudity of the virgins was not shameful—for modesty was present and intemperance was absent—but it implanted plain habits and an eager rivalry for high good health in them, and it imbued in them a noble frame of mind at having a share in *arete* and in pride, whence it came to them to speak and to think as it is said that Gorgo the wife of Leonidas did. When some woman—a foreigner, it would appear—said to her, "Only Spartan women rule men," she answered, "Only Spartan women bear men." [*Lykourgos* 14.2–15.1; A 153]

In this context, a young women's athletics becomes natural, and even if women could not compete in the Olympics they did have competitions. We see portrayals of women athletes running (fig. 238), while Hellenistic poets refer to Spartan girls "who run the same racecourse and oil ourselves down like men beside the bathing pools of the Eurotas River" (Theokritos, 18.22–25). We should note that these references are to mixed exercise and physical training for the two sexes, not to competitions between them. But there is clear evidence of competitions for girls and young women at places other than Sparta, for example the games of Hera in Argos (which were administered the same way as the Nemean Games and by the same people in the Hellenistic period) and other games at Dodona. The best-known competitions for women were the games of Hera held at Olympia itself. As so often, our best information comes from Pausanias (5.16.2–7; A 158):

> Every fourth year at Olympia the Sixteen Women weave a *peplos* [robe] for Hera, and they also sponsor the Heraia competition. This contest is a footrace for virgins of different ages. They run in three categories: the youngest first, the slightly older ones next, and then the oldest virgins last. They run in the following manner: their hair hangs loose, a *chiton* [tunic] reaches to a little above the knee, and the right shoulder is bared as far as the breast. They also use the Olympic stadium, but the track is shortened by one-sixth. The winners receive a crown of olive and a portion of the cow sacrificed to Hera, and they have the right to dedicate statues with their names inscribed upon them. Those who serve the Sixteen Women are, like the sponsors of these games, women.
>
> They trace the competition of the virgins also back to antiquity. They say that Hippodameia, out of gratitude to Hera for her marriage to Pelops, collected Sixteen Women and, with them, sponsored the first Heraia. . . . The Sixteen Women also arrange two choral dances; they call one the dance of Physkoa, the other that of Hippodameia. . . . The Eleans are now divided into eight tribes, and from each they choose two women.

If any proof is needed that Pausanias is describing a venerable situation correctly, we can look at the Roman copy of a Greek statue from about 460 B.C. which shows a female runner dressed exactly as he described (fig. 239). The original of this statue was probably one dedicated at Olympia by a victor in the Heraia, and it indicates that women's athletic competitions were being held in the fifth century B.C.

The games of Hera took place at a different time from the men's Olympic Games, although Pausanias (5.16.8) notes that the Sixteen Women who acted as judges underwent the same ritual ablution as did the *Hellanodikai* before they entered the sacred grove of the Altis. This indicates that the women probably also took the

Fig. 238 A female runner pulling at the hem of her chiton. Bronze statuette, 6th century B.C., from Dodona. Athens, National Museum, inv. no. 135. (photo: © Treasury of Archaeological Receipts).

Fig. 239 A female runner with her right shoulder and breast bare and a chiton belted up to free her legs. The stump support is carved with a palm branch as a victory token. Marble copy of the Roman period from a Greek original of ca. 460 B.C. Vatican, Galleria dei Candelabri, inv. no. 2784 (photo: P. Zigrossi).

long march from Elis to Olympia. Finally, Pausanias (6.24.10) tells us that the Sixteen Women, like the male Hellanodikai, had a special building on the agora of Elis as their headquarters. This, plus the fact that the selection of the Sixteen Women was based on the civic structure of Elis (as was the selection of the Hellanodikai) shows clearly that for both men and women the organization of Olympic training was centered at Elis.

Moreover, at Olympia itself and within the Altis there was a Hero Shrine for Hippodameia to which her bones were transferred from Midea, the place of her death (Pausanias 6.20.7). This shrine has not been located, but its existence, and the fundamental role that Hippodameia played in the foundation of the men's Olympic Games, reveal a strong feminine undercurrent at Olympia and in the games. Women's athletics may have been separate from men's, and never really equal with them, but they did exist and were an important element in Doric society at least.

It is the word "Doric" that may provide the clue to why the nonexistence of women's athletics became accepted wisdom. Dorian women in the literature that survives to us are synonymous with women of loose morals, and Spartan women were the most Dorian of women. They were known as *phainomerides* (thigh showers) at least as early as the sixth century B.C. (Ibykos, frag. 339), and in 426 Euripides could present the stereotypical image of a Spartan women to an Athenian theatrical audience thus: "A Spartan girl could not be chaste even if she wanted. They abandon their houses to run around with young men, with naked thighs and open clothes, sharing the same race tracks and *palaistrai* [wrestling schools] — a situation which I find insufferable. And if your girls are so trained is it any wonder that your Spartan women grow up without knowing what chastity is?" (*Andromache* 595–601; A 154).

The stereotype reappears on the Athenian stage fifteen years later in Aristophanes' *Lysistrata*. Athens and Sparta have been waging sporadic war for a whole generation, and after initial Athenian successes, the Spartans have gained the upper hand, owing in no small part to Athenian excesses. The women of Athens are sick of watching their men march off to war, frequently not to return. They unite under the leadership of Lysistrata and barricade themselves in the Akropolis, where they issue a proclamation to the Athenian men: no more housekeeping, babysitting, or lovemaking until the war ends. They invite the Spartan women to join their cause, and a delegation, led by Lampito, arrives at the Akropolis to be greeted by Lysistrata: "Welcome Lampito, my fine Spartan friend! How deliciously beautiful you look! You could probably throttle a bull!" To which Lampito responds modestly, "Goodness, I suppose I could. . . . It's the exercise. I jump and kick myself in the butt."

The exercise to which Lampito refers is known as *bibasis*: jumping into the air as many times as possible and kicking one's backside with the heels of the feet (Pollux 4.120; A 156). More important for our purposes, however, the interchange between Lampito and Lysistrata perpetuates, for Athenian audiences then and for us now, the image of Spartan women as athletes rather than good women, like the Athenians. Is that image accurate? Are we to believe that Athenian women did not practice athletics? Do Euripides and Aristophanes tell the full story, or is there some poetic and political license in their stereotypes?

Extant written sources, which are almost exclusively Athenian, offer only hints of women's athletics in Athens. Thus, for example, Thucydides (3.104; A 155), writing about the events of 423, suggests that a century earlier women took part in an athletic festival on the island of Delos: "The Athenians first celebrated their quadrennial festival at Delos after the purification [540–530]. There had been a great gathering at Delos in olden times by the Ionians and the surrounding islanders. They made *theorias* [delegations] with their wives and children, even as the Ionians now celebrate the Ephesian Games. There had been a gymnikos agon and a mousikos agon, and the cities sent groups of dancers."

Even this passage suggests, however, that by the time of Thucydides (and Euripides and Aristophanes) Athenian women were no longer involved in athletics. Archae-

Fig. 240 Aerial view of the Sanctuary of Artemis at Brauron, from the northwest (photo: Raymond V. Scoder, S.J., © 1987 Bolchazy-Carducci Publishers, Inc.).

ology tells a different story. On the eastern shores of Attika lies an Athenian township named Brauron, which was famous for its sanctuary to Artemis. Excavations have uncovered an elaborate building with a courtyard and dining rooms (fig. 240), as well as an inscription that mentions a number of other structures including a palaistra. This must have been a wrestling school for girls and women since the Sanctuary of Brauronian Artemis was a strictly female cult center where girls (known as Little Bears because of the affinity of the goddess Artemis to that animal) went through initiation ceremonies.

We have no details of the festival that took place at Brauron, but many fragments of pottery from that site show depictions of girls running, clearly engaged in athletic competition (fig. 241). Fragments of other vases show more young women racing, this time in the nude (fig. 242). In other words, there is clear evidence from Brauron of a women's gymnikos agon. These images, made by Athenian potters and painters, portrayed Athenian women and girls competing in the nude at exactly the same time Euripides was condemning Spartan women for running around "with naked thighs and open clothes." Furthermore, another cult center for Brauronian Artemis was built at this time on the Athenian Akropolis, just a stone's throw from the Parthenon. Women's athletics may not have taken place there, but it offers a direct allusion to them at the religious center of Athens.

We must conclude that even in Athens, women's athletics played a role in society. It is impossible to judge the extent or significance of that role; we know only that

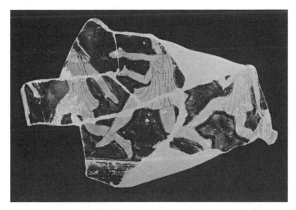 

Fig. 241 Girls racing, clothed in short chitons. Fragment of a red-figure krater, 430–420 B.C. Basel, Collection of Herbert A. Cahn, inv. no. HC 501 (photo courtesy of Walters Art Gallery).

Fig. 242 Young nude women racing. Fragment of a red-figure krater, 430–420 B.C. Basel, Collection of Herbert A. Cahn, inv. no. HC 502a (photo courtesy of Walters Art Gallery).

it was greater than has usually been thought. The problem is that our information comes via Athenians, who were not interested in documenting a practice so closely associated with Sparta. It is not coincidental that fourth-century authors like Xenophon and Plato, who are more sympathetic to the Spartans, place more emphasis on women's athletics.

The problem of assessing the accuracy of written sources continues today. Since 1987, whenever I have taught a course on ancient athletics, I have measured the amount of space given to different topics in the sports section of the *San Francisco Chronicle*. I made these measurements on the day I lectured on women's athletics: October 16, 1987; October 23, 1989; October 26, 1990; October 30, 1992; March 18, 1994; October 30, 1995; October 28, 1996; October 25, 2000; October 26, 2001, and October 29, 2003. The average coverage, measured in square centimeters of print, over these years has been: advertising, 29.37 percent; horse racing, 5.04 percent; men's competitions, 64.10 percent; women's competitions, 1.49 percent. If two thousand years from now these newspapers are the only athletic records that survive, what will historians conclude about the relative importance of women's athletics today?

9

ATHLETES AND HEROES

OUR MODERN CULTURE is filled with sports heroes who have achieved superstar status through talent and accomplishment on the athletic field. Athletes could also be considered heroes in antiquity, but not because of their athletic accomplishments. By ancient standards, a hero was the offspring of humans or of a god and a human who achieved a quasi-divine status. Most important, the ancient hero had to be dead, at which point a hero cult would arise. The hero could then use his intimate connection with the underworld to provide a point of contact for his worshipers, who needed it for, among other things, cursing enemies. (A curse had to be carried to the underworld in order to become effective.) The hero also acquired an aura of magic and the supernatural and was considered especially adept at curing health problems. This is the standard we must use in order to determine whether an individual ancient athlete was rated a hero.

Of all the athletes from the ancient Greek world whose names survive the most famous was probably Milo, from the town of Kroton in southern Italy, a wrestler and *the* strongman of antiquity. His record of success at Olympia began in 536 B.C., when he won in the boys' category, and it continued for the next five Olympiads. He finally lost on his seventh attempt, in 512. He also amassed seven Pythian victories. And his feats outside the wrestling *skamma* elevated him to the level of legend (Pausanias 6.14.5–8; *A 163a*). It was said that he could hold a pomegranate in his hand, daring anyone to take it away, and after each challenger failed, Milo would release the pomegranate unbruised, so great was his control. He would also invite challengers to knock him off a greased diskos, but none could. Milo could tie a cord around his head and then hold his breath until the veins swelled so hard they broke the cord. He could hold his hand out with the fingers held tight together and no one could pry his little finger away from the others. But for all his strength of body, Milo never became a hero, as the manner of his death shows. Walking down a road near Kroton, he happened on a dried-up tree trunk into which wedges had been driven. Milo, arrogant in his strength, stuck his hands into the trunk and began to pull it apart. The wedges slipped

Fig. 243 Head of an athlete, believed to be Polydamas of Skotoussa. Copenhagen, Ny Carlsberg Glyptotek, inv. no. 542.

out and the tree snapped shut on his hands. Milo remained trapped by the trunk until he was devoured by wolves.

Another athlete whose end was similarly foolish became a hero nonetheless. This was Polydamas of Skotoussa, in Thessaly, who won the *pankration* at Olympia in 408 B.C. (fig. 243). Pausanias claims that his statue at Olympia was the work of the sculptor Lysippos, whose career began only about twenty-five years after Polydamas's Olympic victory, and that it was taller than the figure of any other man, presumably reflecting Polydamas's actual height. His strength, like that of Milo, was legendary, and he was credited with the ability to grab a chariot that was speeding past and stop it with one hand. He was also said to have gripped the foot of a large bull so tightly that when it finally broke free his hoof was still in Polydamas's hand. This athlete's ambition to rival Herakles led him to wrestle with a lion on the slopes of Mount Olympos, and his victory over the beast is one of the feats portrayed on the base of his statue at Olympia.

But, as Pausanias warned (6.5.1–9; A 168),

> Those who glory in their strength are doomed to perish by it, and so Polydamas perished through his own might. He entered a cave along with his close friends to escape the summer heat. As bad luck would have it, the roof began to crack, and it was clear that the cave could not hold up much longer and would collapse quickly. Recognizing the disaster that was coming, the others turned and ran out; but Polydamas decided to stay. He held up his hands in the belief that he could prevent the roof from collapsing, that he would not be crushed by the mountain. His end came here.

Despite this ignoble death, Polydamas's statue at Olympia was believed to have magical powers, and Lucian (*Assembly of the Gods* 12; A 165) tells us that it cured worshipers of fever.

Fig. 244 Base of the statue of Euthymos of Lokris displaying a rasura in the second line of its inscription. Olympia, Archaeological Museum, inv. no. Λ527. After O. Alexandri, ed., *Mind and Body* (Athens, 1988), p. 223, no. 114.

The things that could make an athlete a hero in ancient Greece could be even stranger than this. Kleomedes of Astypalaia competed at Olympia in 492 B.C., killing his opponent, Ikkos of Epidauros, in the boxing, for which the *Hellanodikai* convicted him of foul play and stripped him of the victory. Mad with grief, Kleomedes returned home, where he went into a local school and pulled down the roof, killing about sixty children. The townspeople set up a hue and cry, but he hid in a chest in the Sanctuary of Athena. The people could not open the lid and finally smashed in the sides of the chest, but they discovered that it was empty. Puzzled, they went to Delphi to ask the Pythia what had happened to Kleomedes. The oracle responded, "Kleomedes of Astypalaia is the last of heroes. Honor with sacrifices him who is no longer mortal" (Pausanias 6.9.7; A 164). This was one of the more unusual beginnings to a hero cult in ancient Greece.

Another athlete who became a hero was Euthymos of Lokris, in Italy. A boxer, Euthymos was victorious at Olympia in 484, 476, and 472. Pausanias (6.6.4; A 166a) tells us that his father was a man named Astykles but the people of his hometown claimed he was really the son of the Kaikinos River, which bordered their territory. (This was another characteristic of ancient heroes: they were usually endowed posthumously with a divine or at least superhuman father.) The base of Euthymos's statue at Olympia provides evidence that he did indeed make the transition from human to hero (fig. 244). The inscription on the front of the base reads,

> Euthymos of Lokroi, son of Astykles, having won three times at Olympia,
> Set up this figure to be admired by the mortals.
> Euthymos of Lokroi Epizephyrioi dedicated it.
> Pythagoras of Samos made it. [*IvO* 144; A 166b]

However, the second line of the inscription had a different text originally, for the words "to be admired by the mortals" are inscribed in a part of the marble that was erased. When ancient Greeks wished to change an inscribed text, they had to "erase" the original: the stone would be carved down until the inscribed letters disappeared. As a result part of the surface of the stone would be lower than the rest, and within this *rasura* a new text could be inscribed. So although Euthymos acknowledged and continued to acknowledge that his father was Astykles, his image (and therefore he himself) was later removed from the realm of mere mortals.

In 480 Euthymos was defeated at Olympia by another athlete who would become a hero. This was Theagenes from the island of Thasos, in the northern Aegean, who wanted to win both the boxing and the pankration at a single Olympiad. After defeating Euthymos in the boxing, Theagenes was so exhausted that he had no energy to compete in the pankration, which was won by Dromeus of Mantineia *akoniti* ("dustless," uncontested) — the first such victory in the pankration. As a result, the Hellanodikai ruled that Theagenes had entered the boxing to spite Euthymos and fined him a hefty sum — at least $264,000 to be split between Euthymos and Olympian Zeus. Theagenes did not compete in the boxing again at Olympia, but he did win the pankration in 476. His record included three Pythian victories in boxing, and nine Nemean and ten Isthmian victories in boxing and the pankration. In addition to these victories at the *stephanitic* (crown) games, Theagenes is said to have won another 1,376 victories in various *chrematitic* (money) games, including one in the *dolichos*, a long-distance footrace.

Theagenes' athletic success had been foreshadowed by childhood feats of strength: when he was nine he plucked a bronze statue that had caught his eye from its base in the agora and took it home. His posthumous status as a hero, like that of Euthymos, is hinted at by the stories that he was not the son of Timosthenes but the offspring of a phantom of Herakles. The story of his translation to hero status is told by Pausanias (6.11.8 – 9; A 167a):

> After he died, one of his enemies came every night to the statue of Theagenes in Thasos, and flogged the bronze image as though he were whipping Theagenes himself. The statue stopped this outrage by falling upon the man, whose sons then prosecuted the statue for murder. The Thasians threw the statue into the sea, following the precepts of Drako, who, when he wrote the homicide laws for the Athenians, imposed banishment even upon inanimate objects which fell and killed a man. As time went by, however, famine beset the Thasians, and they sent envoys to Delphi, where Apollo instructed them to recall their exiles. They did so, but there was still no end to the famine. They sent to the Pythia a second time and said that although they had followed the instructions, the wrath of

the gods still was upon them. The Pythia responded, "You do not remember your great Theagenes."

The Thasians were then in a quandary, for they could not think how to retrieve the statue of Theagenes. But fishermen who had set out for the day's fishing happened to catch the statue in their nets and brought it back to land. The Thasians set the statue back up in its original position and are now accustomed to sacrifice to Theagenes as to a god. I know of many places, both among the Greeks and among the barbarians, where statues of Theagenes have been set up. He is worshiped by the natives as a healing power.

The heroic status of Theagenes has been confirmed by excavations at Thasos, where the circular base of his monument was discovered (fig. 245). This base was originally surmounted by a circular marble block that served as an altar but also had a cavity within to hold money. Inscribed on the block is the proscription that all who sacrifice to Theagenes must also make a monetary contribution toward the maintenance and upkeep of the shrine. The inscription can be dated to about A.D. 100, so worship of the athletic hero Theagenes was still going strong more than five hundred years after his death.

But such heroes were the exception, and we know of many successful athletes who were failures in later life and were considered as either stupid or bad men. In the former category belongs Dioxippos of Athens, who won the pankration at Olympia in 336 B.C. Later on he was wrongly accused of stealing a gold cup from Alexander the Great. He became despondent and committed suicide, prompting his enemies to declare that it was a real hardship to have great strength of body but little of mind (Diodorus Siculus 17.100–101; A 172a). Dioxippos had revealed his tendency toward emotional overreaction earlier, at the celebration of his *eiselasis* (triumphal return) to his native Athens:

> A crowd gathered from all around and was watching him, hanging on his every move. In the crowd was a woman particularly distinguished by her beauty who had come to see what was going on. The moment Dioxippos saw her he was smitten by her beauty. He could not look away from her and kept turning to keep her in sight. Since he was blushing, it became clear to the crowd that he was not idly staring. Diogenes of Sinope understood what was happening and said to his neighbors, "Look at your great big athlete, throttled by a little girl." [Aelian, *VH* 12.58]

The image of athlete as hero was balanced by the image of athlete as oaf. In addition, there are many examples of incompetent athletes. One such was Charmos, who

Fig. 245 Base of the monument of Theagenes in the agora of Thasos (photo: author).

was said to have finished seventh in a field of six in the dolichos — a friend had run out onto the track to encourage him. Commentators joked, "If he had had five more friends he would have finished twelfth" (*Anthologia Graeca* 11.82; A 174).

Extremely gifted athletes in antiquity, then, were sometimes considered heroes by their contemporaries but for reasons other than their prowess. A modern equivalent might be the baseball player Lou Gehrig, who set a number of records on the playing field but is better remembered as the catalyst for medical research into the disease that killed him, research that continues to bring hope of a cure. Gehrig is thus something of a curative figure similar to ancient heroes.

There were also athletes in ancient Greece of great prowess who never attained the status of heroes — the Babe Ruths, whose fame is limited to their athletic exploits. The majority of ancient athletes, however, like their modern counterparts, were not heroes; they were not even winners. But without them athletics would have no purpose.

10

SPORT AND RECREATION

IN ADDITION TO ORGANIZED athletic competitions the Greeks enjoyed many other physical activities that belong to the broad category of sport and recreation. We can only touch the surface of this subject, but it is important to understand that the sort of games we have considered to this point were part of a much larger field of recreational activities. Most of the games discussed here will seem familiar to us, although equipment has obviously changed, but when we look at ballplaying we shall see that the ancient Greeks had attitudes very different from our own.

Hunting had ceased to be necessary for subsistence long before the Classical period and had evolved into the pastime of the aristocracy, who had ample leisure time and the money to afford the attendant slave-bearers, horses, and dogs. Lion hunting, in particular, was the purview of royalty, and that took it farther and farther away from the egalitarian centers of ancient Greece. It figures in aristocratic art, including decorations on royal tombs, and in dedications at sanctuaries. Next to the Temple of Apollo at Delphi, for example, stood a sculptural group showing Alexander the Great and his companions (prominently Krateros, whose son made the dedication) taking part in a lion hunt. Even when hunters are depicted on foot stalking less exalted prey (fig. 246), we can be confident that we are looking at a sport of the nobility.

Fishing, on the other hand, was a job more than a sport, for fish formed a staple of the ancient diet. Ancient sources mention fishmongers by name, including one man who became an Olympic victor. To be sure, representations of fishing like the image on the Boston cup (fig. 247) could be depictions of a sport, but it is more probable that the aim of this fisherman is to fill his plate.

We might assume that aquatic sports would have played a prominent role in a country so closely tied to the sea, but there are only passing references to swimming, always as a way of training for other sports, and depictions of swimming are rare and

Fig. 246 Deer hunt. Pebble mosaic signed by
Gnosis, ca. 300 B.C. Pella, archaeological site
(photo: © Treasury of Archaeological Receipts).

Fig. 247 A fisherman. Red-figure tondo by the Ambrosios
Painter, ca. 510–500 B.C. Boston, Museum of Fine Arts,
inv. no. 01.8024 (photo: © 2002 Museum of Fine Arts,
Boston, reproduced with permission).

clearly show it as a recreation, not a competition (see fig. 234). A boat race formed part
of the Panathenaic Games, and another took place at Hermione on the Argolid peninsula. The first, and probably both, however, must be understood in the context of military naval training rather than athletics.

Acrobatics were also popular: there are representations of tumblers doing
handstands and somersaults, but these are usually presented as children's entertainment. Certainly there is no evidence that competitions like today's gymnastics took
place. One possible exception exists in the form of a curious pseudo-Panathenaic amphora (fig. 248). On it a small male figure is climbing a pole or doing a pole vault next
to a large horse with a rider looking over his shoulder at a figure in the center of the
frame (the object of everyone's attention), who seems to have just leapt onto the rump
of the horse. Another small male figure apparently beneath the horse wields an ax.
The jumper wears a helmet and carries a pinwheel-decorated shield on each arm. Beneath him is a black object with a broad base that appears to be a takeoff ramp. Standing next to it, a flute player provides accompaniment for the shield-wielding jumper.
Watching all this are spectators sitting on bleachers who are gesturing toward the
jumper. From the mouth of the largest spectator come the words "Good for the
jumper!" Clearly the jumper has just performed some sort of acrobatic stunt. But
there is no evidence that he is engaged in a competition. Rather, the atmosphere con-
jures up images of a circus, where different stunts go on at the same time.

Children had their own games and amusements. Juggling, for example, is depicted as an activity of women and boys (fig. 249). Teeter-totters (*petaura*) and swings
(*aiorai*) appear in similar settings, and one game that is frequently shown is rolling a
hoop (*trochos* or *krikos*; fig. 250). This was usually played in the streets, and was recom-
mended by doctors as a healthy exercise that children could perform by themselves.

Fig. 248 Acrobats performing before a crowd sitting on bleachers. Black-figure amphora, ca. 550 B.C. Paris, Bibliothèque nationale de France, inv. no. 243.

Fig. 249 A seated woman juggles three balls, one of which has eluded her, while two boys watch, one extending a bird as a present. Red-figure kylix by the Sabouroff Painter, ca. 460 B.C. Leiden, Rijksmuseum voor Oudheden, inv. no. PC 77.

The hoops were made of iron, bronze, or, most commonly, wood, with small studs at regular intervals around the edge. These made a loud, easily identifiable noise (always popular for children's toys), which allowed parents (who might otherwise have been less well inclined toward it) to locate their children. The hoop was propelled by a wooden stick or an iron rod (*elater*) and was supposed to stand about chest high. Most representations show it rather smaller, which may mean that the child has grown but is still playing with an early toy.

Fig. 250 Boy rolling a hoop with a stick in his right hand, holding a pillow(?) in his left. An inscription reads, "the boy is kalos." Red-figure tondo by the Colmar Painter, ca. 500 B.C. Oxford, Ashmolean Museum, inv. no. 1886.587.

Fig. 251 Boy playing with a yo-yo. Red-figure tondo, ca. 440 B.C. Berlin, Staatliche Museen — Preussischer Kulturbesitz, Antikensammlung, inv. no. F 2549 (photo: Johannes Laurentius).

Another popular toy was the yo-yo, which appears in several vase paintings (fig. 251). Although it was most commonly made of wood, no examples have survived from ancient Greece. We do have yo-yos made of bronze and terra-cotta, however. It is frustrating that we don't know the ancient name for the yo-yo, nor can we identify any reference to it in ancient literature.

Tops, called *bembikes* (singular, *bembix*), were favored toys. Again, no wooden tops have survived, but there are several terra-cotta and bronze tops, frequently decorated with ivy or palm leaves, branches, birds, and other ornaments. The top was propelled by a rod that had a cord or leather strip on the end similar to the whip used by jockeys (fig. 252; see also figs. 151, 153). This was wrapped tightly around the top and then given a hard pull. There were a number of games, some involving multiple tops, and single tops might be used to predict the future in various imaginative ways.

By far the most common "toys," however, were *astragaloi* and *kyboi* — knucklebones and dice (fig. 253). The former are particularly ubiquitous, frequently found in groups by the dozens, especially in places of communal social and educational gatherings. The Corycean Cave above Delphi, for example, has produced more than twenty thousand astragaloi. They also are frequently found in children's graves and in sanctuaries where children performed a ritual passage to adulthood.

The astragalos is the tarsal bone, or ankle, of a sheep or goat, attached to the shinbone and the radius. It naturally has four sides and two rounded ends. The more elongated end is the foot of the animal; it was called the *keraia* (promontory). The four sides don't match, and each was assigned a different value. One of the two broad sides, characterized by a ridge of bone that separates the ends, was called the *pranes* and had the value of 4; the other broad side was the *hyption* (hollowed) and was valued at 3.

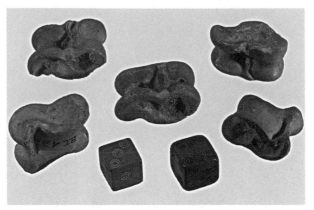

Fig. 252 Woman spinning a top (bembix). The inscription reads, "Hegesibolos made it." White-ground tondo by the Sotades Painter, ca. 430 B.C. Brussels, Musées Royaux d'Art et d'Histoire, inv. no. A 891 (photo: museum).

Fig. 253 Knucklebones (astragaloi) and dice (kyboi). The upper sides of the astragaloi: pranes (upper left), chion (upper right), koon (lower left), and hyption (lower right). In the center is a pranes that has had holes drilled in it so that it can be weighted. Athens, American School of Classical Studies, Agora Excavations (photo: Craig Mauzy).

There are also differences on the shorter sides, one of which has less surface area than the other. The larger of the two was called the *chion* and had the value of 1 while the smaller was the *koon* and had the value of 6. The pairs of sides each had a total value of 7, then, and since the side that landed down was the side that counted, the values were assessed according to the chances of the particular side landing down. For example, the smallest, narrowest and therefore lightest side, the koon, would be the least likely to land down and hence had the greatest value.

With these basic facts in hand, we can imagine a great variety of possible games, some involving a number of astragaloi being thrown at one time, others making the goal be to match a certain number, and so on. The simple and common bone astragaloi were matched by fancier versions made of stone, metal, and glass. And then as now, cheating was not unknown; many bone astragaloi have been found with holes for metal inserts; thus "loaded," the astragalos would land on a specific side. A huge marble astragalos found at Olympia measures more than half a meter in length and was used as the base for the bronze statue of a human figure. It presumably was dedicated because of a victory in some game involving astragaloi, even though they seem out of place at Olympia. Nonetheless, astragaloi were a constant part of the *palaistra*, appearing in what would otherwise seem to be straightforward athletic scenes (fig. 254). Even Sokrates had to interrupt games of knucklebones for his discussions with young Athenians in the palaistra: "I entered the palaistra. We found that the boys had performed the sacrifices already and that the sacred rites were nearly done, and they were playing knucklebones, all dressed to the nines. Most of them were playing outside in the courtyard, but some in a corner of the locker room were playing odds and evens with quantities of astragaloi picked out from little baskets, while others stood around and watched" (Plato, *Lysis* 206E; A 182).

Fig. 254 A young athlete stands in front of a pick holding a diskos while listening to the bearded judge or trainer, who holds the rhabdos in his right hand and an astragalos in his left. Is he scolding the athlete for playing with the astragalos when he should have been training, an accusation denied by the waving finger of the athlete? Red-figure amphora by the Kleophrades Painter, 500–480 B.C. Oxford, Ashmolean Museum, inv. no. 1891.689.

The dice (kyboi) are similar to modern dice and were used in many of the same ways, including games of chance like craps and board games that involved some degree of skill as well as luck. Although kyboi seem to be a later, more sophisticated version of astragaloi, they were already known in the age of Homer: Palamedes, a leader at Troy, was credited with their discovery. But dice existed much earlier in both Egypt and Mesopotamia, and Plato (*Phaidro* 274c–d) specifically credits the Egyptians with the invention. Regardless of their inventor, such games are as old as we and an attribute of our competitive nature. The study of dice is a vast subject and deserves fuller treatment than can be given here.

Ancient Greeks also threw balls and played games with balls, but it is always a source of wonder to modern students that ballplaying was such a minimal part of the athletic scene. It is much easier for us to enumerate the competitive athletics of today's world that do not use some form of sphere than to list those that do. The opposite was the case in antiquity.

Our lack of evidence begins with the names used for the ball. The most common word was *sphaira*, or sphere, which can refer to any spherical object and need not be a ball. *Sphaira* was also used, for example, to designate the padded boxing glove that was worn in practice, as opposed to the long strap, or *himas*. Thus we must examine the context of each ancient writing to see whether a ball or a glove is intended when *sphaira* is used. Further, the word can be used generically of any ball; again, only the context can tell us what kind. In a modern analogy, if "play ball!" were the only words that survived, we wouldn't know whether the game was football, basketball, baseball, or something else.

Specific types of balls can be equally obscure. *Harpaston*, for example, is both a ball and a ball game. This is not surprising—we use "basketball" for both the round object and the game played with it—but again it can be confusing. The harpaston ball was small and hard, apparently covered in leather and stuffed with material (perhaps horsehair). It was about the size of a baseball or a little larger. It could thus be grasped easily, and this may account for the name, derived from the verb *harpazein,* "to snatch," "to grab away from." Another Greek ball was the *palla,* which is rarely mentioned and was probably the equivalent of the Latin *pila,* a lighter, feather-stuffed ball.

There was, in fact, a virtually infinite variety of balls, of all sizes and materials: covered in cloth or leather and stuffed with sand, earth, flour, wool, horsehair, feathers, rags, string, sponge. The larger balls were covered in pieces of leather sewn together; sometimes the pieces were hexagonal and of equal size, giving the ball the appearance of a modern soccer ball. Inflated animal bladders were also used for balls. Balls could be dyed or painted bright colors: red, blue, gold. Our attempts to assign them specific names and functions are frustrated, however, by the use of *sphaira,* modified by some adjective of size (large, medium, small) or color, for almost all of them.

The names of various ball games are somewhat better known, thanks to Pollux, a rhetorician of the second century A.D. (9.103–107 and 119; A 178):

> The names of children's ball games were *episkyros, phaininda, apor-rhaxis, ourania.* Episkyros was also called *ephebike* and commonball. It was usually played with opposing teams of equal number. In the middle a line was drawn with a chip of stone which they called a *skyros.* They set the ball on this line, and each team drew another line behind the opposition. The team that got the ball first threw it over the opposition, whose job it was to grab the ball while it was still moving and throw it back the other way. This would continue until one team had pushed the other over the back line.
>
> Phaininda got its name either from its inventor, Phainindos, or from the word for feinting, since the player fakes a throw to one player while actually throwing to another, and thus deceives the player who expected the ball. This resembles the game with the small ball called harpaston from the word for snatching away. One might call phaininda the game with the soft ball.
>
> Aporrhaxis takes the form of bouncing the ball vigorously on the ground, and dribbling it again and again with the hand. The number of bounces is counted.
>
> Ourania is played with one player bending backward and throwing the ball up into the sky. The others try to snatch the ball before it falls back to the ground. . . . When they dribble a ball against a wall, they count the number of bounces. The loser is called the donkey and has to do whatever he is told. The winner is called the king and gives the orders. . . .
>
> Ephedrismos is played by setting up a stone at a distance and trying to hit it with balls or stones. The one who does not knock it over has to carry the one who did, with his eyes held shut by the other one, until he happens upon the stone, which is called the *dioros.*

Fig. 255 Young athletes playing the ball game known as episkyros or ephebike. Marble statue base with traces of paint, ca. 510 B.C. (see also fig. 143 for another side of this base). Athens, National Museum, inv. no. 3476 (photo: © Treasury of Archaeological Receipts).

These are, for the most part, simple, straightforward descriptions that we can relate to ball games still played today. Some of them can also be recognized in ancient depictions. On one side of the base of a statue six young men are clearly arranged in two groups facing each other (fig. 255). The first man on the left, who is at the rear of his team, prepares to throw a small ball while his teammates take an offensive attitude and the opposition defensive stances. We should probably assume that there is a center line between the two teams and a goal line behind each as in Pollux's description of the episkyros. The alternate name, ephebike, refers to the young citizen-to-be in his late teens whom we have already encountered in the local *chrematitic* (money) games (see Chapter 7), and this fits with the age of the young men depicted here.

The game called ephedrismos, or "sitting on," sounds very curious in Pollux's description, but there are representations of it from the fifth century B.C. (fig. 256). The simplicity and informality of this ball game is as clear as those of the other ball games we have noted.

A ball game not described in written sources, however, does appear on several vase paintings (fig. 257). In each depiction, an older male figure prepares to throw a ball toward pairs of young men. Each pair consists of a larger (older?) young man who carries a smaller (younger?) male piggyback. The "riders" have their hands stretched out to catch the ball, and we are left to imagine the mad dash of the "horses" and the scrambling hands of the riders all converging on the ball after it has been thrown.

Suggestive of modern soccer is the scene on a funerary monument in which a young man (the deceased) balances a large ball on top of his right, raised thigh (fig. 258). The ball is probably a *folis*, an air-filled leather-covered ball that had an animal bladder inside. We should probably imagine that the next step would be for the young

Fig. 256 A game of ephedrismos: one young athlete carries another piggyback while the rider covers the eyes of the carrier with his hands. A third athlete kneels behind the two stones the carrier must find and gestures to them. Red-figure chous by the Schuwalow Painter, 430–420 B.C. Berlin, Staatliche Museen — Preussischer Kulturbesitz, Antiken-sammlung, inv. no. F 2417.

Fig. 257 Trainer or teacher about to throw a ball toward three pairs of young men, one carrying the other piggyback, in an unidentified game. (There are two pairs behind the first one, but they are not visible on this side of the vase.) Black-figure lekythos by the Edinburgh Painter, 500–490 B.C. Oxford, Ashmolean Museum, inv. no. 1890.27 (250).

Fig. 258 Young man balancing ball on his right thigh, holding one hand behind his back and watched by a boy who has an aryballos tied to his wrist and holds a stlengis. To the right is the kampter of a racetrack with the athlete's clothes folded neatly on top. Marble funerary loutrophoros, first half of the 4th century B.C. Athens, National Museum, inv. no. 873 (photo: © Treasury of Archaeological Receipts).

Fig. 259 A face off in some form of field hockey, perhaps called keratizein. Marble base of a statue, ca. 510 B.C. Athens, National Museum, inv. no. 347 (photo: © Treasury of Archaeological Receipts).

man to bounce the ball to his other leg, and so on, back and forth. As easy as it is for us to see and understand the movements and identify the game with our modern soccer, it is frustrating that we do not know what the ancients called it and have no description or even reference to this ball game.

Yet another example of of an ancient game that seems to be a precursor of a modern one can be seen on a marble base in which two athletes face off with curved sticks over a small disc or ball (fig. 259). There is an ancient reference to a young boy using a horn (keras) and it has been thought that this is a representation of such a game, similar to field hockey, called "use the horn" (keratizein). But even if this is the correct interpretation of the reference and the depiction, our lack of information about the game, which is mentioned only in passing, is yet another frustration.

Why are references to and details about ballplaying so rare and, when they do exist, so obscure? Clearly ball games existed in the Greek world, for they are documented in the *Odyssey* and appear in art of the sixth century B.C. Equally clearly, ballplaying was not popular or thought worthy of mention. Why? I believe the answer lies in the absence of, on the one hand, sufficient individuality and, on the other, practical utility. Ballplaying did not prepare the future citizen in any meaningful way for his responsibilities. Furthermore, try to play ball by yourself. To make playing with a ball fun, you generally need at least one other person. But *arete* is an individual characteristic, and it is a function of self-fulfillment, of testing oneself against individual capacities and limits. Arete cannot be best displayed on a team, which is how most ball games are played. It was therefore not central to ancient Greek society and is almost never mentioned. Therein lies one of the most fundamental of the differences between our modern games and the world of ancient Greek athletics.

11

TRAINING: THE WORLD OF THE GYMNASION AND THE PALAISTRA

The Buildings

IT IS TIME TO TURN our attention to the places where athletes trained. The two buildings that served this purpose were the *gymnasion* and the *palaistra,* and they could be found in every city-state; some larger cities had several. Each had a distinct architectural form, but the two were so interconnected physically and functionally that even in antiquity one word, usually *gymnasion,* was often used for both buildings.

The distinction between the gymnasion and the palaistra was kept by Vitruvius, an architect and architectural historian of the Augustan period who wrote a kind of manual of building types. One section of his work was devoted to the palaistra and the gymnasion even though he was a Roman writing in Latin and it was not common to build palaistrai in Italy, as he acknowledges (*On Architecture* 5.11; A 179). If we compare his idealized version to the plan of the actual palaistra at Olympia, however, we find a striking similarity (fig. 260).

Vitruvius begins his specifications for the ideal palaistra with a large central courtyard, open to the sky and surrounded by roofed colonnades. The ancient name of this area was self-descriptive: peristyle (surrounded by columns). Although he does not say so, we know that this area would have been filled with *skammata,* the pits where boxers, wrestlers, and *pankratiasts* practiced. Indeed, the word *palaistra* was derived from *pale* (wrestling), and the connection of the building with wrestling was always understood.

Next Vitruvius prescribes single colonnades on three sides, with a double colonnade on the north to protect the room behind from storms and sun. Behind the single colonnades he set *exedrai* (bays) with seats where classes would be held in philosophy, rhetoric, and other disciplines. One wall of the *exedra* would be open, and this opening usually would have columns to support a roof (fig. 261). There are many of

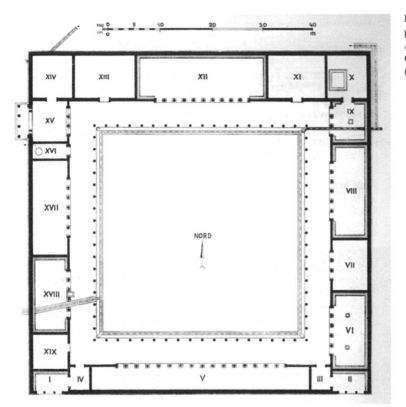

Fig. 260 Plan of the palaistra at Olympia. After A. Mallwitz, *Olympia und seine Bauten* (Munich, 1972), fig. 231.

these in the palaistra at Olympia, some with benches attached to the three solid walls (see fig. 260, rooms VI, VIII, XVIII) and some without (see rooms V, VII, XVII). These introduce us to the fundamental feature of the palaistra-gymnasion; it is a place where the mind as well as the body is exercised and trained.

In the middle of the north side of the courtyard, behind the double colonnade, Vitruvius recommends setting an especially large exedra with seats. This is the *ephebeion,* where the *ephebes* — the young men training to become citizens — receive their lessons about the heritage and traditions of their homeland. This corresponds to room XII at Olympia. To the right of the ephebeion Vitruvius wants three rooms: the *korykeion* (punching-bag room), the *konisterion* (dust or powder room), and (at the corner of the colonnade) the *loutron* (bath). A pool in room X at Olympia shows another point of agreement between that real palaistra and Vitruvius's ideal, but there is only one other room at Olympia (XI) instead of the two that he recommends.

To the left of the ephebeion, Vitruvius places the *elaiothesion* (room for storing oil). This room seems to have gained importance as the city provided oil on an increasingly regular basis for the young men who would become its new citizens. Funds, called *aleimmata* (anointing accounts), were set up and even endowed, and they were probably administered from the elaiothesion. To the left of the elaiothesion is, in

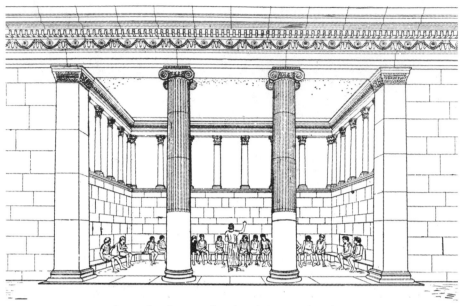

Fig. 261 Reconstruction of an exedra; this example is the Ephebeion in the palaistra at Priene. After M. Schede, *Die Ruinen von Priene* (Berlin, 1934), p. 85, fig. 95.

the Vitruvian account, a cluster of rooms that include a furnace and a hot bath. Here Vitruvius uses Latin words instead of transliterated Greek, thereby betraying the addition of a Roman installation at the northwest corner of his courtyard. These warm baths do not exist in the Greek palaistra at Olympia. It may be that room XIV was the konisterion, which is not located on the other side of the ephebeion, but the entrance of this room, directly from the northwestern entrance of the building, suggests that it probably served as an *apodyterion*.

Vitruvius does not mention the apodyterion (perhaps he reflects the Roman prejudice against nudity), but this undressing room is listed in other sources as a standard feature of the palaistra, and we can assume that one was located in every palaistra whether specifically mentioned or not. Room V in the palaistra at Olympia (fig. 262) has also been suggested as some kind of undressing room, a suggestion supported by its location between the two entrances at the southern corners of the building. Some palaistrai also had another room Vitruvius does not mention, a *sphairisterion* (ball room). The image of something resembling a handball court comes to mind, but we do not really know what the room was for (exercise or storage), and we do not know what architectural requirements were necessitated by its function. Room XIX in the palaistra at Olympia may be a sphairisterion, but there seems no way to identify it positively.

The picture of the palaistra that emerges from the text of Vitruvius and the physical remains at Olympia indicates that it was the ancient equivalent of the school-

Fig. 262 View from apodyterion of the palaistra at Olympia across the southeast corner of the court toward rooms VI–VIII (see fig. 260) (photo: author).

house, a place where body and mind were trained. This is why we sometimes hear of a palaistra existing independent of the gymnasion; the latter was more specifically, if not exclusively, for physical exercise. At the same time, the distinction between the words and the buildings were frequently blurred, and references to a "gymnasion" may actually mean a palaistra or a palaistra-gymnasion complex.

We should recognize, however, that the palaistra took different forms depending on its location. At Delphi, influenced at least in part by the rugged terrain, the palaistra has no large central courtyard (see fig. 186), but the builder placed great emphasis on the bath, whereas the bath at the Olympia palaistra is only subsidiary. The difference probably has to do with the relative lack of water at Olympia (although there was a bathing establishment just southwest of the palaistra) in contrast to the plentiful water supply at Delphi. Whatever the reason, the loutron in the Delphi palaistra was truly monumental (see fig. 184). A massive, well-built wall holds the terrace above, while a channel cut through the length of the wall brought water to a series of holes, from which it flowed into tubs mounted along the base of the wall. This is similar to the arrangement at Nemea (see fig. 194), although the circular pool has a different shape and larger capacity than the pool at Nemea; the Delphic pool has a diameter of 9.7 meters and a depth of 1.9 meters.

The holes along the wall that brought water to the tubs were masked by lions' heads whose mouths provided ornamental spouts. We see such "shower heads" in vase paintings of the sixth and fifth centuries B.C. (fig. 263). It would therefore appear

Fig. 263 Two athletes shower beneath lion-head spouts in a fountainhouse, flanked by pairs of athletes oiling themselves. Black-figure hydria by the Antimenes Painter, ca. 520 B.C. Leiden, Rijksmuseum voor Oudheden, inv. no. PC 63.

that the fourth-century tubs at Delphi and Nemea were a relatively late development. Indeed, it is possible that the showering athletes of the vase paintings are using a fountainhouse intended for common use, not just for athletes, and that the loutron was a late-classical-period development in palaistra architecture.

Vitruvius describes the ideal gymnasion as a building composed of three colonnades surrounding an open space; the fourth side is open. A double colonnade adjoins the back (north) wall of the palaistra, with two single colonnades a *stadion* (about 200 meters) in length perpendicular to the first on the other sides. The single colonnades are called *xystoi,* and they provide a covered track for running in bad weather. Outside, parallel to each xystos is an open-air track called the *paradromis.* The situation at Olympia once again strongly resembles the Vitruvian ideal. Set against the back wall of the palaistra is a single colonnade, longer than the back wall of the palaistra (fig. 264). At right angles to it is a gateway, which forms the main entrance to the gymnasion, and immediately next to (north of) it begins a xystos, which is, indeed, a stadion long, as was proven by test excavations at the northern end based on the Olympic stadium. There, some 150 meters north of the last excavated section of the xystos the end of the building was discovered. The remainder of the xystos has never been excavated, which is unfortunate since we know both that the official list of Olympic victors was kept there and that excavations in the xystos at Delphi in the 1980s uncovered plaster from the wall painted with lists of Pythian victors. The Olympian xystos differs from Vitruvius's ideal in having a double colonnade (fig. 265). Perhaps more athletes used it than frequented an ordinary gymnasion. The xystos on the other side of the open space was washed away by the Kladeos River, although a few traces indicate that it did exist.

Although Vitruvius does not mention it (nor does any other written source), the large open space between the three colonnades must have been the practice area for javelin and diskos throwers. One xystos and its corresponding paradromis may have been for sprinters and the other for long-distance runners, and there must have been an area set aside for the jumpers. Thus the palaistra and the gymnasion provided exercise and training space for all the festival events.

Fig. 264 Model of Olympia with the gymnasion and its xystos (X) extending out of the photo to the left at the base of the Hill of Kronos, with the palaistra (P) adjacent to its right (south) end (photo: © The British Museum, neg. inv. no. PS 254952).

Vitruvius's final words as he closes his chapter on the palaistra-gymnasion are significant: "Behind a xystos the stadium is to be planned so that large crowds can watch the athletes in comfort." The significance of this will become clear when we move from the palaistra-gymnasion at festival centers like Olympia and Delphi to the ones in city sites, at least in the Hellenistic period. A prime example can be found in Delos, which was always important as the birthplace of Apollo, and particularly flourishing as a commercial center in the second and early first century B.C. The Delian palaistra has a central court with a variety of rooms opening off it on three sides. The most immediately recognizable is the northern exedra, which must be the ephebeion (fig. 266). A marble bench runs around its walls, and we can imagine young men sitting there learning, willy-nilly, about their civic responsibilities (see fig. 261). The gymnasion which is attached to the palaistra at Delos consists of a xystos or covered track, as we would expect, but the paradromis is actually slightly separated from it, at a lower level. The slope between the two was intended to accommodate spectators, who would come to watch competitions. In other words, the paradromis also served as a stadium.

The same architectural arrangement can be seen at other sites, including Priene (fig. 267), and from it we can understand Vitruvius's final statement. At city sites, the practice track was also used for the competition stadium, conserving space and using facilities more efficiently. At festival centers, on the other hand, the stadium and the gymnasion are separate buildings because space is not as great a problem and the officials place more emphasis on pomp and ceremony than on the efficient use of facilities. Further, the significance of a victory at Olympia could never be approached by one at a city, and a separate stadium symbolizes that greater significance.

Fig. 265 Xystos of gymnasion at Olympia with its double colonnade, from the south. Late 4th–early 3rd century B.C. (photo: author).

The palaistra-gymnasion would be equipped with a variety of gear, and we could guess at the nature of some of this equipment. The names of the rooms given by Vitruvius indicate that oil and powder were stored there, as well as utensils for applying them. Punching bags were also present. We are especially fortunate, however, to have a list of the valuables in the building at Delos. In the second century B.C. annual inventories were made of the movable wealth of the city-state, and these inventories were made building by building, including the gymnasion (as the Delian palaistra-gymnasion was termed; *ID* 1417AI.118–154; *A 180*). The list mentions only valuable objects (specifically items made of bronze), so it does not identify everything that was in the building, but it does give an idea of the furnishings. For example, a total of ninety-eight shields, scattered in various rooms, is given. These shields were used in the local *chremetitic* (money) games in the *hoplitodromos,* the *hoplomachia,* the *pyrrhiche,* and the *apobates.* On the other hand, the list mentions only one helmet box, and it is described as "archaic with copper inlay, without inscription." Probably the owners of the helmets, which were made to fit their own heads, took them home while the state provided the shields for the competitions.

There were also a number of torches in the building. Torches are associated with the torch races (*lampadedromia*), and the ones on the list are actually dedications by victors, indicating that the palaistra-gymnasion also functioned as a trophy room. Twelve different torches are listed along with the name of the victor who dedicated each, and many are described as "on the wall." In these cases we can visualize a stone block embedded in the wall and jutting out from it on which sits the torch trophy (fig. 268). There were also "many dedicatory plaques" in the building at Delos that were probably victory trophies from competitions other than the lampadedromia.

More utilitarian, at least in some sense, were the three elevated tubs, the ten tubs on the floor, and a semicircular stool that are listed for the loutron of the palaistra-gymnasion. The custodian's office contained two water jugs, two jars, an urn, and a basin for holy water. (The last resembled the one depicted in figure 20.) Elsewhere were two amphoras and two sundials. One of the latter was in the sphairistera, which was presumably a closed room and therefore not sunlit. Still, keeping time was important in the palaistra-gymnasion.

Fig. 266 Aerial view of the palaistra-gymnasion of Delos from the northeast. The ephebeion (E) opens left onto the courtyard of the palaistra, while the xystos (X) and the paradromis (P) of the gymnasion continue off the photograph toward the lower right (photo: © H. R. Goette, Berlin).

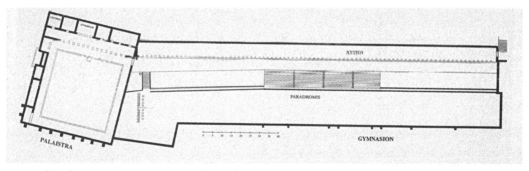

Fig. 267 The palaistra-gymnasion at Priene with seats for spectators between the xystos and the paradromis-stadium. Drawing by author.

Statues and statuettes, all apparently of bronze, are also in the inventory. Six of these are not identified, although the names of the dedicators are frequently given, as is a brief description: "a totally nude male statue," "a totally nude male statue holding a staff," "a female statue holding a drinking cup in her hands," are typical examples. Perhaps the person making the inventory was unable to identify the figure portrayed. The statues that are identified are of divinities: three of Herakles, two of Eros (one of which is aping Herakles, holding a lionskin and a club), one of Apollo, and one of Pallas Athena. Each of these deities has a role to play in the typical palaistra-gymnasion and their presence is not surprising. Herakles is the hero-god associated with the heavy

Fig. 268 The wall support for a torch trophy.
The roughened surface marks the portion of the
marble block that was embedded in the wall;
the smoothed surface projected from it. This
projection has a socket on top into which the
torch trophy was set, and an inscription on the
front recording the name of the victor-dedicator
and other information, such as the date of the
victory. In this case a certain Antiochos won
the "epitaphia" torch race in the annual Hermaia
when Apolexides was archon (ca. 7 B.C.), and
when Philios and Apollonides were the paidotribai
and Demetrios was the assistant paidotribes.
Athens, Epigraphical Museum, inv. no. 8626
(IG II² 2997) (photo: author).

events of wrestling, boxing, and the *pankration*. Apollo supervised lessons in music, and
Athena in letters, while Eros assisted in the sexual education of young men.

The Delian inventory lists forty-one stone herms in the custodian's office, and
this requires special comment. The herm in its best-known form was a semi-aniconic
or quasi-anthropomorphic statue of the god Hermes (fig. 269): a square stone pillar
surmounted by the bearded human head of the god. Small square stubs of stone projected at the sides to imply shoulders, and an erect phallus was attached to the front of
the pillar somewhere near the middle. Herms can be found at entries throughout the
ancient world, but they were especially appropriate to the palaistra-gymnasion for
Hermes was the god of speed, worshiped by runners and pentathletes.

Several herms have been found at the palaistra-gymnasion at Delos (fig. 270).
These may actually be some of the forty-one listed in the inventory, but they are not
necessarily portrayals of Hermes. Many herms carried the heads of *gymnasiarchoi*,
leaders of the gymnasion, whose portraits were sometimes set up by their grateful
students (see, for example, fig. 278).

These are the key items of the Delian inventory, but there must have been hundreds of other pieces of equipment and furnishings in the palaistra-gymnasion that
were not valuable enough to be listed in the annual inventories. Chairs, stools, writing
tablets and styli, diskoi, and javelins were all surely available in the building, and there
must also have been large pots into which the athletes dumped the mixture of dust
and sweat (*gloios*) they scraped off their bodies.

Finally, a word about size. As we have seen, the gymnasion was a large area
defined on two sides by xystoi or covered colonnades that were at least 200 meters
long. The distance between them, to judge from the remains at Olympia, was at least
100 meters so they occupied some 20,000 square meters. The fourth side seems to
have had no strict architectural limit. Large as this area seems, we know that in at least
two cases the gymnasion was popularly considered to extend over an even greater
area. Both gymnasia were in Athens: the Akademy at the northwest of the city, and

Fig. 269 A beribboned athlete crowning a herm, which shows on its side the kerykeion (caduceus) of Hermes. Nike prepares to tie a ribbon on its head. Red-figure krater, ca. 430 B.C. Agrigento, Museo Archeologico, inv. no. R178/a.

Fig. 270 The base and the shaft of a herm from Delos. Note the socket for the phallus and the various inscriptions, including the relief portrayal of a victory crown. Marble, 2d century B.C. Delos, palaistra-gymnasion (photo: author).

the Lykeion to the east. In both cases we should envision something like a college campus with areas of trees and grass surrounding buildings—the palaistra and the gymnasion in the narrow technical sense described above. The total area of these sprawling suburban schools is not known, but the Akademy has been estimated at about 180,000 square meters.

Both the Akademy and the Lykeion were training grounds where young athletes prepared for competition. But not only athletes studied in these palaistrai-gymnasia—or at least it is hard to believe that certain young men were considered athletic (fig. 271). Rather, these were training grounds for every young man and for every aspect of the man. Successful athletes emerged from the playing fields of the Akademy and Lykeion, and successful poets, playwrights, politicians, and philosophers emerged as well. Here young legs and young minds were stretched and prepared for all life's competitions. Here Plato and Aristotle and many before and after them engaged young men in the total human experience. We should always remember that Plato's Akademy and Aristotle's Lykeion—terms which came to represent types of philosophical schools—were first and last gymnasia and that there is no inherent reason to separate the activities of the mind from those of the body.

Fig. 271 Young men in the gymnasion. From left, a runner in the starting position, a fat boy holding an ankyle or a himas, a stool with piled-up clothes, a javelin thrower, and a diskos thrower. All, including the fat boy, wear crowns. The inscription reads, "Pheidippos painted it." Red-figure kylix by Pheidippos, ca. 510 B.C. London, The British Museum, inv. no. E 6 (GR 1846.5–12.2) (© The British Museum).

The People

The buildings where athletic training took place are, of course, meaningless without the people: those who trained there and those who trained them. The officials varied by place and time, but by the Hellenistic period the record allows us to reconstruct the staff of a city gymnasion.

The gymnasiarchos was, as the name suggests, the leader of the gymnasion, the man in charge of the building, its staff, and the program of education. Gymnasiarchoi were elected annually and had to be a certain age, usually over forty and under sixty. The gymnasiarchos is probably the figure pictured on vase paintings holding a cane and watching the lessons (fig. 272).

The gymnasiarchos was assisted by a *paidonomos,* who was appointed to the post; he had to be more than forty years old. The paidonomos decided which boys had completed their studies satisfactorily and could advance to the next year's lessons. He helped the gymnasiarchos in the selection of some of the staff and settled disputes among the teachers about the number of students in their classes.

The size of the teaching staff and the specialties of each teacher (*didaskalos*) obviously depended on the size of the city and what was considered suitable for public education. A third-century B.C. inscription from the island of Teos gives a detailed breakdown of the school staff there. (Note that my equivalences for the sums of money may not be accurate, but the relative values are.)

Fig. 272 Lessons in the palaistra-gymnasion: aulos and aulos singing (left) and recitation or spelling (center). The gymnasiarchos at the right supervises the whole. On the wall hang various musical instruments and scrolls (books? music?). The inscription at the top reads, "Hippodamas is kalos." Red-figure kylix by Douris, ca. 480 B.C. Berlin, Staatliche Museen — Preussischer Kulturbesitz, Antikensammlung, inv. no. F 2285B (photo: Johannes Laurentius).

1. At the end of the annual election of the magistrates and after the election of the secretaries three grammar teachers will be hired to teach the *paides* [boys] and the girls; the annual salary of the one elected on the first round is to be $13,300, of the one elected on the second round $12,100, and of the one elected on the third round $11,000.

2. Two *paidotribai* [physical trainers] will be appointed whose annual salary is to be $11,000 each.

3. Either a *kitharistes* [kithara player] or a *psaltes* [kithara singer] will be appointed with an annual salary of $15,400 for the one elected, who is to teach any paides who have advanced to the next level, and of those whom he teaches each year, the younger ones will be taught music in general and how to be either a kitharistes or a psaltes, but the epheboi will be taught only music in general. The paidonomos will decide about the age limits of these paides. If there should be an intercalary month an additional month's salary will be paid.

4. After notification to the demos the paidonomos and the gymnasiarchos will hire an infantry drillmaster and an instructor of archery and the javelin who will teach the epheboi and the paides who are enrolled in the music lessons. The salary of the instructor of archery and the javelin will be $5,500 and that of the infantry drillmaster $6,600. The infantry drillmaster will teach not less than two months each year.

The paidonomos and the gymnasiarchos must see to it that the paides and the epheboi are carefully exercised in the lessons set out for each in the laws. If the grammar teachers argue about the size of their classes, the paidonomos will settle the dispute, and they must abide by his decision. The grammar teachers will produce the customary exhibitions in the gymnasion and the music teachers in the *bouleuterion* [council house], <and the paidotribai in the stadium>. [*SIG*³ 578; A 184]

Among the interesting aspects of this document, the priorities in educational staff are especially noteworthy. We can recognize the emphasis on reading and writing from the position of a grammar teacher at the head of the list. Similarly, the competition among the various teachers implicit in the fact that they are elected and that their pay differs indicates the relative value placed on different aspects of education. On the other hand, apparently only the children (paides) received instruction in reading and writing. Was the emphasis on attaining a basic level of skill, then, but not on developing it further? Moreover, the teaching of this subject to girls is, as far as I know, unparalleled, and it raises a number of questions: Were girls educated when they were the same age as paides and in mixed classes? Were they also educated in the palaistra? Any answers I might have to these questions would be based on my own impressions, so I prefer to pose the questions but not answer them until more evidence is available.

The teachers known as paidotribai are the physical instructors or trainers. Their ranking below the grammar teachers, with smaller salaries, reveals the relative value placed upon them by the citizens of Teos. On the other hand, they rank higher than the music teachers, even though their salaries are smaller. Apparently music was not considered as important as verbal and physical skills, but good music teachers commanded higher salaries. Note, too, that the music teacher was either a kitharistes or a psaltes. The flute (*aulos*) player seems not to have been as highly esteemed; as we see in the vase paintings (such as fig. 272) the flute player accompanies the young singer but does not train him in the aulos itself. The kitharistes, on the other hand, taught students to play the kithara. We should also note that the aulos player in figure 272 is significantly younger than the kitharistes on the other side of the same vase (not shown here), perhaps another indication of their relative importance.

Finally, the selection of instructors in infantry maneuvers and use of bow and arrow and javelin by the gymnasiarchos and the paidonomos (rather than by election by the people), as well as the placement of these instructors at the end of the list, the size of their salaries, and the stipulation that they have to teach at least two months all show that military training was the lowest priority, though still recognized as necessary. It is also clear that military training was given only to advanced older students and epheboi, who were older still and were preparing for their enrollment as citizens. The selection of these instructors in addition to the paidotribai shows yet again that

Fig. 273 Young men preparing for exercise. A boy watches a young man disrobe while another young man oils himself. At the left a boy works on the ankle of a young man. Note the labels next to the men identifying them by name (from left): Hippomedon, Traxon, Egesias, and Lykon. The boy to the far right has no label, but between Egesias and Lykon is the familiar "Leagros is kalos." Red-figure krater by Euphronios, ca. 510 B.C. Berlin, Staatliche Museen — Preussischer Kulturbesitz, Antikensammlung, inv. no. F 2180 (photo: Johannes Laurentius).

athletics was not considered (an adequate) training for war. Specialized instructors were needed for both physical and military training.

Another person who was present at the palaistra, although he may have gotten only as far as the front door, was the *paidogogos* (literally "the boy leader"). This was typically a man of advanced years—a grandfather or long-time slave—who was responsible for bringing the boy to and from school. We can imagine a cluster of paidogogoi hanging around outside the palaistra, chatting and waiting for their charges. We do not know when boys stopped needing this escort—it probably varied from family to family—but teenagers surely make the trip by themselves.

Along with lists of people we would expect to find at a palaistra-gymnasion, we have evidence indicating who was not allowed in. In addition to the obvious—women—a second-century B.C. inscription from Verroia, in Macedonia, lists in its law regarding the organization of the gymnasion certain types of people who are prohibited: "No slave is to disrobe in the gymnasion, nor any freedman, nor their sons, nor cripples, nor homosexuals, nor those engaged in commercial craft, nor drunkards, nor madmen" (*SEG* 27.261; *A* 185). Perhaps the authorities who mandated these prohibitions were concerned about such people receiving the free oil (*aleimmata*) provided by the state; elements of society who did not contribute to the common good should not receive state benefits. Or perhaps they feared that such people would corrupt the city's youth. Thus, we hear that in fourth-century Athens schoolrooms opened only after sunrise and closed before sunset, and no older person was allowed in the schoolrooms with the paides except the didaskalos and his immediate relatives. Entering a classroom illegally was punishable by death (Aischines, *Against Timarchos* 9–12; *A* 183). Further, the *choregos* (producer) who paid for the training of paides for public performances had to be over the age of forty "in order that he might have reached the most self-controlled time of life when he encounters our paides."

Such regulations suggest that the palaistra-gymnasion provided opportunities for homosexual behavior, which the city fathers sought to curb. Obviously, when

Fig. 274 Young men in the palaistra. The youth on the right is goosing the central youth, who is dipping into a large krater (for wine? water? gloios?) while the third young man empties a pitcher and waves at the gooser. Red-figure kylix, 510–500 B.C. Warsaw, National Museum, inv. no. 198514.

Fig. 275 Older men making advances at young men in the palaistra. In one pair, the older man offers a hare as a love gift and touches the knee of the young man, who appears to be responding positively to the approach. On the wall hang two kitharas and a kit with aryballos and sponge. Red-figure kylix by Douris, ca. 480 B.C. Malibu, Calif., The J. Paul Getty Museum, inv. no. 86.AE.290 (photo: Penny Potter).

young men of different ages are nude together, as they were when they exercised in the gymnasion, and especially when the exercise requires physical contact, erotic situations can arise. A krater showing naked young men disrobing and oiling themselves in the company of boys, labeled with the names of real people and bearing the words *Leagros kalos* (Leagros is beautiful; fig. 273) has strong sexual undercurrents. These are probably being given expression in another vase painting showing the age-old locker-room antics of teenage youths (fig. 274) or the painting showing older men approaching young men with love offerings (fig. 275).

Occasionally the erotic connection between an older man and a boy is made explicit (fig. 276), and there can be no doubt about the existence of homosexuality in the

Fig. 276 An aroused teacher has abandoned his stick and fondles a boy, still holding his kit, who caresses the man's head. On the wall hang a stlengis, an aryballos, and a sponge, identifying the setting as the palaistra. Red-figure tondo by the Brygos Painter, ca. 480 B.C. Oxford, Ashmolean Museum, inv. no. 1967.304.

Fig. 277 Young men and boys in the gymnasion. The young men are marked as teachers or leaders by their sticks. The boy on the right seems to be doing stretches for his teacher, while the boy on left holds a diskos and is about to be crowned by his leader. The boy in the center is being embraced by his leader. Red-figure amphora by the Dikaios Painter, 510–500 B.C. Paris, Musée du Louvre, inv. no. G 45, Réunion des Musées Nationaux / Art Resource, New York.

palaistra-gymnasion. We might assume that these were simply portrayals of transgressions of the prohibition of older men and homosexuals in the schoolhouse. But specific homosexual relations are also shown between young men of slightly different ages in the palaistra-gymnasion, and it is clear that some depict young men offering physical and emotional guidance to boys (fig. 277). The interplay includes but is not limited to homosexual acts.

A better understanding of the situation comes from Plato's *Lysis* (203a–211a; A 182), in which Sokrates, on his way from the Akademy to the Lykeion, is drawn into a palaistra by a group of young men whose behavior suggests that they are in their late teens. Sokrates asks one of them, Hippothales, whether he has a boyfriend and, if so, who he is.

> He reddened at the question and I said, "Hippothales son of Hieronymos, there is no need to say whether or not you are in love—I see for myself that not only are you in love but that the passion is already far advanced. I may be a dummy and useless in other things, but god has given me the ability to recognize immediately a lover and a beloved."
>
> He reddened even more when he heard this, and then Ktesippos said, "What a joke, Hippothales, that you blush and hesitate to tell Sokrates his name. If Sokrates spends another ten seconds with you he will be bombarded with the name by you in any case. Let me tell you, Sokrates, that our ears are numb from being hit with 'Lysis this and Lysis that'; and if

Hippothales has had a bit to drink, we are apt to be roused from a deep sleep with the name 'Lysis' ringing in our ears. And his talk about Lysis is bad enough, but he drowns us with his poems and love letters. But worst of all is when we have to listen to him singing—in his fine voice—the praises of his boyfriend. And now he blushes at a question from you?"

"I guess this Lysis must be a newcomer," I said. "At least I don't recognize his name."

Sokrates inquires about Lysis and his background, and finds that Hippothales has been too timid to approach Lysis, so Sokrates sets out to show Hippothales how to make himself interesting to Lysis.

Taking Ktesippos along, I entered the palaistra. We found that the boys had performed the sacrifices already and that the sacred rites were nearly done, and they were playing knucklebones and all dressed to the nines. Most of them were playing outside in the courtyard, but some in a corner of the locker room were playing odds and evens with quantities of knucklebones picked out from little baskets, while others stood around and watched. One of these was Lysis, who stood among the boys and young men wearing a garland on his head and had a distinct appearance, worthy to be called not just beautiful [kalos], but imbued with *kalokagathia*.

Many points emerge from these passages. The students are divided by age, boys and young men (paides and *neaniskoi*). Further, they often wore garlands, which were not, in such a context, victory prizes from the games but decorations (see fig. 271). A physically attractive male was *kalos*, "beautiful," but the quality of spiritual goodness, *agathos*, was also recognized in the compound *kalokagathia* (*kalos kai* [and] *agathos*). Most significant, however, is the fact that Sokrates (and Plato and his audience) accepted—as an expected and positive part of the palaistra experience—a love relationship between a young man and a boy. This behavior was so integral to ancient life that ancient authors did not feel the need to write discourses on its origins or significance, although these can easily be surmised.

Bonding between two human beings is a natural occurrence, and it can have a positive social impact. It creates a sense of responsibility toward another person, especially if the older protects and the younger is sheltered, the older teaches and the younger learns. We know that the Thebans especially relied on such relationships, pairing warriors so that each would be particularly careful to look out for his partner. Philip of Macedon, who spent his youth at Thebes, also understood the benefits to be derived from male partnerships. If this male bonding resulted in sexual bonding, this could ensure that the connection was solid.

At the same time, it is clear that the ancient Greeks put emphasis on emotional bonds, a loving relationship that would result in permanence and stability. Profligate homosexuality was scorned and condemned. Hence, when the people of Verroia included homosexuals in the list of people banned from the gymnasion, they were forbidding perverts and prostitutes, not men who would create a caring homosexual relationship that included the erotic. Zeno the Stoic and others were cited: "Eros is a god who helps with the safety of the city-state. That other philosophers, older than Zeno, also recognized that Eros is holy and removed from all evil as shown by the fact that he is established in the gymnasia along with Hermes and Herakles, the former in charge of speech, the latter in charge of strength. When they are united, friendship and harmony are born, and through them the most beautiful freedom grows for their partakers" (Athenaeus 13.561C–D; A 181).

We may also note another social benefit of homosexuality. Property ownership was (and is) fundamental to society, and the peaceful, legal transfer of property from one generation to another was an important issue in ancient Greece. Lines of inheritance needed to be clear. This is why a man typically did not marry until into his thirties or even his forties (Aristotle, *Politics* 1335a, recommends thirty-seven as the ideal age), once the most dangerous period of military duty had been passed, lessening the possibility that his children would be orphaned. (Orphans were liable to become the responsibility of the state.) But if a man was not to wed until his thirties, he might well produce illegitimate offspring. Illegitimate children were a threat to orderly property transfer and a destablizing factor in society. Homosexuality allowed young men to deal with sexual impulses without fear of producing bastards. But when a man married, he was expected to restrain his tendencies toward homosexual erotic relations, and this is why the age limits for the gymnasiarchos and the choregos were typically set at forty. Homosexuality among the students in the gymnasion was, then, accepted, common, and regulated by tacit rules of conduct.

But sex was only one aspect of life at the gymnasion. At least once a year the students took part in competitive festivals. They were divided into age groups, typically the paides and the neaniskoi, and competed in festivals known as the Hermaia and the Mouseia. The latter included displays of musical achievement, while the former were physical competitions (almost always including a lampadedromia) which emphasized conditioning, coordination, and training. We should probably understand these festivals as a kind of annual review of what had been learned, a final exam.

One more area of education was offered, in part, in the gymnasion. This was the *ephebeia*, the two-year training for young men about to become citizens. Although this kind of training existed in most, perhaps all, Greek cities, most of our evidence comes from Athens, especially from Aristotle (*Constitution of the Athenians* 42; A 186). The young men had to have reached the age of eighteen, and they would spend the next two years first in training and then in active military service. These young men,

Fig. 278 Portrait herm of the kosmetes Sosistratos. Marble, A.D. 141/2. Athens, National Museum, inv. no. 385 (photo: © Treasury of Archaeological Receipts).

the epheboi, were organized according to their fathers' membership in one of the ten tribes of Athens. Each year each tribe selected a man of forty years of age or older to be the *sophronistes* (teacher-trainer) of their epheboi—a kind of master sergeant who organized the common meals and training of his troop. The year's program was overseen by yet another elected official, the *kosmetes,* who together with the sophronistai organized tours of the temples and shrines throughout Attika so that the epheboi could get a good grasp of their heritage. It is not specifically stated in our sources, but given the need of a citizen to be literate, this was the time when every young man was tested to make sure he could read and write. We are told that the epheboi attended lectures in the gymnasion and listened to philosophers in the Akademy and the Lykeion.

The city provided two paidotribai to oversee the epheboi's exercises, and this was as close as the epheboi came to using athletics as a military preparation, for their other teachers taught them infantry drills and the use of the bow, the javelin, and the sling. At the end of the first year the epheboi were issued a shield, a spear, a *chlamys* (heavy cloak), and a *petasos* (broad-brimmed hat; see fig. 222) and sent on border patrol around the territorial boundaries of Athens. Some years the epheboi were exceptionally talented, and the city would officially congratulate them and their leaders, especially the kosmetes. One record of such honors paid to a group notes that they took the initiative to repair an old catapult and learn how to use it (*IG* II², 1006; A 187). The group is especially praised for its *philotimia* (love of honor) in its behavior toward the city and the kalokagathia acquired from the kosmetes, Dionysios. He, meanwhile, is praised for his leadership and his arete. (Note that the term "arete" cannot be applied to a group but only to an individual.) Further, his epheboi honored him with a gold crown and a bronze statue. In other cases, the epheboi honored their kosmetes with a marble portrait herm (fig. 278; see also fig. 270).

As important as the ephebeia was to the life of the gymnasion and in preparing the young men for competition in the local Panathenaic Games, it played only a supporting role for athletics. Athletics were important to the individual because they offered a chance to display arete, to society for their entertainment value, and to the city-state for their propaganda value, but athletic competitions were not essential to the health and welfare of the city.

12

ATHLETICS AS ENTERTAINMENT IN THE HELLENISTIC AND ROMAN PERIODS

ALEXANDER THE GREAT and his Macedonian army changed the world as they pushed south to the Nile and east to the banks of the Indus River, creating an empire that was the largest ever known, although it collapsed after Alexander's short life came to an end. Even after his death, however, a veneer of Hellenism lay over his former empire, and his successors—from the Attalids in Pergamon to the Ptolemies of Egypt—maintained their Greek customs and defended their Greek heritage in the world we call Hellenistic, "Greekish," rather than Hellenic, "Greek."

The most important result of Alexander's conquests was the spread of Greek as the common language, which served as a binding force for hundreds of years. Hence, for example, the New Testament was first written in Greek, so that its gospel could more easily be spread throughout the Hellenistic world. So, too, Greek athletics were exported as part of the Hellenic tradition, a custom Alexander encouraged. During the course of his conquests Alexander held games along the way for a variety of reasons. In his *Anabasis* Arrian describes Alexander's expedition chronologically, specifically mentioning the various games. These can be tabulated as follows:

Soli (Cilicia = southeast Turkey)	gymnikos and mousikos
Tyre (Lebanon)	gymnikos and lampadedromia
Memphis (Egypt)	gymnikos and mousikos
Memphis (Egypt)	gymnikos and mousikos
Tyre (Lebanon)	gymnikos and mousikos
Susa (Iran)	gymnikos and lampadedromia
Zadrakarta, (Iran)	gymnikos
Alexandria Ultima (Uzbekistan)	gymnikos and hippikos
Taxilia (India)	gymnikos and hippikos

Hydaspes River (India)	gymnikos and hippikos
Hyphasis River (India)	gymnikos and hippikos
Karmania (Pakistan)	gymnikos and mousikos
Ekbatana (Iran)	gymnikos and mousikos
Babylon (Iraq)	gymnikos and mousikos

When we think of these Greek soldiers marching out to the limits of their world, through nation after nation of people who had no notion of Greek athletics, and bringing their games with them, we can understand how important these competitions were to them.

These games were staged to entertain Alexander's troops. But were they staged *by* his soldiers? In other words, were the soldiers also athletes? Athenaeus notes that two of Alexander's comrades, Perdikkas and Krateros, "were such lovers of gymnic exercise that they brought along a *stadion*'s-worth of goatskins on the march, beneath whose shade—after they had grabbed a place in the encampment—they exercised. They also brought along many wagonloads of the kind of *konis* [dust or powder] used in the *palaistra*" (*The Gastronomers* 12.539C; A 190).

But there is no explicit reference to Perdikkas or Krateros or any of Alexander's soldiers winning his various competitions. Of course, the names of the winners were not recorded at all, so this is hardly decisive evidence. On the other hand, it is clear that when the games included the *mousikos agon* the competitors were professional musicians, and the competitions were held to entertain the troops. The games included acting competitions as well, and the whole amounted, in reality, to the ancient Greek equivalent of a USO concert. The musicians and actors were members of professional guilds or unions, and as we can see from the list of games they did not accompany Alexander on his easternmost expedition. It is interesting, though perhaps coincidental, that the musicians and actors were never with Alexander's army when the Pythian Games, the most important of their competitions, were going on.

Athletic guilds, probably came into existence during the time of Alexander. We know, for example, that there were men in his army whose job was to be athletes, not soldiers. The best evidence is the case described in Chapter 9 of Dioxippos, the Olympic *pankration* victor in 336 who fell out of favor with Alexander and committed suicide. The reason for Alexander's displeasure is revealing. A Macedonian, Koragos, in a drunken snit challenged Dioxippos to a duel. Dioxippos accepted.

> Alexander set the day for the battle, and when the time came for the duel thousands of men assembled for the spectacle. Because he was one of their own, the Macedonians and Alexander rooted for Koragos, while the Greeks favored Dioxippos. Koragos came onto the field of honor clad in the finest armor while the Athenian was naked, with his body oiled and carrying a well-balanced club.

Both men were marvelous to see in their magnificent physical condition and their desire for the fight. The spectators anticipated a veritable battle of gods. The Macedonian looked like Ares as he inspired terror through his stature and the brilliance of his weapons; Dioxippos resembled Herakles in his strength and athletic training, even more because he carried a club.

As they approached each other, the Macedonian hurled his spear from the proper distance, but Dioxippos bent his body slightly and avoided it. Then the Macedonian poised his long pike and charged, but when he came within reach the Greek struck the pike with his club and splintered it. Now Koragos was reduced to fighting with his sword, but as he went to draw it, Dioxippos leapt upon him, grabbed his swordhand in his left hand, and with his other upset his opponent's balance, knocking his feet from under him. As Koragos fell to the ground, Dioxippos placed his foot on the other's neck and, holding his club in the air, looked to the crowd.

The spectators were in an uproar because of the man's incredible skill and superiority. Alexander motioned for Koragos to be released, then broke up the gathering and left, clearly annoyed at the defeat of the Macedonian. [Diodorus Siculus 17.100–101; A 172a]

This duel not only has all the trappings of spectacle rather than a competition, it clearly sets the soldier against the athlete as his antithesis, and there is an underlying tension between these two different breeds of professional. It had long been recognized that the training of the athlete was detrimental to the training required of the soldier. As early as Euripides' time, about 420, the difference between the athlete and the soldier was recognized: "What man has ever defended the city of his fathers by winning a crown for wrestling well or running fast or throwing a *diskos* far or planting an uppercut on the jaw of an opponent? Do men drive the enemy out of their fatherland by waging war with diskoi in their hands or by throwing punches through the line of shields? No one is so silly as to do this when he is standing before the steel of the enemy" (*Autolykos,* frag. 282; A 230).

In other words, it is highly unlikely that Dioxippos was serving in Alexander's army as a fighter and much more probable that he was there as an entertainer, an athlete called upon to perform for the amusement of the troops. About a century later the distinction between soldier and athlete is expressed cogently by Plutarch:

Since Philopoimen [ca. 253–182] seemed well formed for wrestling, some of his friends and advisers urged him into athletics. But he asked them whether anything about athletics could impinge on his military training. Then they told him the reality: that the athletic body and lifestyle are different in every way from the military, and that the diet and exercise are especially different since athletes were always fortifying themselves with a lot of sleep, perpetual stuffing of their stomachs, and fixed periods for motion and rest, guarding their condition against every lapse or deviation from the habitual that might change it for the worse. The soldier, on the contrary, has to be experienced in every sort of wandering and irregularity, and especially to be able to bear easily lack of food and sleeplessness. When Philopoimen heard this he not only avoided athletics and made fun of them but later, when he was a general, he rejected all athletics with dishonor and abuse as making the most useful bodies worthless for the truly necessary contests. [*Philopoimen* 3.2–4; *A 208*]

The development of the athlete as entertainer parallels and is closely tied to the foundation of dozens of new *stephanitic* (crown) games around the Hellenistic world. Thus, for example, the Aitolian League established new games called the Soteria (savior) after the Aitolians saved Delphi from an invasion by Gauls in 278. They established these games as *isoPythian* (equivalent to the Pythian Games) in the mousikos agon, and *isoNemean* in the gymnikos agon and the hippikos agon with regard to age categories and prizes. The Aitolians then sent embassies throughout the Greek world seeking official recognition of their Soteria Games, urging especially that citizens of the different city-states "who compete and win at the Soteria have the same honors as those written in the law for victors at the Pythia and Nemea" (*SIG*³ 402; *A 191*). We shall examine in the next chapter the practical significance of receiving "the same honors." For now it is important to see what type of games figured in the spread of Greek athletics. The four ancient stephanitic games always retained their preeminence, but a second tier of international competitions developed. A century after the Soteria Games were founded, for example, the Amphiktyonic Council of Delphi itself accepted as stephanitic the new Nikephoria Games of King Eumenes II of Pergamon. These were to be isoPythian in the musical competitions, and *isOlympic* in the nude and equestrian competitions, again with regard to age categories and prizes.

Yet another example comes from Judaea, where King Herod the Great finished his new capital, Kaisareia Sebaste, in 10 B.C. The architectural monuments included a theater and next to it a handsome stadium by the sea (fig. 279). Although the artificial embankments have now been embellished with stone seats, the tunnel entrance from the locker room (*apodyterion*) is still a standard feature of this architectural form (fig. 280). As a major part of his celebration of the completion of his new capital, Herod announced games with gymnikoi, mousikoi, and hippikoi agones, and to this he added gladiatorial bouts. He dedicated these Sebasteia Games to the Roman emperor Augustus and made them stephanitic and quadrennial—another addition to the larger cycle of crown games (Josephus, *Jewish Antiquities* 16.136–141; *A 198*).

Fig. 279 The stadium at Kaisareia Sebaste with a wooden protection over the tunnel, viewed from the southeast, 10 B.C. (photo: author).

A few years later, in 2 B.C., Augustus himself established a new festival in Naples (an old Greek city), the Italic, Roman, Augustan, IsOlympic Games and Festival. The regulations of these new games were inscribed at Olympia, perhaps to legitimatize the title isOlympic (*IvO* 56.11–28; *A 199*). On the other hand, the Naples games included sacrifices to the emperor and cash prizes for the musical competitions. These were surely not elements of the Olympic Games and indicate that *isOlympic* refers only to certain parts of the contest.

We should not imagine that the indigenous people throughout the extended Hellenistic world all adopted Greek culture, including Greek athletics. There were confrontations, and one of the best documented occurred in Jerusalem in 175 B.C. Antiochos Epiphanes, one in a line of successors to Alexander and a promoter of Hellenism, had become king of Syria. A certain Jason bribed his way into the position of high priest of Jerusalem and asked permission to

> set up a *gymnasion* and an *ephebeion* and to enroll those in Jerusalem as citizens of Antioch. When the king granted this and Jason became leader, he straightway converted his countrymen to Greek customs. . . . He happily founded a gymnasion right under the akropolis and organized the best of the *epheboi* to wear a *petasos* — such was the extent of Hellenism . . . that the priests no longer wanted to perform liturgies at the altar but disdained the temple and neglected the sacrifices in their haste to participate in the illegal activities in the palaistra whenever the diskos drew them. The leaders no longer set stock in their ancestral honors but sought Greek glories. . . .

Fig. 280 Northern support wall of the stadium at Kaisareia Sebaste with the tunnel entrance and the area (unexcavated) of the apodyterion, viewed from the northeast, 10 B.C. (photo: author).

> When it was time for the quadrennial agon at Tyre, at which the king was to
> be present, the abominable Jason sent as *theoroi* from Jerusalem those who
> had become citizens of Antioch. [Maccabees 2.4.9–15 and 18–19; A 193]

In other words, the Jews of Jerusalem were being Hellenized, and the way it was being done was through the physical and intellectual training of the palaistra-gymnasion and participation in Greek games at Tyre. The Maccabees were outraged, but for us the significance is the omnipotence of athletics as a force of Hellenization.

Athletics were less favorably and less successfully received in the west because the Romans were highly suspicious of nudity. Nonetheless, the initial diplomatic contact between Rome and Corinth in 228 B.C. resulted in Roman participation in the Isthmian Games (Polybius 2.12.8; A 194). But Greek athletics were still a novelty in Rome a generation later when, in 186, Marcus Fulvius Nobilior held games in the capital to celebrate his capture of the city of Ambrakia in northwestern Greece. For this celebration "many actors came from Greece to pay honor to him. Then also for the first time an athletic competition was put on as a spectacle for the Romans" (Livy 39.22.1; A 195). So by this time athletes were enlisted as entertainers not just in the Hellenic world but in foreign lands as well.

To be sure, the Etruscans, who exerted so much influence over the development of early Rome, had had contact with Greek athletics. Indeed, many of the Greek vases that portray athletics were found in Etruscan tombs (see, for example, figs. 7, 8, 11, 70, 76). But this is largely because Etruscans collected Greek vases, and the tombs also contain many that portray subjects other than athletics. Furthermore, it seems clear that the Etruscans, like the Romans, were ambivalent about nudity, and it has been suggested that all the vases on which *perizomata* (loincloths) were painted over the athletes' genitalia were made or adapted for the Etruscan market (see, for example, figs. 4, 5). Wall paintings on an Etruscan tomb known as the Tomb of the Biga appear to show naked Greek athletes, but close analysis reveals that the subjects of the paintings were borrowed from vase paintings without direct contact with or knowledge of Greek athletics. For example, one athlete holds his javelin as if it were a pole for vaulting, and the *rhabdos* (whip) of the judge looks like a piece of limp pasta that couldn't make a scratch. There is no evidence that either the Etruscans or the Romans had any direct knowledge of Greek athletics in the sixth, fifth, or fourth centuries B.C.

Greek athletics remained a novelty to the Romans down to imperial times. In 45 B.C., Julius Caesar, like Marcus Fulvius 140 years earlier, brought in athletes to stage competitions in a temporary stadium built for the purpose in the Campus Martius. In addition to being temporary, these games were only a part — and a small part — of the larger celebration that included "a gladiatorial combat, stage plays in every quarter of Rome performed in every language, chariot races in the Circus, athletic competitions, and a mock naval battle" (Suetonius, *Julius Caesar* 39; A 201).

Nero's passion for all things Greek included the games, although it is doubtful that any Romans were persuaded by his example to adopt Greek competitions. In A.D. 67 Nero visited Greece and won 1,808 victories at various festivals. Suetonius gives a detailed description of Nero's Hellenic tour of triumph, from which we can understand something of the situation in Greece as well as the character of this emperor. The trip was undertaken because

> the Greek cities which sponsored regular music contests had adopted the policy of sending him every prize for kithara playing. . . . This led him to say, "Only the Greeks are worthy of my genius, for they really listen to music." So he sailed off to Greece and after he landed made the rounds of all the festivals.
>
> Most contests were held only at long intervals, but he ordered them all to be held during his visit, even if it meant repeating them after an irregular interval. He broke tradition at Olympia by introducing a music contest in the athletic games. . . .
>
> No one was allowed to leave the theater during his performances, however urgent the reason, and the gates were kept locked. There are stories of women in the audience giving birth, and of men being so bored that they would sneak out by jumping off the wall at the back of the theater, or by playing dead and being carried away for burial. . . .
>
> Once, while acting in a tragedy, he dropped his scepter and quickly picked it up, terrified of being disqualified. The accompanist who played the flute and served as prompter for his lines swore that the slip had not

been noticed because the audience was listening enraptured, so he took heart again. Nero insisted on announcing his own victories and this led him to enter the competitions for *kerykes* [heralds]. In order to destroy every trace of previous winners in his contests, he ordered that all their statues be pulled down, dragged away, and dumped into public latrines.

He took part in the chariot racing on several occasions, and at Olympia he drove a ten-horse team, a novelty added to the festival just for him. However, he lost his balance and fell out of the chariot and had to be helped into it again. Nonetheless, even though he did not run the whole race and quit before the finish, the judges awarded him the victory crown. On the eve of his departure for Rome, he gave the whole province where Olympia is located its freedom and granted Roman citizenship as well as large cash rewards to the judges. He announced these benefactions himself from the middle of the stadium on the day of the Isthmian Games.

Returning from Greece to Naples, where he first landed, he entered with white horses through a part of the wall that had been torn down, as is the custom for victors at the sacred games. Then he entered Antium in the same way, then Albanum, and then Rome; but at Rome he entered in the same chariot that Augustus had used to celebrate his triumph long ago, wearing a purple robe embroidered with golden stars and a *chlamys* [heavy cloak], with the Olympic crown on his head and the Pythian in his right hand. The other crowns were carried before him with legends telling where they had been won and whom he had defeated. [Nero 22–25; A 203]

Embedded in this story are many details about the games that we have already examined and others we shall look at presently (such as tearing down the walls of the city). Perhaps the most important information this story provides, however, is the clear indication that the athletic festivals of Greece might have been undermined by Nero, but they were very much alive and in good operation in his day.

Despite the thorough adoption of Greek philosophy and literature in Rome by the time of Augustus, it was the emperor Domitian, a philhellene who was as despised as—and more feared than—Nero, who made Greek athletics a part of the Roman scene with the establishment of the Capitolian Games in A.D. 86. This was a quadrennial contest in honor of Jupiter Capitolinus with music, equestrian, and gymnic competitions typical of Greek games, but it also offered a race of maidens and competitions in prose recitation in Greek and Latin. To give his games a permanent home, Domitian built an odeum, or closed music hall, and a stadium in the Campus Martius. These monuments have left their footprints on the plan of modern Rome, especially the stadium, today's Piazza Navona (fig. 281). Soon after Domitian's death, however, the buildings were used for gladiatorial shows and the stadium was flooded for mock naval battles. Greek athletics simply did not excite the Romans.

Fig. 281 Aerial view of the Piazza Navona, which lies over (and retains the shape of) Domitian's Stadium, Rome.

During the Hellenistic and Roman periods, the athletic guilds took on an important role. A letter from Mark Antony of 33/2 B.C. to the Commonwealth of Greeks in Asia sets out special favors for his friend and *aleiptes* (masseur) Artemidoros, who is described as working with the priest of the Synod of Worldwide Winners of Sacred Games and Crowns, which must have been a sort of alumni club for successful athletes (*PLond* 137 [CR 7 (1893) 476]; A 209). Certainly, to judge from the favors offered by Mark Antony — including exemption from military service, public duties, and the billeting of troops — the group had clout.

By the late first century A.D., we hear of other guilds, for example the Loyal, Patriotic, Reverent, and Itinerant Synodos of the Alexandrians, which had as its high priest a successful athlete (*IG* XIV, 747; A 210). Another group had the equally grandiose name of the Xystic Synodos of the Heraklean Athletic Winners of Sacred Games and Crowns (*IG* XIV.1055b; A 212). This union was located in Rome and in A.D. 143, it received a *curia athletarum* (meetinghouse of athletes) located near the Baths of Trajan from Emperor Antoninus Pius. Union halls for athletes have also been documented at Olympia, where excavations southwest of the Altis have uncovered massive remains of the Roman period. It is also likely that something similar to a curia athletarum is pictured on a terracotta relief that shows a statue of Herakles flanked by athletes set in an architectural frame (fig. 282). So by this time athletes have established their professional identity, status, and place in society.

Another development of the Hellenistic and Roman period is the creation of titles to demonstrate the superiority of a given athlete. In an era where athletic times and distances were not recorded, the number and types of victories indicated the star per-

Fig. 282 Herakles (identified by his club and skin of the Nemean lion) stands in the central section of a building that consists of a colonnade behind an arcade with a pediment above. In the pediment two tritons hold a central shield. Within the colonnade to the right of the statue of Herakles are two boxers, and to the left are an athlete scraping himself down and a victor with a palm branch. Terracotta relief of the 2d century A.D. Brussels, Musées Royaux d'Art et d'Histoire, inv. no. A 125 (photo: museum).

formers. Thus, in 212 B.C., when Kapros of Elis won the *pale* and the *pankration* at the same Olympics, he was given the special title of Successor of Herakles, and six athletes after him also received this title. Leonidas of Rhodes won the stadion, the *diaulos,* and the *hoplitodromos* and was hailed with the title Triastes (tripler). It is difficult to begrudge him this title since he won those events at the Olympics of 164, 160, 156, and 152!

Another title appears in the Hellenistic period for the first time, although it was applied retroactively to earlier athletes. This was *periodonikes* (circuit winner): an athlete who had been victorious at least once at Olympia, Delphi, Isthmia, and Nemea. The idea of having, and winning, a Grand Slam certainly enhanced the reputation of the athlete, but the title may also have been a means of protecting the reputation of the old stephanitic festivals in the face of the newly established crown games like the Soteria at Delphi and the Nikephoria at Pergamon.

Perhaps the most fulsome praise given an athlete appears in a biographical text set up in Naples in A.D. 107 for Titus Flavius Archibius of Alexandria (*IG* XIV, 747; A 210). He is called a "victor incomparable" and his many victories (forty-six are mentioned specifically) are listed in excruciating detail. In eight cases he is said to be "the first of mankind" to accomplish a given sequence or combination of victories. Let us end with a brief sampling of his other exploits:

> At the Pythian Games he won the pankration in the *ageneios* [youth] category, and at the next Pythiad he won both the pale and the pankration in the men's category, and at the next Pythiad he won the pankration in the men's category, the first of mankind to do so. At the Nemean Games he

won the pankration in the boys' category and the pankration in the men's category three times in a row, the first of mankind to do so. . . .

At the sacred four-year games at Antioch he won the pankration in the boys' category and at the next festival four years later he won the pale and the *pyx* in the ageneios category, and at the next festival he won the pankration in the men's category, and at the next festival again he won the pankration in the men's category, the first of mankind to do so. . . .

At the sacred four-year games at Alexandria he won the pankration in the ageneios category and four years later he won the pankration in the men's category and again at the next festival he won the pankration in the men's category and at the next festival he won the pale and the pankration in the men's category, the first of mankind to do so . . .

13

PROFESSIONALS AND AMATEURS

MODERN ATHLETICS, particularly the Olympics, exhibit an ambivalence on the question of professionalism in sport. The desire for amateurism — competition for its own sake — runs smack into economic realities: athletes must eat, and they also have to find a way to pay for their training. Antiquity is frequently invoked to justify one position or the other, but how well do ancient athletic practices really support either advocates of professionalism or those of amateurism?

It will be obvious from the previous chapter that by the Roman period athletes were professional in every sense of the word. Athletes competing in the Italic, Roman, Augustan, IsOlympic Games and Festival at Naples had to appear a month before the festival but each received a daily *obsonion* (food allowance) during the training period as well as a place to sleep. A century later the obsonion had become a pension for victorious athletes at the so-called *eiselastic* games. These games entitled the victorious athlete to a grand procession when he returned home, and a section of the town wall was torn down for him to pass through — the *eiselasis*, an ancient equivalent to being given the key to the city. Pliny the Younger, serving as imperial representative in northern Asia Minor, debated some of the problems created by this professionalism in an exchange of correspondence with the emperor Trajan in A.D. 111. Pliny was having bureaucratic difficulties about the payment of the obsonia:

> Sir, the athletes are constantly complaining that they ought to receive the obsonia you established for the eiselastic games from the day they are crowned. They maintain that what counts is not when they were led triumphantly into their native city but when they actually won the contest for which they get the obsonia. Since I have to countersign the obsonia payments with the notation "eiselastic account," it is my strong inclination that only the date when they make their eiselasis should be considered.

The athletes are also asking for the obsonia for victories in the games you designated eiselastic even when their victories at those games came before your designation. They maintain that this is only reasonable since the obsonia have been stopped for their victories at games which have been dropped from the eiselastic list even though their victories at those games came while the games were still on the list. I seriously question whether such retroactive awards should be given, and I therefore beg you to instruct me on the intention of your benefactions.

Trajan's response could have been foretold:

I do not think that anything is owed the victor in an eiselastic contest until he has made the eiselasis in his own city. No retroactive obsonia are owed the athletes who won victories at the games I have been pleased to place on the eiselastic list if the victories antedate the games becoming eiselastic. It is no argument that they no longer receive the obsonia for their victories in games I have removed from the eiselastic list. Although the status of those contests was changed, I did not demand that they refund what they had already received.

One wonders at the nerve of the athletes in daring to haggle with the emperor, but even more important is the fact that the coffers of the empire were expected to provide pensions for victors at a number of *stephanitic*—the crown as opposed to money (*chrematitic*)—games. These athletes were professionals, and they depended upon athletics for their livelihood. To be sure, a successful athlete would become financially secure if he won enough eiselastic victories, for his multiple obsonia would be the equivalent of several meals a day and what he did not spend on food could go to rent, clothes, and other needs. Further, there were jobs open to athletes after their competitive careers had ended. Markos Aurelios Asklepiades, for example, in about A.D. 200, became director of the Imperial Baths and president of his union (*xystarches* for life of the Sympas Xystos; *IG* XIV.1102; *A* 213). But these success stories were the exception. Galen, writing about twenty years earlier, offers a very different picture, one that probably was more accurate about the conditions, if not the abilities, of the average athlete:

All natural blessings are either mental or physical, and there is no other category of blessing. Now it is abundantly clear to everyone that athletes have never even dreamed of mental blessings. To begin with, they are so deficient in reasoning powers that they do not even know whether they have a brain. Always gorging themselves on flesh and blood, they keep their brains soaked in so much filth that they are unable to think accurately and are as mindless as dumb animals.

Perhaps it will be claimed that athletes achieve some of the physical blessings. Will they claim the most important blessing of all—health? You will find no one in a more treacherous physical condition. . . . Athletes overexert every day at their exercises, and they force feed themselves, frequently extending their meals until midnight.

Their sleep is also immoderate. When normal people have ended their work and are hungry, athletes are just getting up from their naps. In fact, their lives are like those of pigs, except that pigs do not overexert or force feed themselves. . . .

Furthermore, the extreme conditioning of athletes is treacherous and variable, for there is no room for improvement and it cannot remain constant, so the only direction they can go is downhill. Thus their bodies are in good shape while they are competing, but as soon as they retire from competition degeneration sets in. Some soon die, some live longer but do not reach old age.

Since we have now considered the greatest physical blessing— health—let us go on to the physical blessings which remain. With respect to beauty it is clear that natural beauty is not improved a bit for athletes; many athletes with well-proportioned limbs are made exceedingly fat by the trainers, who take them and stuff them with blood and flesh. Indeed, the faces of some are battered and ugly, especially of those who have practiced the *pankration* or the *pyx*. When their legs are finally broken or twisted permanently out of shape or their eyes gouged out, I imagine that the beauty resulting from their way of life can most clearly be seen! While they are healthy this is the beauty they have the good fortune to possess, but when they retire the rest of their bodies go to pot and their already twisted limbs are the cause of real deformities.

But perhaps they will claim none of the blessings I have mentioned so far but will say that they have strength—indeed, that they are the strongest of men. But in the name of the gods, what kind of strength is this, and what is it good for? Can they do agricultural work such as digging or harvesting or plowing? Perhaps their strength is good for warfare? Euripides will answer that, for he said, "Do men fight battles with *diskoi* in their hands?" Are they strong in the face of cold and heat? Are they rivals of Herakles so that they too, summer and winter, go barefoot, clad in a skin, and camp out under the heavens? In all these respects they are weaker than newborn babies.

I think that it has become abundantly clear that the practice of athletics has no utility in the real business of life. You would further learn that there is nothing worth mention in such practice if I tell you the myth some talented man put into words. It goes like this: if Zeus decided that all the animals should live in harmony and partnership, and the herald invited to Olympia not only men but also animals to compete in the stadium, I think that no man would be crowned. In the *dolichos* the horse will be the best, the *stadion* will belong to the hare, and the gazelle will be first in the *diaulos*. Wretched men, nimble experts, none of you would be counted in the footraces. Nor would any of you descendants of Herakles be stronger than the elephant or the lion. I think that the bull would be crowned in the pyx and the donkey would, if he decided to enter, win the kicking crown. And so it shall be written in the pankration: "In the 21st Olympiad which was won by Brayer."

This myth shows quite nicely that athletic strength does not reside in human training. And yet, if athletes cannot be better than animals in strength, what other blessing do they share in?

Perhaps someone will say that they have a blessing in the pleasure of their bodies. But how can they derive any pleasure from their bodies if during their athletic years they are in constant pain and suffering, not only because of their exercises but also because of their forced feedings? And when they reach the age of retirement, their bodies are essentially if not completely crippled.

Are athletes perhaps to be worshiped like kings because they have large incomes? Yet they are all in debt, not only during the time they are competing but also after retirement. You will not find a single athlete who is wealthier than any business agent of a rich man. . . . Finally, athletes have big incomes while they are actively competing, but when they retire money quickly becomes a problem for them and they soon run through their funds until they have less than they started with before their careers. Does any one loan them money without property for security? [*Exhortation for Medicine* 9–14; A 215]

When did this situation begin? We have noted the presence of athletes as entertainers in Alexander's army, and it is surely relevant that a new architectural form develops for festival competitions at about the same time. This was a stadium that had earthen embankments for spectators, a vaulted underground entrance tunnel, and a locker room. We have seen it at Olympia, Nemea, Epidauros, and Athens, all within the period from about 340 to 320. We cannot be certain of the purpose of the new form, but we can see clearly its effects. Athletes and spectators were divided into two distinct groups, and we see therein the first physical evidence for the athlete as entertainer, complete with (un)dressing room, where his costume of nudity was put on.

Once it started being possible to make a living in athletics, a whole sector of ancient society started trying to do so, including the *gymnastai* (trainers), who increasingly acted as agents for their protégés. We see this as early as 257 B.C., in a letter from a schoolmaster named Hierokles to the protector (Zenon) of a boy named Pyrrhos, who is attending boarding school in Alexandria (*PZenon* 59060; *A 207*). Hierokles is acknowledging his instructions to train the boy as an athlete only if he shows promise, and relates that the gymnastes thinks the boy is a potential winner. Hierokles explains that he is therefore going ahead with Pyrrhos's athletic training, adding, "I have every hope that he will win a crown for you."

The letter clearly shows the profit motive that underlies athletic training, but it does not describe the whole role of the gymnastes, nor does it indicate the potential for corruption. We see that later, in a report by Philostratos of a bribe that seems to have occurred in his own day (ca. A.D. 230) but that probably reflects a situation that had been developing for centuries:

> A luxurious lifestyle . . . led to illegal practices among the athletes for the sake of money. I refer to the selling and buying of victories. I suppose that some surrender their chance at fame because of destitution, but others buy a victory which involves no effort for the luxury it promises. There are laws against temple robbers who mutilate or destroy a silver or gold dedication to the gods, but the crown of Apollo or of Poseidon, for which even the gods once competed, athletes are free to buy and sell. Only the olive at Elis remains inviolate, in accordance with its ancient glory. Let me give one of many possible examples that will illustrate what happens at the other games.
>
> A boy won the pale at Isthmia by promising to pay $66,000 to his opponent. When they went into the gymnasion the next day, the loser demanded his money, but the winner said that he owed nothing since the other had tried after all to win. Since their differences were not resolved, they had recourse to an oath and went into the sanctuary at Isthmia. The loser then swore in public that he had sold Poseidon's contest and that they had agreed upon a price of $66,000. Moreover, he stated this in a clear voice with no trace of embarrassment. The fact that this was announced in front of witnesses may make it more truthful, but it also makes it all the more sacrilegious and infamous; he swore such an oath at Isthmia before the eyes of Greece. What disgrace might not be happening at the games in Ionia and Asia?
>
> I do not absolve the gymnastai of blame for this corruption. They came to do their training with pockets full of money, which they loan to

the athletes at interest rates higher than businessmen who hazard sea trade have to pay. They care nothing for the reputation of the athletes; rather, they give advice about the sale or purchase of a victory. They are constantly on the lookout for their own gain, either by making loans to those who are buying a victory or by cutting off the training of those who are selling. I call these gymnastai peddlers, for they put their own interests first and peddle the *arete* of their athletes. [*On Gymnastics* 45; A 214]

With descriptions like these of corruption in the Roman period, a corruption whose roots lay in the Hellenistic, many admirers of Greek athletics have laid the blame on money. Money, they assert, breeds professional athletes, which breeds corruption; only through strict amateurism can the true value of sport be realized. This has led, in turn, to the belief that the athletics of ancient Greece, at least before the time of Alexander the Great, were amateur competitions. Is this true? Were the athletes of the sixth and fifth centuries B.C.—Arrhichion, Milo, Theagenes, Kleomedes, Euthymos, Polydamas—amateurs? To answer that, we must first define *amateur* and *professional*.

These two words are frequently perceived as antitheses: an amateur is the opposite of a professional, and vice versa. The amateur is one who is not compensated with money; the professional is. But these are not really accurate definitions of either word, and we must turn to the words' linguistic roots to understand their meaning. First, both terms derive from Latin, not Greek, words. There is no ancient Greek equivalent for the word *amateur*, although *idiotes* can sometimes be translated that way. But *idiotes* refers to a private person as opposed to a public official and has no connotation that comes close to the idea of someone who is not paid. *Amateur* is the French derivative of the Latin *amator* which comes, as every student of Latin I knows, from *amo*: an amator, "amateur," is a lover, a person who does something out of love. It has nothing to do with money: one can do something for love and still get paid for it. There are, and always have been, fortunate people who spend their lives doing a job they enjoy, for which they receive a salary.

Professional, on the other hand, comes from the Latin *professio*, a public declaration or acknowledgment. *Professio* also gives us *professor*, and it comes ultimately from the verb *profiteor*, "to declare publicly"—and it has nothing to do with profit, as most professors can attest. Again, there is no monetary implication in the term *professional*, and it is not the antithesis of *amateur*. One can perform a task out of love on a professional level. The confusion arises in part from our word *profit*, which derives from the Latin *proficio*, "to make progress" or "to gain an advantage," hence to "profit" monetarily, socially, politically, or in some other way.

If we recognize that *amateur* and *professional*, as applied to athletics at least, are modern concepts and that the Greeks had no equivalents for them, we can see that the presence of money in athletics was not in itself a problem. Money was not the reason for the change in emphasis we see beginning at about the time of Alexander. After all, we have seen that money was part of ancient athletics from the beginning. The Homeric games of Patrokles offered prizes of real cash value, and the chrematitic games were by definition games with hefty monetary rewards.

Theagenes of Thasos, discussed in Chapter 9, clearly shows the kind of money a successful athlete could earn in the first half of the fifth century B.C. Pausanias (6.11.2 – 9; *A 167a*) tells us that Theagenes won a total of 1,400 victories, and he lists 24 of these as occurring in the stephanitic games. Thus, his remaining 1,376 victories must have been in various chrematitic games. We don't know the cash value of each of those victories, but, as noted in Chapter 7, a Panathenaic victory in the pyx and the pankration (Theagenes' favored events) was probably worth at least $25,000. This means that Theagenes won something in the neighborhood of $44,400,000 during his career. There was big money to be made in athletics even in the earlier, "amateur" days.

Neither can we cling to the stephanitic games as exemplars of sport for sport's sake. By the fifth century athletic competitions had become extremely important. Hence we learn that a long-distance runner, Dromeus of Stymphalos, who won twice at Olympia (484 and 480) and Delphi, three times at Isthmia, and five times at Nemea, invented a new diet to improve his performance (Pausanias 6.7.10; *A 217*). Whereas athletes earlier made cheese the basic element, Dromeus substituted meat, and his success launched the tradition of athletes gorging on meat. At the end of the century a *paidotribes* (trainer) named Herodikos was said to have used a combination of physical exercise and diet to prolong his life beyond the point of usefulness (Plato, *Republic* 406a–b; *A 218*). Specialized diets and training for athletes suggests rewards beyond those of glory.

In Athens at this same time the reward that awaited the returning Athenian athlete who had been victorious at any of the four stephanitic games was a free meal at state expense in the prytaneion (town hall) each day for the rest of his life (*IG I³* 131; *A 221*). This lifelong extension of the victory banquet given at the Prytaneion in Olympia showed the financial underpinning to athletic competition, and multiple winners won multiple dinners. Here is the basis for the obsonia of the Roman period that was regulated by the emperor. The triumphal eiselasis was an important honor, but the free meals were an enduring economic benefit.

Awards for returning victors may date as far back as the early sixth century. At that time the Athenian lawgiver Solon reportedly established cash prizes for Athenian athletes who won at Olympia and Isthmia (Plutarch, *Solon* 23.3; *A 223*). The difference in the amount of the awards (an Olympic victor received five times more than someone who won at Isthmia) and the lateness of the source (about six hundred years after Solon's death) have made scholars dubious about whether these prizes really existed at this early date. But it is at exactly such an early date that a bronze tablet was inscribed at Sybaris in Magna Graecia (*SEG* 35.1053; *A 220*). From it we learn that Kleombrotos the son of Dexilaos has dedicated a tenth of his victory at Olympia to Athena. This can hardly apply to the olive wreath that was the only tangible thing he would have won at Olympia, and it strongly suggests that his hometown of Sybaris rewarded him with something more substantial than vegetable matter. In gratitude, Kleombrotos had shared a tenth of that reward with the goddess.

In the second half of the sixth century we hear of Demokedes of Kroton, a medical man and trainer, who worked for two years at Aigina (Herodotus 3.129–133; A 216). In his second year he received a salary equivalent to $132,000. The next year he was hired away to Athens for the equivalent of $220,000, and the following year Samos snagged him for $264,000. After capture by the Persians and various other adventures, including saving the life of King Darius by means of his medical knowledge, Demokedes, now even wealthier, returned to Kroton and married the daughter of the renowned athlete Milo. Since marriages usually took place between families of more or less equal socioeconomic status, Demokedes' marriage implies that Milo also counted among the wealthy, although it does not prove that Milo's wealth derived from his athletic triumphs.

Money, then, including both direct and indirect economic benefits to athletes, played a key part in the athletic world from early days. If getting paid for a good performance on the track is our criterion for determining the "professional" status of an athlete, we would be forced to conclude that all ancient athletes were professional from the beginning of organized athletics. If, however, we define a professional as a man who pursues one activity as the sole source of his income, and is trained in that activity to the exclusion of all others, then the changes that occurred in the time of Alexander the Great do herald the advent of athletic professionalism.

The reason for the change is not difficult to see. With the conquests of Alexander, masses of wealth came into the Greek world, encouraging specialization in a number of occupations, including athletics, which developed athletic entertainers to meet the growing demand for entertainment. The spread of stephanitic games after Alexander's death shows that Hellenistic society could support athletic entertainment and that athletes could reasonably hope to make a living from it. The issue is not the presence of money, but the amount of money present. Greater economic benefits and greater opportunities to reap such benefits were the causes of abuses that arose from exploitation by trainers and parents willing to gamble the future of the young athlete for their own security.

At the same time, people in Hellenistic and Roman society were willing to trade the enjoyment of entertainment by professional athletes during their prime for the burden of supporting athletes who were crippled and in poor health for the remainder of their short lives. But the athletes themselves clearly bought into the promises and ignored the dangers. Some indeed became champions, gaining financial security for themselves, their parents, and their trainers. But for every winner there were dozens of athletes lost along the way. We catch only glimpses of them, in the grafitti on the stadium entrance tunnel at Nemea and the occasional accounts like the story of Marcus, a *hoplitodromos* who was "mistaken by the custodians for one of the statues that line the track when they locked up for the night. The next day they opened the stadium and found that Marcus had finished the last lap" (*Anthologia Graeca* 11.85; *A 175*).

In Greek athletics there was one winner but many losers. If the losers trained in athletics alone, what was left to them? Hence Galen, in his advice about the kind of profession to enter, warns against useless or evil career choices. He is "suspicious only of the pursuit of athletics, which might trick some youth into thinking that it is an art because it promises strength of body and reputation among the masses and a grant of money each day from the public treasury." Galen's final advice is still sound: "If any of you wants to prepare to make money safely and honestly, you must train for a profession which can be continued throughout life" (*Exhortation for Medicine* 9–14; *A 215*).

14

POLITICS AND THE GAMES

In the distant past, the games were part of religious rites dedicated to gods on snow-clad Mt. Olympus to substitute peace for war and a truce during the festivities.

— Richard Stout, *Christian Science Monitor,* January 14, 1980

ASIDE FROM its all-too-common confusion between Mount Olympos and Olympia—which puts nude athletes shivering on those snow-clad slopes—the sentiment expressed above is one most of us would like to believe. To a large extent it was even true. We may doubt that the games were originally planned as a substitute for war, but they certainly developed into a positive political force in the Panhellenic world during the time of the festivals. Nonetheless, one of the ironies of the ancient Olympics is still with us today. The games brought all the Greeks together (to the exclusion of all non-Greeks, to be sure) and, in some sense, promoted international (that is, inter-polis) communication and understanding, albeit on a much more restricted level than today. By bringing together citizens of different city-states at a religious festival focused on athletics, the political rivalries that divided them could be ignored for a few days. At the same time, by their insistence that competitors be certified as legitimate representatives of a particular city-state, and in the proclamation of both each competitor's affiliation at the start of the events and the victor's city-state at the end, the games promoted competition and rivalry between the city-states.

This competition is still expressed today: athletes have to be certified representatives of their countries, and these affiliations are proclaimed at each event. And the lists ranking countries by the number of medals won had their counterpart in ancient Greece as well. Many cases are known of an athlete being hired to represent another city, to the dismay of his original hometown. One of the first recorded is that of Astylos, a double Olympic victor (in the *stadion* and *diaulos*) in three successive Olympiads (488, 484, and 480; Pausanias 6.13.1; A 224), who also won the *hoplitodromos* in 476

216

(*POxy* II.222; *A 129*). Astylos first competed as a citizen of his native Kroton, but he subsequently ran for Syracuse. After his switch, citizens in Kroton pulled down his statue and turned his house into a prison.

Syracuse was notorious for trying to lure star athletes onto its national team. Antipater, winner of the boxing for boys in 388, resisted the temptation of a bribe to become a Syracusan (Pausanias 6.2.6; *A 225*), but Dikon did not (Pausanias 6.3.11; *A 226*), as we know from the three statues of him at Olympia, one for each of his victories there. The first victory was in the boys' stadion in 392, and the statue identified him as Dikon, son of Kallibrotos, from Kaulonia. But the two subsequent victor's statues listed him as being from Syracuse. The first of this latter group surely was erected after his victory in 388, an Olympiad that, as we saw in Chapter 6, was particularly scandal ridden. The practice was not confined to Syracuse; in the Olympiad of 384 the *dolichos* was won by Sotades of Crete (Pausanias 6.18.6; *A 227*). At the following Olympiad, however, Sotades took a bribe and announced that he was from Ephesos. It is not surprising that the Cretans exiled him.

An athlete might change his citizenship for reasons other than bribery, but these were also political. Ergoteles of Knossos had been exiled because of internal civic strife; he moved to Himera, in Sicily (Pausanias 6.4.11; *A 228*). When he won the dolichos twice at Olympia (472 and 464), he was identified as being from Himera, which was also listed as his hometown on his victory statue.

The case of Kroton, a Greek city in southern Italy, is noteworthy. The absolute dominance of athletes from Kroton in the *gymnikos agon* during the sixth and early fifth centuries has long been a source of wonder to students of ancient athletics. Between 588 and 488 there were twenty-six victors in the stadion race at Olympia. Since these victors gave their names to their Olympiad, we know who they all were and where they came from. And eleven of those twenty-six runners came from Kroton. Kroton's next closest rivals are Elis and Kerkyra, which each provided two victors in the stadion during this period.

From this same period we know the names of the victors at Olympia in seventy-one different events of the gymnikos agon: twenty of them are Krotoniates. That a single polis could produce some 28 percent of the Olympic victors is phenomenal — and let us not forget that one of Kroton's most famous athletes, Phaÿllos, skipped the Olympics to fight against the Persians. Since he never won at Olympia, I did not count him in these statistics. Further, the most famous medical trainer of the same period, Demokedes, was also from Kroton. As an ancient proverb had it, "He who finishes last of the Krotoniates is first among the rest of the Greeks" (Strabo 6.1.12).

It is no wonder that modern scholars have labeled Kroton a "jock factory," but the source of this Olympic dominance is not clear. Was it something in the water? Was Kroton buying athletes? Were its training methods so far advanced over those of other states? We have seen the violent reaction of the people of Kroton when one of their own, Astylos, was hired away by Syracuse. In the next chapter I shall advance my own theory for this dominance, but whatever its source, its result was that Kroton's fame and influence were spread far and wide, and it is reasonable to assume that Krotoniates found this result desirable and devised policies to bring it about. Athletics were clearly a tool of ancient political aggrandizement—just as they are today.

As we have seen, the city-states felt that victories in the games were so important that they gave the victor a free meal every day for the rest of his life for each victory he won. They also granted winners a front-row seat (*proedria*) at local games and frequently offered tax exemptions as well as exemptions from other services to the polis. This state of affairs already existed by around 525 B.C., as we learn from Xenophanes' criticism of it (fragment 2; A 229):

> Even if a man should win a victory in the sanctuary of Zeus at Olympia in the footraces or the pentathlon or the *pale* or the painful *pyx* or in the dreadful struggle which men call the *pankration,* even if he should become a most glorious symbol for his fellow citizens, and win proedria at the games and his meals at public expense as well as some especially valuable gift from the state, even if he should win in the horse races, and even if he should accomplish all of these things and not just one of them, he still would not be as valuable as I am. For my wisdom is a better thing than the strength of men or horses. The current custom of honoring strength more than wisdom is neither proper nor just. For the city-state is not made a bit more lawabiding for having a good boxer or a pentathlete or a wrestler or a fast runner, even though running may be the most honored event in the games of man. There is little joy for a state when an athlete wins at Olympia, for he does not fill the state's coffers.

Xenophanes was swimming upstream with his criticisms, for there are many indications that the state thought that it was made a great deal better for having an Olympic victor, even if its coffers were not filled thereby. In fact, coins were frequently used to advertise victories at Olympia and other games. Philip of Macedon displayed his *synoris* victory at Delphi on a gold issue, and his Olympic victory in the *keles* (supposedly reported to him on the same day as the birth of his son, Alexander) on a long-lived silver issue (fig. 283). This silver coin was so popular that it continued to be issued in Macedonia many years after Philip's death. Elis, which administered the Olympics, also used the games as a promotional tool, issuing coins with the cult statue of Olympian Zeus on one side. And a nicely minted series from Kos with a *diskobolos* and a tripod cauldron advertised local games dedicated to Apollo (fig. 284).

If the games were ever a means of promoting international understanding and peace, we would expect to find that relationships between the sanctuaries where the

Fig. 283 Silver tetradrachm of Philip II of Macedon referring to his victory in the keles in 356 B.C. (note the palm branch in the jockey's hand), minted 315–295 B.C. at Amphipolis. Athens, Numismatic Museum, inv. no. 1383 (photo: © Treasury of Archaeological Receipts).

Fig. 284 Tridrachma of Kos showing a diskobolos with tripod cauldron, 480–450 B.C. Athens, Numismatic Museum, inv. no. 1903/4 KΘ′1 (photo: © Treasury of Archaeological Receipts).

games were held was tranquil, and usually they were. Indeed, Olympia and Delphi seem to have had a mutual support system. Recall that the winner in the flute playing at the Pythian Games became the honorary *auletes* for the jumping event of the pentathlon at the next Olympic Games. And when Kallippos of Athens was caught bribing his competitors at the Olympic Games in 332 B.C. Delphi refused all Athenians access to the Pythian Oracle until his fine was paid to Olympia (Pausanias 5.21.5; A 236).

Nonetheless, there are signs of stress between some of the sanctuaries. We are told that the crown of victory at Isthmia was changed from pine to wild celery because of Isthmia's jealous rivalry with Herakles, which must be a reference to Nemea and the Nemean Games (Plutarch, *Moralia* 675D–676F; A 235). The most serious and long-lived rivalry, however, was between Olympia and Isthmia, and it involved the "curse of Moline" (Pausanias 5.2.1–2; A 232).

The story begins with a war between Herakles and Augeas of Elis. With the help of the sons of Aktor, Augeas was routing the forces of Herakles, when it was time to announce the sacred truce (*sponde*) for the Isthmian Games. The sons of Aktor went as *theoroi* (delegates who announced the truce) to the games, but they were ambushed and killed by Herakles in the territory of Kleonai, which administered the Nemean Games on behalf of Argos. Moline, the sister of the youths (in some traditions, the mother) demanded justice from the Argives since Herakles was living in their territory at Tiryns. The Argives refused. The Eleans next tried to persuade the Corinthians to exclude the Argives from the Isthmian truce. After the Corinthians also refused, Moline put a curse on her countrymen, swearing that they would never compete at the Isthmian Games. Convoluted as this story is, with many layers of possible significance, the one sure element is that Elean athletes did not, in fact, compete at Isthmia. We know, for example, that Hysmon the pentathlete won at Olympia and at Nemea around 384, and another pentathlete, Timon, won at all the games around 200 (Pausanias 6.3.9 and 6.16.2; A 233 and A 234, respectively). Neither ever won at Isthmia, however, because neither ever competed there.

Indeed, an Elean was excluded, by birth, from the ranks of the *periodonikai* (circuit winners), and there must have been a continuing resentment of the Isthmian Games by Elis. Modern scholars have felt so sorry for the Elean athletes that they have created a new category: the three-quarter periodonikes. The absence of Elean athletes from the Isthmian Games must have made a noticeable gap in the competition, and an undercurrent of political interest is probably to be recognized in it.

There could also be rivalries between city-states and the festivals. At least, this is one way to interpret the Olympics of the Macedonians, set up at the base of Mount Olympos but modeled on the games at Olympia. More explicit is the case of Sybaris, which tried to eclipse the Olympics around 512 B.C. (Athenaeus 12.521F; A 237). The city-state offered huge cash prizes for games it put on at the same time as the Olympics in an attempt to lure the best athletes. (It didn't work.)

More typical are the numerous instances of political friction that found expression at the *stephanitic* centers of supposed international understanding. Not surprisingly, many of these concerned the city-state that administered the games. For example, in 420 B.C., the Olympic truce was broken by the Lakedaimonians (Spartans), at least according to the Eleans. The Eleans assessed a fine against the Lakedaimonians as demanded by Olympic law, but when the latter refused to pay, "they were excluded from the sanctuary, the sacrifice, and the contests, and sacrificed by themselves at home" (Thucydides 5.49 and Pausanias 6.2.2; A 238). However, Lichas the son of Arkesilaos "was flogged by the *rhabdouchoi* because when his team of horses won but was announced as belonging to the people of Boiotia since he had no right to compete, he had run up and tied [a *tainia* (victory ribbon) on] the charioteer to make clear that the chariot was his. Thus everyone was in a great state of fear, and it seemed that something was going to happen. But the Lakedaimonians kept their peace and the celebration was completed."

The Olympics of 420 were thus preserved, but bitterness lingered among the Lakedaimonians, and in 399/8 (not an Olympic year) they invaded the Altis (Xenophon, *Hellenika* 3.2.21–22). The Eleans defended themselves by climbing onto the tops of the temples and other tall buildings. One Elean soldier died up there, and his corpse was discovered 550 years later in the rafters of the Temple of Hera, where it had been preserved safe from heat and cold alike. The corpse was then buried with its weapons outside the Altis (Pausanias 5.20.5; A 239). After this battle, Lichas set up a statue of himself as winner of the 420 *tethrippon*, but the official Elean records continued to list the polis of Thebes as the winner.

It cannot be a coincidence that shortly before the Olympics of 420 Elis had concluded a treaty with Athens, Argos, and Mantinea against the Spartans. Hence the Elean excommunication of the Lakedaimonians was surely influenced by the hostilities that had been openly declared between the two city-states as part of the ongoing Athenian-Spartan conflict. And the Olympiads preceding the games of 420 show another aspect of this rivalry. In 448 Spartans began a domination in the tethrippon competitions that lasted for the next eight Olympiads. The single non-Spartan winner came in 436, when Megakles of Athens took the victory. As we have seen, the tethrippon always had a special function in the games as a way to display wealth and power. The stadion victor might give his name to the Olympiad, but the tethrippon victor acquired a particular aura that reflected on his hometown. The score in 420, then (Spartans 7, Athenians 1), must have galled the Athenians. It was at the next Olympiad, in 416, that Alkibiades entered his seven chariots, finally breaking the stranglehold of the Lakedaimonians.

Alkibiades, and probably many other Greeks, saw his victory as a sign of Athens's continued power and a forecast of an Athenian victory in the Peloponnesian War. So it is that the Athenian Alkibiades can claim, according to Thucydides (6.16.2),

> My deeds, which make me the object of public outcry, actually bring glory not only to my ancestors and myself but also to my country, and this glory is mixed with practical advantage as well. The Greeks who had been hoping that our city was exhausted by the war came to think of our power as even greater than it is because of my magnificent embassy at Olympia. I entered seven tethrippa, a number never before entered by a private citizen, and I came in first, second, and fourth.

Politics and political violence were not unique to Olympia. The Nemean Games were removed from Nemea after a destruction that can be dated to about 415 B.C. The violence is documented by a widespread layer of architectural debris mixed with ash and carbon, discolored stone blocks, and vitrified roof tiles, all indicating that a fire was a central feature. Another feature, even more central, were the dozens of bronze arrowheads and iron spear points indicating that the destruction had human origins. Through archaeology we have retrieved evidence of violence that is recorded in none of our extant ancient authors, but written sources do tell us that the military maneuvering of the Spartans in campaigns against Argos in 419/8 and 415/4 included forays through Nemea (Thucydides 5.58–60 and 6.95). Either of these could have been the occasion of the destruction, which did not necessarily take place during the games, although it played an important role in their history.

More clearly described in the written sources and documented in the archaeology are the disastrous events of 390 at Isthmia. The Argives had pushed their frontiers until they included Corinth within the city limits of Argos, and they and their Corinthian sympathizers had gone to Isthmia to celebrate the Isthmian Games. The Spartan king Agesilaos suddenly appeared on the scene with his army augmented by the Corinthians who had refused to accept the Argives. The Argive sympathizers left in fright, and the Corinthian exiles conducted the sacrifices to Poseidon and then put on the games. As soon as they left, the Argive sympathizers returned and celebrated the Isthmian Games all over again. "And in that year some athletes lost twice and others were twice proclaimed victors. . . . During the night four days later it became clear that the Temple of Poseidon was burning, but no one saw who started the fire" (Xenophon, *Hellenika* 4.5.1–2. 4; A 240).

Perhaps even more egregious was the armed battle in the Altis during the Olympic Games of 364 (Xenophon, *Hellenika* 7.4.28; A 241). The Arkadians and their allies had captured Olympia the previous year, and when it became time for the games, they prepared to celebrate them. During the pentathlon the Eleans, who were not known as particularly warlike or militarily gifted, suddenly invaded the sanctuary and pushed the Arkadians back across the Altis until they had suffered so many losses that they retired. The Arkadians continued the games, but the Eleans refused to acknowledge the result and referred to those games as an Anolympiad (Non-Olympiad). The Arkadians subsequently relinquished control of Olympia, but the deaths suffered during the games remained part of the history of the site.

More than a century later, in 235, another violation of the truce occurred, this time in association with the Nemean Games. The Nemean Games had been moved to Argos in 271, but a political leader and an enemy of Argos, Aratos of Sikyon, decided that he would run games at Nemea as an alternative to the games at Argos (Plutarch, *Aratos* 28.3–4; A 242). Aratos controlled the territory north of Argos, and he captured and sold into slavery any athlete he caught traveling through that territory to compete in the Nemean Games at Argos rather than at the Nemean Games at Nemea. This was reckoned a great sacrilege against the truce, and we have to feel sorry for the athletes who were caught in the middle of the political conflict between Aratos and Argos.

In addition to such episodes of politically inspired violence at the sanctuaries, the athletic festival centers were also used to celebrate military victories by one city-state over another. There are many examples; perhaps the following will suffice. In 457 the Spartans defeated the Athenians and their allies at the Battle of Tanagra. This victory was celebrated by the dedication of a shield at the top of the pediment of the Temple of Zeus at Olympia. The shield was mounted on a base bearing the following inscription:

> The Temple has a golden shield from Tanagra,
> The Lakedaimonians and their allies dedicated it:
> A "gift" from Argives and Athenians and Ionians
> A tithe from victory in war. [Pausanias 5.10.4; A 243]

It seems unlikely that much international understanding or peace was inspired in the defeated "contributors" who passed beneath this inscription on their way to see the cult statue of Zeus.

At Delphi the Athenians, in their turn, built a stoa from the booty they gained in a battle, probably in 429. The dedications within the stoa included the prows of ships and shields, which were listed as victory dedications from Elis, Lakedaimonia, Sikyon, Megara, Pellene in Achaia, Ambrakia, Leukas, and Corinth (Pausanias 10.11.6; A 244). Were the citizens of those cities filled with warm and tender thoughts about the Athenians as they walked up the Sacred Way at Delphi to the Temple of Apollo?

Of all the cities and people who used the athletic festival centers for political purposes, none was more successful than Philip II of Macedon. His activities began on an innocuous note when he celebrated his Olympic victory in the keles on his coins. Philip's status as an Olympic victor was enhanced by two subsequent victories in the tethrippon. Yet another equestrian victory, this time in the synoris, was celebrated on a gold series (see fig. 155). Although it is not certain whether this victory was at Olympia or at Delphi, the propaganda value is clear. Philip was a major player at — and with — the games.

Philip was also a protector of Olympic tradition and law, as we see in the case of Phrynon of Athens. Phrynon was on his way to the Olympic Games in 348 when he was seized by Philip's troops during the Sacred Month and robbed of all his possessions. When remonstrances were made to Philip, he "received them in a kindly and friendly way and returned to Phrynon everything that his soldiers had robbed and more in addition from his own pocket, and apologized that his soldiers had not known that it was the Sacred Month" (Demosthenes, *De falsa legatione*, Hypoth. 335; A 89).

The next step in Philip's campaign to use the athletic centers was gaining de facto control of Delphi. On behalf of the Amphiktyonic Council, Philip defeated the city-state of Phokis, which had taken over the Sanctuary of Apollo. The council "chose" Philip because in his takeover of the lands of Thessaly he had come to control half its members. Now, after his military victory, the Olympic victor was given Phokis's seat on the council, solidifying his power. He presided over the Pythian Games of 346, and it was probably at that time that his statue was erected at Delphi. Subsequently, his henchmen ran Delphi on his behalf. One of the most prominent of these was Daochos of Pharsalos, a descendant of Olympic victors, as he proudly proclaimed in statue dedications (see figs. 182–183). Another of Philip's friends, Epichares of Sikyon, supplied wood for the reconstruction of the Temple of Apollo (*FD* III[5] 36.6.8; Demosthenes, *Corona* [18] 295). Not surprisingly, Demosthenes complained that the Pythia was Philippizing (Plutarch, *Demosthenes* 20.1).

The ultimate value of Philip's maneuvering came in 339, when the Amphiktyonic Council, which controlled Delphi (but was controlled by Philip), invited Philip to lead the Fourth Sacred War. Philip's victory the following year in the Battle of

Fig. 285 Reconstruction of the Philippeion in the northwestern corner of the Altis at Olympia with the gate to the gymnasion at the left and the western end of the Temple of Hera at the right. Drawing from F. Adler et al., *Die Baudenkmäler von Olympia* (Berlin, 1896), pl. 131.

Chaironeia was directly attributable to his political control of the athletic festival centers. Philip had also won the allegiance of Elis by 343, and Olympia was already in his column. It is natural that Philip would immediately celebrate his victory over the other Greeks at Chaironeia by constructing a monument at Olympia (fig. 285). This elaborately decorated circular building stood by the entrance at the northwestern corner of the Altis between the Prytaneion, the Temple of Hera, and the Shrine of Pelops. Every visitor to the site passed by it and every victor emerging from his banquet in the Prytaneion saw it immediately. Its location could hardly have been more prominent if it were on top of the Great Altar of Zeus. Inside were chryselephantine statues of Philip's father and mother, his wife, and his son. The kind of statement made by the Philippeion was not new at Olympia, but its size, location, and ornamentation set it as far above the other victory monuments as the Battle of Chaironeia set the Macedonians above the other Greeks.

Philip, who recognized the value of the stephanitic athletic festival centers as a means of advancement, also saw their continued importance as a way to consolidate power. He established a league, with himself as leader, which was to meet in rotation at the four sites at the time of the stephanitic games. In each of the sites excavation has documented large new building programs, as well as the return of the Nemean Games to the site for which they were named. Now, with the power of the individual city-states broken, the stephanitic games could truly be used to promote international understanding. References to politically inspired violence at the sites after the time of Philip's son, Alexander, are reduced to mere whispers as the games increase in entertainment value for the spectators, and the percentage of true participants dwindles. The athlete on the track, always a surrogate for his hometown, becomes a surrogate for his hometown's soldiers as well.

It should not surprise us that politics, and even occasional violence, played a part at the games. What is more surprising is that the episodes were so infrequent, and that the games went on nonetheless. The Olympic Games of ancient Greece lasted for more than a millennium, and they were never canceled. In 480, with the Persians on the doorstep, the games went on. In 364 two city-states fought a battle within the Altis itself, and the Eleans refused to recognize the results of the competitions, but the games went on; we even know the names of several of the victors. In 80 Elis and Olympia were both broke and couldn't afford to stage the games for the men's events, but the boys were invited, and the games went on; the victor in the boys' stadion gave his name to that Olympiad. Nero forced the delay of the Olympics that should have occurred in A.D. 65 to 67, and the program was drastically changed to suit his vanity, but the games went on.

The modern Olympics are just over a century old. In that time one was almost destroyed by murder (Munich, 1972), and three by major boycotts (Montreal, 1976; Moscow, 1980; and Los Angeles, 1984), all for political motives. And the games of 1916, 1940, and 1944 did not go on at all because of the political situation. Perhaps we do need to study ancient practices more closely, after all.

15

ATHLETICS AND SOCIETY

SOME OF THE INTRICATE connections between athletics and ancient society have emerged in the discussion of various aspects of the games. But athletics played a positive, even fundamental, role in society in a number of ways that still affect how we live and what we know about ourselves. History, art, literature, law, and government all owe something to the world of ancient Greek athletics.

Let us start with the Olympic victors' list, the compilation, Olympiad by Olympiad, of the names of winners in the various events at the Olympic Games. The first edition is credited to Hippias of Elis in about 420 B.C. He probably began the practice of naming the Olympiad after the victor in the *stadion*. The list was straightforward, consisting of the name of the victor, his hometown, and the event, as we know from papyrus fragments of copies of the list that survive in Egypt (see, for example, *POxy* II.222; *A* 129). Throughout antiquity, the list was revised and updated; its editors included Aristotle (ca. 330), Eratosthenes (ca. 225), and Phlegon of Tralles (A.D. 141). By the time of Pausanias — and probably several hundred years earlier — the official updated register was maintained by the Eleans in the *gymnasion* at Olympia. (Excavations in the 1980s in the gymnasion at Delphi produced fragments of wall plaster with a list of Pythian victors from the Roman period.) Where it is possible to check the extant versions of the list with independent records, it proves remarkably accurate, and the discovery of fragments in Egypt shows how widespread the register of Olympian victors was.

Some modern scholars have questioned the accuracy of the early part of the list: What evidence did Hippias and his successors have for their compilation? Is it likely that there was documentation more than three hundred years before Hippias, when writing was in its infancy? What proof is there that the Olympics were originally quadrennial: might they have been annual local festivals? In that case the four-year span given to each of the first fifty victors should be reduced to a year each and the beginning date of 776 B.C. be "shrunk" to about 630. Whatever the answers to those questions (and we should note that the traditional date of 776 conforms to the archaeological record), the fact remains that from about 600 the list can be verified, and it is correct from then on. The chronological framework of the Olympic register is secure.

The importance to the study of Greek history of a securely based chronological outline is tremendous. In ancient Greece each city-state kept its own records in accordance with its own institutions and its own calendar. Thus, for example, the annually elected archon of Athens provided an ongoing chronological framework for Athenian record keeping: "In the archonship of so and so, it seemed best to the council and the people to do thus and so . . . " By maintaining a list of the archons, the ancient Athenians established a relative chronology, which ultimately allowed scholars to write their history by placing events in their correct sequential and consequential order. But such a system was idiosyncratic to Athens and could be reconciled only with great difficulty, if at all, with the system at Corinth or at Argos or at Thebes—or anywhere else. Further, although all calendars were lunar, the names of the months varied from city to city (though the same names frequently occurred in several cities). Local adjustments to the lunar months to keep them attuned to the solar year meant that a month with the same name in two different cities could, and did, occur at two different seasons of the same solar year.

The Olympic register, however, was international and independent of local variations in the calendar. However great its importance was for reckoning time within the Greek world is arguably insignificant compared to its importance to the whole Western world as a means of relating Greek events to those of other cultures. Thus a series of scholars including the early Christians Eusebius (ca. 320) and Jerome (ca. 410) could begin to synchronize events throughout the ancient world. The purpose of these synchronizations was largely to establish the chronologies of biblical events, but the effect was to unite the world in a recognizable and ultimately widely accepted system that is still in use today. How do we know that Sokrates drank hemlock in 399 B.C.? How do we know how many years passed between the death of Sokrates and that of Jesus Christ? How do we know how long it was after the burning of the Akropolis by the Persians that Muhammad was born? In the final analysis, we know because of the register of ancient Olympic victors.

Athletics also played an important role in the evolution of art. Today, thanks to the camera and other devices, we take for granted the ability to portray our world in a naturalistic and realistic way. But the first efforts to make such portrayals came in Greece in the sixth century B.C. by means of vase painting and, especially, sculpture. Until about 600 B.C. there is no evidence of life-sized or even semi-life-sized sculptures of human beings. But about that time we begin to see a series of portrayals of young men, called *kouroi,* who clearly owe their inspiration to centuries-old sculptural traditions of Egypt. Rigid figures with legs close together but one foot forward, arms straight down at the sides, facial features and anatomical details stylized and based more on some notional portrayal than on observation, all look back to large-scale figures from Egypt (see fig. 180). There is, however, one very obvious difference: the Greek kouroi are nude.

Fig. 286 Diskophoros. Marble Roman copy of original by Naukydes of Argos, ca. 400 B.C. Paris, Musée du Louvre, inv. no. MA89 – 9840323 (head in the Capitoline, Rome), Réunion des Musées Nationaux / Art Resource, New York (photo: Herve Lewandowski).

From about 600 to 480 or so, we can trace a clear progression in the portrayal of the human body toward the ever more anatomically correct. The body appears flexible even as the stone from which it is carved is transformed into the flesh of the real person. The same evolutionary process can be seen in vase painting; compare, for example, the portrayal of the anatomies of the runners in figure 3 with those of figure 52, painted about two hundred years later.

It is, of course, possible to explain much of this progress as owing simply to greater observation and curiosity about the world. Muscles are muscles and can be portrayed without recourse to athletes. But the ability to portray the whole of the male body correctly obviously depends upon the opportunity to observe it, and the custom of athletic nudity provided such opportunities and the beauty of the well-conditioned body might well have aroused interest in portraying it accurately.

The custom of setting up victory statues at Olympia and the other games sites also promoted the development of artistic portrayal. Hundreds of victor statues documented at Olympia provided a clear motive for sculptors to carve nude male bodies, and for other young men, who might never become victors, to wish to appear in the pose of a nude athlete. And another key aspect of athletics played its part: motion. As

Fig. 287 Diskobolos. Marble Roman copy of bronze original by Myron, ca. 460 B.C. London, The British Museum, inv. no. S 524 (GR 1814.7–4.43) (photo: © The British Museum).

Greek artists developed their ability to show the human body realistically, they started trying to show motion. This was much easier for vase painters, but sculptors tried to solve the problem of motion portrayal as well, and athletes offered them the best opportunity to study it. Most of their work was in bronze and is preserved to us only in marble copies of the Roman period, but we can still appreciate the implicit motion of a *diskophoros* (diskos holder) who steps toward the line, preparing to cock his arm and twist his body into the corkscrew position that will help his throw (fig. 286).

Perhaps the most famous of all these attempts to introduce motion into lifeless marble was the Diskobolos by Myron (fig. 287). Many copies of this statue survive today, and they show the incipient motion of the diskophoros has been carried a step further. The body is twisted, the diskos raised at the top of the backswing, the arms and legs balanced in untenable positions—the athlete must spin forward or fall, and the viewer mentally completes the motion. Myron, noted for his athletic sculpture, brought from the stadium many advances in sculptural composition that would affect other artistic fields through the ages.

Within a generation of Myron, Polykleitos of Argos was expounding his philosophical definition of the "perfect" in the principle of *symmetria* (commensurability of

Fig. 288 Diadoumenos. Marble copy (done about 100 B.C.) of a bronze original by Polykleitos, 440–430 B.C. Athens, National Museum, inv. no. 1826 (photo: © Treasury of Archaeological Receipts).

the parts) in a written treatise that does not survive. But several of his statues do survive in the form of Roman copies, and we can see that Polykleitos chose the athlete as a visual manifestation of his philosophy. The Diadoumenos (fillet-binder; fig. 288) shows a nude athlete with his clothes hanging on a bush (functionally, a support for the statue) wrapping a victory fillet (*tainia*) around his head. One leg is straight, bearing his weight as the other is about to push forward into the next stride — motion and stability in balance. His elbows are bent, and the direction of the gaze from the bent head as well as the missing bits of the tainia reinforce the diagonal line of the shoulders and upper arms. That line is in opposition to the line of hips and knees. This balance of the lines of composition and the similar balance between motion and stability represent Polykleitan symmetria, in a statue that was originally set up as a dedication by a victorious athlete.

A century later, Lysippos added posthumous portraits of Agias (see fig. 183) and Polydamas (see fig. 243) to the athletic genre. The deeply set, brooding eyes evoke an emotion that does not depend upon the athletic nude for inspiration but shows a more general trend in fourth century portraiture. Portrayals of athletes in the Hellenistic era more typically display the brutality of modern life rather than philosophical justifications for sculptural systems (see figs. 85–87). The contribution of athletics to the development of art was over, but the gifts of the Classical period were recognized in antiquity, for example this anonymous poem in honor of the famous runner Ladas, Olympic victor in the *dolichos* in 460 (*Anthologia Graeca* 16.54–54A; A 254):

> As you were in life, Ladas, flying before
> wind-foot Thymos,
> barely touching the ground with
> the tips of your toes,
> just so did Myron cast you in bronze,
> engraving all over your body
> expectation of the crown of Pisa.
> He is full of hope, with the breath on
> the tips of his lips
> blowing from within his hollow ribs;
> bronze ready to jump
> out for the crown—the base cannot
> hold it back;
> art swifter than the wind.

Literature of the Classical period also owes something to athletics. A favorite genre was the victory ode, or Epinikian poetry, at which Pindar and Bacchylides were particularly adept. We learn from these odes details about athletes and competitions, but we also see the larger role played by athletics in expressing the values of contemporary society. Perhaps the following example from the victory ode of 450 for the wrestler Aristomenes of Aigina will show what I mean:

> In Megara you have a prize already, Aristomenes,
> and in the plain of Marathon, and three victories
> in Hera's games in your home of Aigina.
> But now you fell heavily and from high and with malice aforethought
> upon the bodies of three opponents.
> For them there was at Delphi no decision
> for a happy homecoming like yours,
> nor did happy laughter awaken pleasure in them
> as they ran home to their mothers.
> They slunk through the back alleys, separately and furtively,
> painfully stung by their loss.
> But he who has won has a fresh beauty and

is all the more graceful for his high hopes
as he flies on the wings of his manly deeds
with his mind far above the pursuit of money.
The happiness of man grows only for a short time
and then falls again to the ground,
cut down by the grim reaper.
Creatures of a day, what is a man? what is he not?
Man is but a dream of a shadow.
But when a ray of sunshine comes as a gift from the gods,
a brilliant light settles on men,
and a gentle life. [Pindar, *Pythian* 8.70–98; A 249]

But this obvious connection between athletics and literature does not begin to show the intricate use of athletic metaphors in other types of literature. Some are obvious, some not, and the subject has not been studied thoroughly, but the imagery elicited by the use of athletic terms was vivid, and understood by all audiences, such as Euripides' use of *diauloi* to describe the waves in *Hecuba* ("Now I lie on the shore, now in the surf of the sea, unmourned, unburied, washed back and forth by the many diauloi of the waves"). When Euripides wrote these lines, he had no doubt that the audience in the theater would understand this allusion to the back-and-forth movement of the race. *Diaulos* was not a strange technical term, but a word that was part of everyday life.

Not surprisingly, the works of Plato, who spent the better part of his life in and near the *gymnasion* known as the Akademy, are filled with athletic metaphors. At one point in his discourse with Protagoras, who is credited with being the first professional educator of antiquity and the originator of the maxim "man is the measure of all things," after Protagoras has made a telling point, winning the applause of their auditors, Sokrates admits, "At first I felt as if I had been socked by a good boxer as darkness, and dizziness came over me from his words" (*Protagoras* 339E). Earlier, when Kallias had begged Sokrates to stay and continue the discussion, Sokrates made use of an extended athletic metaphor (335E–336A): "Now I fear that you are asking me to keep pace with Krison of Himera at the peak of his career, or with some dolichos runner or a *hemerodromos*. And I wish that I could keep up with them, but I can't. If you want to see me and Krison running together, you will have to ask him to change his pace for, even though I cannot run fast, he can run slow." Then as now, athletics, the language of athletics, and intellectual inquiry were inseparable.

Perhaps the most important contribution of athletics, at least in my opinion, was its creation of the concept of equality before the law, *isonomia,* the foundation on which democracy is based. In a Darwinian world of survival of the fittest, the notion of isonomia is unnatural, and it was not the first social concept developed, yet it had clearly been formed by the early sixth century B.C., just at the time the *stephanitic* cycle was completed with the addition of the festivals of Delphi, Isthmia, and Nemea to the Olympic festival. Within these competitions, the artificial preeminence of the *gymnikos agon* over the Sport of Kings, the *hippikos agon,* has been noted, as well as the fact that this situation in the early sixth century reverses the dominance of the chariot races in the earlier Homeric world. The preeminence of the gymnikos agon at the stephanitic games carries with it other characteristics we have noted: winners are determined strictly on the basis of objective criteria—a form of isonomia—and committers of fouls are flogged regardless of social or economic status, another form of it. The last, most obvious equalizer of men in this athletic setting is the fact that they are all nude. Social position cannot be easily discerned in the locker room; economic privilege does not propel one set of legs faster than another. The participants in the gymnikos agon are democrats striving to excel with their beings, not their possessions.

It is, then, no coincidence that Kroton, which developed one of the first democracies, became such a powerhouse in the gymnikos agon. In fact, one of the earliest, perhaps the earliest, uses of the word *isonomia* comes from the sixth-century physician Alkmaion of Kroton. And it is significant that Kroton has no recorded Olympic victories in the hippikos agon. Horse racing belonged to those with money and rank, and it was exactly for this reason that Alkibiades " held the gymnic games in contempt since he knew that some of the athletes were lowborn and from small city-states and poorly educated." The gymnikos victories of Kroton were embedded in the Krotoniates' concepts of democracy.

The vase painting of Athens, which has been so important to our study of the details of individual competitions, provides yet another insight into the connection between athletics and democratic institutions. The year 508/7 B.C. marks the advent of Athenian democracy, although the forces that brought it about had been building for some time. The triumph of democracy can, in some ways, be associated with the defeat of the Persians in 480 and 479 at Salamis and Plateia and the period of recovery thereafter. By the middle of the fifth century, Athenian democracy had begun to take another turn with the establishment of the Delian League, a euphemism for Athenian imperialism. If we look at the portrayals of the gymnikos agon in Attic vase painting (omitting Panathenaic amphoras) we find that nude athletic scenes begin to make up an ever larger proportion of the representations at about 520–510, and the number continues to grow until about 460, when athletic scenes fall off dramatically, a progression that parallels the rise and decline of Athenian democracy. (It was also during the 470s and 460s that one of the most famous trainers of antiquity, Melesias of Athens, was in his prime [Pindar, *Olympian* 8.54; *Nemean* 4.93 and 6.65].)

That the popularity of athletics parallels the flourishing of Athenian democracy is no coincidence: the gymnikos agon was for every man—and everyman—and this is the significance of one of the best-known stories about Sokrates. The year was 399 and Sokrates had just been found guilty of impiety and corrupting the youth of Athens. The jury had to decide whether he should suffer the death penalty or an alternative, to be proposed by him. Such alternatives usually included exile, financial penalties, and disenfranchisement. Sokrates made his proposal:

> What is a fitting penalty for a poor man who is your benefactor and who needs leisure time for advising you? There is nothing more fitting, men of Athens, for such a man than that he be given free meals for the remainder of his life in the *prytaneion*. And that is much more fitting than such a reward for one of you who has won the *synoris* or the *tethrippon* at the Olympic Games. He makes you think you are happy; I make you happy. And he does not need free meals; I do. If, then, I have to be penalized in accordance with my just worth, I should be penalized with free meals in the prytaneion. [Plato, *Apology* 36d–e; A 231]

The jury disagreed with this logic, and Sokrates was sentenced to death. Let us note, however, that in his proposal he contrasts his situation with that of men who win in the hippikos agon. At the same time, he says nothing about the gymnikos agon, even though we know that its victors also enjoyed free meals in the prytaneion and had done so for many years. It seems to me that Sokrates, the poor democrat, is disassociating himself from the wealthy equestrian competitors and, by his silence, even identifying himself with the athlete in the gymnikos agon. This is, in other words, a subtle reminder to the Athenian jury of his humble social status, which can be considered the equivalent of that of the athlete in the gymnikos agon. All three — jury, athlete, and Sokrates — are democrats.

16

ARETE

WE WANT OUR ATHLETES to be better than they are. We want to follow their exploits and rejoice when they win or break records. They are an extension of ourselves and an unrelinquished claim on our youth, an eternal source of memories of the days when we could run fast and jump far, when our muscles stretched and grew. We look at them and see ourselves as we would want to be seen, and sometimes we fool ourselves that we might have been as good at games as they. They represent an undying hope that we have a share in immortality, and they allow us to step outside ourselves from time to time so that we can return refreshed and revived to our everyday lives.

Our feelings are not new. Was it Plato the philosopher or Plato the sports fan who happily shared a tent with strangers at Olympia? Was it Aristotle the scientist or Aristotle the sports-statistics nerd who revised the list of Olympic victors? Who researched and created the first list of Pythian victors? The mythologizing of athletes we see today in the figures of Michael Jordan, Pelé, and Ronaldo—and dozens of others—can equally be seen in Milo, Phaÿllos, and Theagenes. We have accomplices in our modern mythmaking: sports writers, sportscasters, and sports photographers. Ancient athletes had their own versions of these.

In 464 B.C. the boxing event at Olympia was won by an athlete named Diagoras of Rhodes. This apparently was the culmination of his career for Diagoras, who had already won twice at both Delphi and Nemea and four times at Isthmia in the *stephanitic* festivals, as well as at a number of *chrematitic* games including the Panathenaia. His victor's statue was made by a sculptor named Kallikles of Megara and was set up at Olympia; its base has been found. His victory was also celebrated in a Pindarian ode, part of which I quote here:

> *As when a man takes up in his wealthy hand*
> *a drinking cup brimming with the dew of the vine,*
> *and gives it to his new son-in-law,*
> *toasting his move from one home to another*

to the joy of his drinking companions,
and in honor of his new alliance, and thus makes him,
in the presence of his friends, an object of envy
for the true love of his marriage bed;
just so do I send my liquid nectar, gift of the Muses,
sweet fruit of my talent to the prize winners,
and please the winners at Olympia and Pytho.
Truly blessed is he who is surrounded by constant good repute,
for the Grace who gives the bloom to life now favors one, then another
with both the sweet-singing lyre and the variegated notes of the flute.
To the accompaniment of both have I now come
with Diagoras to his land while singing of
Rhodes, daughter of Aphrodite, bride of Apollo.
I have come to honor his fighting form and his skill in boxing
and the great man himself, who was crowned by the Alpheios
and by the Kastalian spring and to honor his father, Damagetos.
....
Twice crowned with the laurel has been Diagoras,
and with his good fortune four times at famed Isthmia,
and again and again at Nemea and at rocky Athens.
Nor is he a stranger to the bronze shield at Argos,
nor to the prizes in Arcadia and at Thebes.
And he has won six times at Pellana and Aigina,
while at Megara the stone tablet tells the same story.
O father Zeus, give honor to this hymn for a victor at Olympia,
and to his now famous arete in boxing.
Grant him grace and reverence among his townsfolk and among foreigners.
He travels the straight path which despises hubris,
and he has learned well the righteous precepts of good forefathers.
[Olympian 7.1–16 and 80–93; A 248]

In addition to singing the praises of Diagoras's father and his fatherland, and listing the many victories of this boxer, Pindar interjects two words that are loaded with significance: *arete* and *hubris*. In crediting Diagoras with the possession of one and the lack of the other, the athletic excellence of striving for arete and the moral virtue of avoiding hubris are balanced; together they will steer Diagoras through society as a good man, not just a famous athlete.

Pindar's glorification of Diagoras befits this athlete, who was to found an Olympic dynasty. His eldest son, Damagetos, won the *pankration* at Olympia in 452, just twelve years after his father's boxing triumph. At the next Olympiad, Damagetos won again, and this time he was joined by his brother Akousilaos, who won the box-

Fig. 289 Diagoras of Rhodes on the shoulders of his sons, all of whom were Olympic victors. Bronze statue by Nikolaos, ca. A.D. 1970. Olympia, International Olympic Akademy (photo: author).

ing. They took a joint victory lap carrying their father on their shoulders — an event celebrated in antiquity and again today in a modern rendition of the story (fig. 289). Diagoras's third son, Doreius, was also an Olympic victor in the pankration in 432, 428, and 424. Doreius was in fact a three-time *periodonikes* (circuit winner), for he also had four victories at Delphi, eight at Isthmia, and seven at Nemea. Diagoras had two daughters, Kallipateira and Pherenike, each of whom produced a son. One, Eukles, was victorious in the boxing at Olympia in 404 and the other, Peisirodos, in the boys' boxing at Olympia, probably in the same Olympiad. Statues of these six Olympic victors stood together in a group at Olympia.

Here, then, is an ancient Olympic dynasty whose patriarch was renowned as graceful, reverent, and righteous. It is little wonder that Diagoras lives on today, in the name of a professional soccer team from the island of Rhodes. To be sure, there were some black sheep in the family: both Doreius and his nephew Peisirodos were exiled from Rhodes. But there is no reason to doubt the picture Pindar paints. Nonetheless, we must realize that Pindar was hired to write for Diagoras, and he was not about to add the warts. Pindar himself admits the profit motive when he says that his muse is a

Fig. 290 Portrait of Aristotle. Marble copy of the Roman period. Vienna, Kunsthistorisches Museum, inv. no. ASI 246.

profiteer and hired hand, and that there are "sugared soft-voiced songs silver-plated for sale by Terpsichore" (*Isthmian* 2.18; *A* 251). Indeed, Pindar reputedly charged fees for odes in excess of $66,000, and one gift he received in appreciation for a line of poetry in which he praised Athens earned him more than $220,000.

So, too, the wonderful sculptures of athletes hardly tell the whole story. Lysippos, commissioned by Daochos to make a statue of his ancestor Agias (see fig. 183), presumably leaves out the scars that the pankratiast must have had. The perfect marble images create an illusion that is far from the oily, sweaty, dusty athletes in whom the arete resided.

What of this arete? The word is used so frequently in the context of athletics or to describe athletes that it sometimes seems that this excellence or virtue—as the word is frequently translated—carries strictly athletic connotations. To be sure, arete can most easily be recognized on the playing field, where outstanding performance can be judged quickly and succinctly. But arete was not the exclusive possession of the winner. Anyone who exceeded the performance reasonably expected of him could be said to have shown his arete, and arete was essentially an individual, rather than a collective, characteristic.

Nonetheless, the precise definition of *arete* was not even agreed on in antiquity. Aristotle (fig. 290), discussing the proper educational system for the young, argues:

> It is clear that there ought to be legislation about education, and that education ought to be conducted on a public system. But one must not forget what the nature of education is, and what ought to be taught. At present there are disagreements about these questions. Not everyone agrees about what the young ought to learn and whether the goals should be arete or the

good life, nor is it clear whether studies should be directed toward the development of intellect or of character. Troublesome questions arise from the current status of education, and it is not clear whether the student ought to study those things that are useful for life, those that lead toward arete, or those that are theoretical. Each of these has its supporters. Nor is there even agreement about what constitutes arete, something that leads logically to a disagreement about the appropriate training for arete.

It is at least clear that the young must be taught those utilitarian things that are absolutely necessary, but not everything utilitarian. A distinction must be made between liberal pursuits and those that are not liberal; that is, the student ought not to participate in the utilitarian pursuits that lead to vulgarity. It is necessary to define as vulgar any pursuit, craft, or science which renders the body, soul, or mind of free men useless for the practice of arete. Thus we call vulgar crafts that deteriorate the condition of the body and employments that earn wages, for they make the mind preoccupied and degraded. Even liberal sciences are liberal only up to a point, for to devote oneself to them too rigorously and completely can have the damaging result of vulgarity. The purpose of one's pursuits or studies also makes a great difference. If the purpose is for the inherent joy of the project or for friendship or for arete, it is not illiberal. He who does the same thing, however, because of other people would seem to be acting as a servant or a slave. [*Politics* 1337a–1339a; A 189]

Aristotle thus considered arete something that was neither a practical nor a theoretical matter but a way of leading an excellent and virtuous life. Further, all parts of the human—body, soul, mind—were needed to practice arete. Hence, arete is not solely an attribute of the athlete. In fact, though Aristotle strongly favors physical education, he condemns athletic overdevelopment:

Since it is clear that education by habit must precede education by reason, and that education of the body must precede education of the mind, it is clear that the children must be turned over to the *gymnastai* and the *paidotribai,* for the one works with the condition of the body, the other with its actions.

At the present time some of the states with the greatest reputation for attention to their children produce such an athletic condition in them as to detract from the form and growth of the body. The Spartans, although they have avoided this mistake, turn their children into little animals through their labors, which they think contribute to manliness. But as has often been said, attention must not be paid to just one virtue, nor even to one virtue before all others. Indeed, they do not even consider whether

Fig. 291 Portrait of Plato.
Marble copy of the
Roman period. Berkeley,
Calif., Hearst Museum,
inv. no. 8–4213 (photo:
Therese Babineau).

their training leads to that virtue. For we see in these cases of animals and
of foreign races that courage and manliness do not belong to the wildest
but rather to the more gentle and lionlike temperaments. There are many
foreign races inclined toward murder and cannibalism who have no share
in manly courage. Nobility rather than animalism should play the leading
role, for neither a wolf nor any other animal will risk a noble danger, but
only a good man. Those who train their children in athletics to the exclusion of other necessities make their children truly vulgar and available to
the state for only one kind of work; and they actually train them worse for
this one job than others do.

It is, then, agreed that we should make use of physical education and
how we should make use of it. Until puberty lighter exercises should be
applied, and forced diets and required work forbidden in order that there
be no impediment to growth. There is no small proof that such training
can stunt growth. In the list of Olympic victors we can find only two or
three who have won in both the boys' category and the men's category.

Mind, body, and soul must all be engaged, must all be conditioned to lead a life
filled with arete. Athletics must be present, but not dominant, in the whole man. It is
no coincidence that the Akademy of Plato was first and foremost a place of exercise
for the body, and that the best-preserved portrait of Plato (fig. 291), whom we think of
as a thinker, a philosopher, and a man of letters, appears on a herm from his gymnasion and that he wears the ribbon of an athletic victor. But even Plato knew (*Protagoras*
361A) that "arete cannot be taught."

GLOSSARY

All italicized words are transliterated from the Greek unless otherwise noted.

abaton–Untrodden, inaccessible. When describing holy sites, "not to be trodden."

ageneioi (s. *ageneios*)–Literally, "beardless ones"; used to designate an age category for competitors between the *paides* and the *andres*. The specific age limits for the ageneios category varied from place to place, but it was generally confined to the late teens. By the Hellenistic period nearly all the games, including the Pythian, Isthmian, and Nemean, had the ageneios category, but it was never adopted at Olympia, which continued to divide competitors into the two basic categories of paides and andres. See also *neaniskos*

agon (pl. *agones*)–Gathering, assembly. In an athletic context, "competition," "games."

agonothetes (pl. *agonothetai*)–The sponsor, producer, or manager of games. The agonothetes was responsible for the conduct and smooth functioning of the games, and at times also underwrote them.

agora–The marketplace of a city, usually an open square surrounded by buildings, which served as the commercial and civic and political center.

aiora (pl. *aiorai*)–Swing or hammock; occasionally of a chariot equipped with springs.

akon (or *akontion*)–A light spear or javelin, distinguished from the *dory*, the heavier military or hunting spear.

akoniti–Literally, "dustless"; used to designate a victor who has won without a contest, usually because his opponents were physically or psychologically unable to compete. Initially used exclusively for the heavy events: wrestling, boxing, and the *pankration*.

alabastron (pl. *alabastra*)–An oil jar shaped like an elongated *aryballos*; like it, the alabastron had no resting surface or base.

aleimma (pl. *aleimmata*)–Literally, "something used for anointing," such as an unguent or oil; in athletic context, a fund that provided oil for young athletes.

aleiptes (pl. *aleiptai*)–Literally, "one who anoints," an "oiling man"; used to designate a trainer who specialized in massages.

Altis–The sacred grove at Olympia surrounding the Temple of Zeus, defined in the fourth century B.C. by a wall. In theory, everything within the Altis was sacred, and all secular activities and buildings were outside this open square.

amphotis (pl. *amphotidai*)–Literally, "something around or over the ears"; used for ear protectors for boxers.

anabates (pl. *anabatai*)–Literally, "one who mounts," a rider; sometimes used as a synonym for its opposite, *apobates*.

anakeryxis–A proclamation or announcement made by a herald (*keryx*); referred especially to the declaration of the name of the winner at the conclusion of a competition.

andres (s. *aner*)–Men. Used to designate the oldest age group at the games. See also *ageneios; paides*

anephedros–Literally, "without a seat" or "without sitting," the negation of *ephedros*; used to describe a victor who had competed in every round—that is, "without sitting one out."

ankyle (Latin, *amentum*)–A rawhide thong, nearly 2 meters long, used in throwing the *akon*.

ankyrzein–To hook with the leg, to trip; technical term used in wrestling.

anthipassia–A mock cavalry fight in which the emphasis was on maneuvers between teams of horsemen.

apene–A wagon or cart drawn by mules; for a relatively brief period it was one of the equestrian events at Olympia.

aphesis–Literally, a "letting go" or a "sending forth"; used generically of the starting line for both the footraces and the horse races.

apite–The oral command "Go!" used to start the footraces.

apobates (pl. *apobatai*)–Literally, "one who dismounts"; used to designate participants in a race in which an armed warrior jumped from a moving chariot, ran alongside it for a while, and then jumped back on again; sometimes used as a synonym for *anabates*.

apodyterion (pl. *apodyteria*)–An undressing or locker room, usually in a *palaistra* or *gymnasion*, where the athletes disrobed before practice. Before competitions athletes disrobed in special buildings, also called apodyteria, outside the stadium as at Epidauros, Olympia, and Nemea.

aporrhaxis–The name of a ball game, apparently a sort of handball.

apoxyomenos (pl. *apoxyomenoi*)–Used to describe an athlete scraping the *gloios* off his body.

arete–A word for which we have no simple equivalent in English. *Arete* includes the concepts of excellence, goodness, valor, nobility, and virtue. It existed, to some degree, in every ancient Greek and was, at the same time, a goal to be sought by every Greek.

aryballos (pl. *aryballoi*)–A small vessel, usually ceramic and round with a wide lip around a small mouth, which held the athlete's daily allotment of oil.

astragalos (pl. *astragaloi*)–Knucklebones; bones from the joints of animals used for various games of chance.

athletes (pl. *athletai*)–One who competes for an *athlon*.

athlon (pl. *athla*)–A prize given at a contest.

athlothetes (pl. *athlothetai*)–Literally, "one who sets out a prize"; the title of the person who organized games with prizes, an ancient "promoter." Essentially synonymous with *agonothetes* and, sometimes, *Hellanodikes*.

auletes–One who plays the *aulos*.

aulos (pl. *auloi*)–Can be any woodwind but is usually a flute.

balbis–An area in the stadium track marked off for the *diskos* throwers. Sometimes used to designate the starting line for the runners.

bater–Something which is trod upon, like a threshold. Used to designate the taking-off place for the *halma* (jump) and, more generally, the starting line in the stadium.

bembix (pl. *bembikes*)–A top. Used metaphorically for whirlpools and cyclones.

bibasis–An exercise or competition consisting of leaping straight up and kicking one's backside with the heels of the feet.

bomonikes (pl. *bomonikai*)–Literally, "an altar winner"; used at Sparta to designate young men who endured the greatest flogging.

boule–The council or senate of a city-state. The Olympic boule consisted of fifty Eleans who had control over the Olympic festival.

bouleuterion–The place where the *boule* met.

caestus–The boxing glove of Roman times. It consisted of a leather strap wrapped around the hands, usually loaded or studded with pellets of lead or iron.

chiton–Thin unisex undergarment like a long tunic or T-shirt.

chlamys–A heavy cloak or mantle worn especially, but not exclusively, by cavalrymen; the "uniform" of the *epheboi*.

choregos–A private citizen who sponsored a festival or a team in a competition.

chrematitic–Used to designate games where the prizes were either money or had monetary value as, for example, the Panathenaic Games at Athens. The name derives from *chrema*, "money."

chryselephantine (Greek, *chryselephantinos*)–Something made of gold (*chrysos*) and ivory (*elephantinos*); the most precious material a cult statue could be made of.

circus (Latin)–Circle; used to designate the elongated oval horse-race track in Roman times. The most famous of these was the Circus Maximus at Rome.

curia athletarum–The Latin phrase for the "council house of the athletes," or the athletes' union hall.

demes–Territorial subdivisions of Attica and elsewhere. A township is the best modern analogy; membership in a *deme* was a prerequisite of citizenship.

demos (pl. *demoi*)–The people of a given city; its citizens as a body politic, as in "the demos of the Athenians": the citizens of Athens as a group.

diadoumenos (pl. *diadoumenoi*)–Used to describe an athlete wrapping or tying a *tainia* around his head.

diaitater (pl. *diaitateres*) – An arbitrator, an umpire. Used for the judges at Olympia before *Hellanodikes* was adopted as their official designation.

diaulos – A footrace that was twice a *stadion* in length, that is, a sprint down and back the length of the track.

diazoma (pl. *diazomata*) – A loincloth. Synonymous with *perizoma*.

didaskaleion (pl. *didaskaleia*) – Literally, "the place of the *didaskalos*"; a classroom, a place where the mind was trained.

didaskalos (pl. *didaskaloi*) – A teacher; generally a master of a particular subject in which he trained students.

dioros – The stone target in the game called *ephedrismos*.

diskobolos – A thrower of a *diskos*.

diskophoros – A carrier or bearer of a *diskos*.

diskos (pl. *diskoi*) – Originally a weight of unformed stone or metal, it came to be shaped more or less like the modern discus and to have the same function in athletic contexts. In other contexts, a diskos could be anything shaped like a disk.

dolichos – The long-distance footrace. The length is uncertain, even at Olympia, where the evidence is better than elsewhere, but it was probably twenty-four lengths of the stadium there, or close to 5,000 meters.

dromos – A race or a race track; sometimes used as a synonym for the *stadion*.

eiselasis – A "driving into" or an entrance. Used to designate the triumphal entry by an athlete into his hometown after a victory in the Panhellenic games.

ekecheiria – Literally, "a holding of hands." Usually referred to a cessation of hostilities or a truce, especially the sacred month-long truce of the games.

elaiothesion – A room in a palaistra where oil was stored and athletes oiled themselves.

ephebeion – A room or a recessed bay (*exedra*) in a *palaistra* set aside for the use of the *epheboi* in their classroom training for citizenship.

ephebos (pl. *epheboi*) – A young man who had reached the age (eighteen) of training for and ultimately admittance to citizenship. The training was called ephebic (*ephebike*) and was crucial to the state's revival and in the creation of a citizens' military reserve.

ephedrismos – A game in which stones or balls were aimed at a target.

ephedros (pl. *ephedroi*) – Literally, "on the seat"; used to designate a competitor who had drawn a bye and therefore did not have to wrestle or box as many rounds as his competitors. See also *anephedros*

ephippios – Used with *dromos* to signify a footrace (rather than a horse race) that was four *stadia* in length. See *hippios*

epipola – Argive term for a flat, open space; used of the sacred area around the Temple of Zeus at Nemea.

episkyros – A ball game played by teams that resembled soccer or American football in general, though not in the shape or size of the ball.

episphaira (pl. *episphairai*)–A pad on the end of an object, such as the tip of a sword, used to blunt blows. Hence, a padded boxing glove used in practice.

euandria–Manliness, physical fitness. It was also a competition in the local games, for which the civic self-image was personified in the city's young men.

exedra (pl. *exedrai*)–Architectural term for a large recess or a room with one wall open, usually with benches around the other three sides. A common room in the *palaistra*, where it was used for lectures.

follis (diminutive, *folliculus*)–A type of ball in Roman times made of skin or a bladder and inflated with air.

gloios–The mixture of sweat, oil, and dirt scraped off the body of an athlete after exercise by means of a *stlengis*. These scrapings, specifically the mixture of sweat and oil, were used medicinally as an ointment for inflammations of the vulva and the anus, for condyloma, for muscle pains, sprains, and inflamed joints.

gymnasiarchos–Literally, "the leader of the *gymnasion*"; the man responsible for overseeing the training of the students and the functioning of the staff, not unlike an American high school principal.

gymnasion (pl. *gymnasia;* Latin, *gymnasium*)–A place where nude exercises took place. Technically, it differed from the *palaistra,* although the two buildings were often physically connected and their names confused. In the narrow sense, the gymnasion consisted of a covered practice track, or *xystos,* one *stadion* long. Parallel to this, in the open air, was the uncovered practice track, the *paradromis.* Practice for the *akon* (javelin) and the *diskos* took place beyond the *paradromis.*

gymnastes (pl. *gymnastai*)–Literally, "a trainer of nude exercises"; later used to designate a trainer or coach—sometimes even an agent—for a professional athlete.

gymnikos agon (pl. *gymnikoi agones*)–Competitions performed in the nude, generally the track and field and the heavy events, like wrestling, boxing, and the *pankration.*

gymnos–Nude, naked.

halma (pl. *halmata*)–A leap, spring, or bound; in athletic contexts, the jumping event of the pentathlon. It resembled the modern long jump, except that the competitors carried weights (*halteres*) and jumped to the accompaniment of an *aulos* player.

halter (pl. *halteres*)–A small weight usually shaped like a dumbbell used in jumping.

harpaston (pl. *harpasta*)–The name of both a ball game and the relatively small stuffed leather ball with which it was played.

hedran strephein–Literally, "to turn the seat" or "to turn the buttocks"; in wrestling, the cross-buttocks throw.

Hellanodikaion–The place for the *Hellanodikai,* a judges' building or stand.

Hellanodikes (pl. *Hellanodikai*)–A "Greek judge"; the judge or umpire who officiated at the Olympic and other games.

hemerodromos–Literally, "running through the day"; used to designate a courier, a messenger runner.

Herm–A quasi-anthropomorphized statue of a man, originally the god Hermes, in the form of a square pillar representing the torso with a human neck and head above; the pillar usually had rectangular projecting stubs for shoulders and an erect phallus. Used as the base for portrait statues, especially of men associated with the *gymnasion,* in Hellenistic and Roman times.

Hermaia–Competitions dedicated to Hermes representing the physical side of education in the *gymnasion,* as contrasted to the Mouseia.

himas (pl. *himantes*)–An oxhide thong wrapped around the knuckles, wrist, and forearm to serve as a boxing glove. The earlier, more simple himantes were called "soft" to distinguish them from the "hard" himantes of the Hellenistic period that had protruding layers of leather which increased the protection for the wearer but not for his opponent.

hippikos agon (pl. *hippikoi agones*)–The equestrian competition. The name derived from the word for horse (*hippos*).

hippios–Used with *dromos* to signify a footrace in the Nemean Games four *stadia* in length. See *ephippios*

hippodrome–Track for the horse races.

hoplites–Man in arms. Also used for the *hoplitodromos.*

hoplitodromos–A footrace the same length as the *diaulos* that was run in armor. The competitors originally wore helmets and shin greaves and carried shields. The greaves were later dropped from the equipment.

hoplomachia (pl. *hoplomachiai*)–A "battle in arms"; a duel by infantrymen in local, civic games.

hubris–Wanton insolence, arrogance, the cause of many a man's downfall.

hydria (pl. *hydriai*)–A water jar or pitcher that characteristically has two handles on opposite sides of the shoulder for carrying the vessel and a third, vertical handle from the shoulder to the rim for pouring.

hysplex (pl. *hyspleges*)–The mechanism or the rope or gate part of the mechanism used for starting the foot and the horse races.

idiotes (pl. *idiotai*)–A private person, an individual, as opposed to the state or *demos.*

isOlympia–"Equivalent to Olympia"; used to designate games or parts of games that were modeled on the Olympic games.

isoNemean–"Equivalent to Nemea"; used to designate games or parts of games that were modeled on the Nemean games.

isonomia–Equality before the law, equality of political rights.

isoPythian–"Equivalent to the Pythian"; used to designate games or parts of games that were modeled on the Pythian games.

kalokagathia–A composite derived from the Greek *kalos kai agathos*, "beautiful and good" signifying physical and moral excellence.

kalos–"Beautiful." When applied to a young man, *kalos* expresses admiration for his physical beauty.

kalpe–An equestrian event held at Olympia for a brief period. The evidence indicates that it was either a race for mares or a race in which the rider jumped off his horse and ran beside it for a part of the race. These two possibilities are not, of course, mutually exclusive.

kampter (pl. *kampteres*)–The post where the turn was made in the footraces and the horse races.

keles–A riding horse and the name of the horseback race. The length of the race seems to have been six laps, or twelve lengths, of the hippodrome.

keleustes (pl. *keleustai*)–One who urges or orders, specifically the boatswain who gives the beat to oarsmen.

keras (pl. *kerata*)–Horn or anything made of horn, perhaps including a club resembling a hockey stick that was used in a game. The verbal form *keratizein* seems to refer to the use of the keras in such a game.

keryx (pl. *kerykes*)–A herald; in athletic contexts, the winner of the heraldry competition at Olympia, who was rewarded with the honor of announcing events and victors.

kithara–A harp or lyre.

kitharistes (pl. *kitharistai*)–A *kithara* player; used to designate teachers of the kithara.

klados phoinikos–A branch of the palm tree, one of the preliminary awards given to the victorious athlete; generally, a symbol or token of victory.

kleros (pl. *kleroi*)–A lot, the casting of lots, or the allotment itself.

konis–Dust; sometimes used to designate a kind of powder, like talc, that was applied after bathing. *Konis* is frequently mistranslated as "sand."

konisterion–The room in a *palaistra* where athletes powdered themselves.

korykeion–A room in the *palaistra* for the punching bags.

korykos–A leather bag or sack, used in the *palaistra* as a punching bag.

kosmetes (pl. *kosmetai*)–An official at Athens elected annually to be in charge of the *ephebike* training.

kouros (pl. *kouroi*)–A boy, lad, youth, young warrior; used generically to designate statues of nude young men.

krikos (pl. *krikoi*)–A ring, circle, loop; used to designate a hoop rolled by children.

krypte esodos–Literally, the "hidden entrance"; the entrance tunnel to the stadium at Olympia. The name has been applied by modern scholars to similar tunnels in the stadiums at Nemea, Epidauros, and Athens.

kybos (pl. *kyboi*)–A cube; used to designate gaming dice.

kynodesmes (pl. *kynodesmai*)–Dog leash; a nickname for the string used to tie up the foreskin of the penis.

lampadedromia–A torch race used as a part of civic and religious ceremonies and competed in by the different tribes of *epheboi*.

lampadephoros–Literally, a "torch bearer"; used as another name for the *lampadedromia*.

loutron–A bathing establishment or a bath chamber within a *palaistra*.

lygos (pl. *lygoi*)–A willow bush (*agnus castus*) from which came the switches (*rhabdoi*) used to flog athletes who committed fouls and spectators who misbehaved.

mastigophoros–A whip or switch bearer, who helped keep control at the games.

meson echein, meson labein–Literally "to have the middle," "to seize the middle," that is, the waist. Technical wrestling terms for waist locks.

metretes (pl. *metretai*)–A measurer, a measurer of liquids, a liquid measure equalling 38.88 liters.

mitra (pl. *mitrai*)–A waistband or a headband, including a chaplet awarded to victors at the games, perhaps to hold the *tainia* in place.

Mouseia–Competitions dedicated to the Muses representing the intellectual side of education in the *gymnasion*, as contrasted to the Hermaia.

mousikos agon (pl. *mousikoi agones*)–The musical competition.

myrmex (pl. *myrmikes*)–Ant; used to designate the *himantes* (boxing glove) that "bit" like an ant.

neaniskos (pl. *neaniskoi*)–A young man, a youth; also used in the plural to designate an age group older than the *paides*, more or less the equivalent of the *ageneioi* (mid- to late teens).

nomophylax (pl. *nomopylakes*)–A guardian of the laws. Used at Elis for the officials who trained the *Hellanodikai* for their duties at the Olympic Games.

nyssa (pl. *nyssai*)–A largely poetic (especially Homeric) equivalent of *kampter* (turning post).

obsonion (pl. *obsonia*)–Literally, "foodstuffs," things eaten with bread, provisions, or the funds to cover the expenses of food. In Roman times the name of the pensions given to athletes who had won at a "sacred game" (so-called because the emperor had so called it) after the celebration of an *eiselasis* by the athlete.

odeum (Latin; Greek, *odeion*)–A building (usually enclosed) for musical performances, a recital hall.

ourania–Heavenly; the name of the muse of astronomy and a ball game that involved throwing the ball in the air (heavenward).

paidagogos–Literally, "leader of the boy"; a tutor and chaperon for a young boy, frequently a slave or servant who took him to and from school.

paides (s. *pais*)–Boys; in athletic contexts, used to designate the youngest group allowed to compete at the games or exercise in the *gymnasion*; the age limits were generally confined to the early teens.

paidonomos–An official in the *gymnasion*, second to the *gymnasiarchos*, who supervised the educational curriculum.

paidotribes (pl. *paidotribai*)–Literally, a "smoother of the boy" or "boy polisher";
   a trainer for physical activities, including athletic exercises and military drills.

palaistra (pl. *palaistrai;* Latin, *palaestra*)–The wrestling school. See also *gymnasion*

pale–Wrestling, both the event and the exercise.

palla (pl. *pallai*)–A ball, type unknown. It may resemble the *pila*, which appears in
   Latin sources.

pankration–The "all-powerful" contest, a combination of boxing and wrestling.

panselinos–The full moon, which marked the central day in the Olympic festival.

paradromis (pl. *paradromides*)–Uncovered practice track. See *gymnasion*

pentathlon–Competition involving five exercises: *stadion, diskos, halma, akon,* and *pale*.
   The order of competition is not clear, and the method of determining the
   victor is still much debated. We do know that an athlete who won three of
   the five would be the winner.

peplos (pl. *peploi*)–A heavy woolen garment for women, worn pinned at the shoulders
   and belted at the waist.

periageirmos–A leading or drawing around, in a circuit. Used to designate the
   athlete's victory lap.

peribolos (pl. *periboloi*)–A throwing around, surrounding. The official term for the
   Sacred Area at Delphi and at Isthmia.

periodonikes (pl. *periodonikai*)–Literally, a "circuit winner"; title given to an athlete
   who had won at least one time at each of the Panhellenic sites (Olympia,
   Delphi, Isthmia, Nemea).

perizoma (pl. *perizomata*)–Clothing worn around the loins, an apron, girdle.
   In athletic contexts, a loincloth, synonymous with *diazoma*.

petasos–A broad-brimmed hat worn by *epheboi*, a virtual badge of their position.

peteuron (pl. *peteura;* Latin, *petaura*)–A pole, a spar, a springboard; used in later
   sources for teeter-totters.

phaininda–A ball game resembling keep away.

phainomeris (pl. *phainomerides*)–Showing the thigh, a thigh revealer; used pejoratively
   of women of loose morals, as was the term "Spartan women."

philotimia–Literally, "love of honor," but with a basic meaning of "pride."

phyllobolia–Literally, "throwing of leaves"; in athletic contexts, showering the victor
   with flowers and leaves as he takes his victory lap.

pila (pl. *pilae,* Latin)–A medium-sized ball stuffed with feathers.

poda para poda–Literally "foot by foot"; the call to runners to prepare for the race by
   getting their feet set in the *balbis* (starting blocks).

polikos–Adjective derived from *polos* to designate races restricted to young horses.

poloi (s. *polos*)–Foals, whether colts or fillies; used to designate the category of
   young horses. A four-legged version of the *paides*.

proedria–The right to sit in reserved front-row seats in the theater, at the games, and
   elsewhere, given to distinguished guests of the state and accomplished citizens.

prytaneion–A building in the ancient city-state that housed the eternal flame of the city where new citizens were enrolled and guests of the state were invited for free meals.

psaltes (pl. *psaltai*)–A singer with *kithara* accompaniment; a music teacher.

pygmachia–Synonym for *pyx*.

pygme–Synonym for *pyx*.

pyrrhiche (pl. *pyrrhichai*)–A war dance; a competition in the civic games in which both defensive and offensive moves with weapons were used, especially in groups.

pyx (also *pygmachia, pygme*)–Boxing.

rhabdos (pl. *rhabdoi*)–A rod or wand; the switches used by the judges at the games to punish fouls. See *lygos*

salpinktes (pl. *salpinktai*)–A trumpeter; in an athletic context, the winner of the trumpeting contest at Olympia, who won the honor of signaling the athletic and equestrian events to the crowd. The salpinktes worked closely with the *keryx*.

semeion (pl. *semeia*)–A sign or signal; used to designate the markers that indicated the length of the jumps and throws of the athletes.

skamma (pl. *skammata*)–Literally, "that which has been dug," a pit, or a trench; the pit where the jumpers in the *halma* landed, as well as the wrestling "ring," where the softened earth helped break falls.

sophronistes (pl. *sophronistai*)–Literally, "one who makes something moderate," a chastiser, a softener. Sophronistai were annually elected officials at Athens, one from each of the ten Athenian tribes, who were charged with the supervision of the training and of the welfare of the *epheboi* of their tribe.

sphaira (pl. *sphairai*)–A ball, glove, or sphere. The word occurs in athletic contexts as a ball for games and as a padded practice glove for boxing. Some modern scholars believe that the gloves were used in actual boxing competitions, but the evidence for this is slight.

sphairisterion (pl. *sphairisteria*)–A room in the palaistra for playing ball.

spina (pl. *spinae*, Latin)–Backbone or spine; the divider down the middle of the race track in the *circus*.

spondai (s. *sponde*)–The sacred rites used to begin a treaty or truce; subsequently used for the truce itself.

spondophoros (pl. *spondophoroi*)–Literally, "a truce bearer"; an official at Olympia and elsewhere who traveled throughout Greece to announce the festival truce. See also *theoros*

spongos (pl. *spongoi*)–A sponge, part of an athlete's equipment.

stadion (pl. *stadia*)–Originally a unit of measurement of 600 ancient feet. (The ancient foot varied in length from place to place from about 0.296 to 0.320 meters.) Later used to designate the footrace that was a stadion long: a sprint down the length of the track. Finally, it also designated the place where the race was held, the stadium.

stele (pl. *stelai*) – A block of stone, usually in an upright position, that can be either a thin slab or a square pillar. Used generically as another name for the *kampter* (turning post).

stephanitic – Originally used to designate the four Panhellenic games at Olympia, Isthmia, Delphi, and Nemea, where the only victory prize was a crown (*stephanos*). Later other, lesser festivals were stephanitic as well.

stlengis (pl. *stlengides*) – A strigil. Usually made of bronze, it was shaped like a celery stalk in cross-section, bent below the handle; the athlete used it after exercise to scrape the accumulated oil, sweat, and dirt (*gloios*) off his body.

synodos – Literally, "an assembly" or "a meeting"; in later times, used in a more technical sense for a guild or union.

synoris (pl. *synorides*) – A team of horses, a two-horse chariot, and the race for the two-horse chariot that was eight laps or sixteen lengths of the hippodrome.

systasis (pl. *systaseis*) – A bringing or standing together. In wrestling, the starting position.

tainia – A ribbon, used specifically as a noun and in verbal forms to refer to the ribbons tied around the head, arms, and legs (and occasionally the waist) of a victor in the games.

Taraxippos – Literally, "the frightener of horses." An obstacle, apparently mainly psychological, in the hippodrome at Olympia.

taurotheria – Bull-hunting.

terma (pl. *termata*) – Literally, "an end" or "a boundary"; used to designate the finishing line and the turning post in the stadium and hippodrome. It could also be a mark or goal.

tethrippon (pl. *tethrippa*) – A team of four horses, a four-horse chariot, and the race for the four-horse chariot which was twelve laps or twenty-four lengths of the hippodrome.

theoria – Literally, "a looking at" or "a viewing" of something; a delegation, embassy, or mission sent on behalf of a city-state to oracles or other city-states or the Panhellenic festivals.

theorodokos (sometimes spelled *thearodokos*) – A "*theoros*-receiver," or hometown representative of a festival. When the theoroi of the festival arrived at his town, the thearodokos was responsible for greeting them, providing them with hospitality, and expediting their work.

theoros (pl. *theoroi*) – A messenger; a delegate sent on behalf of a festival to announce the sacred truce.

trachelizein – To bend or twist someone's neck. In wrestling, a neck hold.

triakter (pl. *triakteres*) – A "three-timer"; used to designate the victor in wrestling because he has thrown his opponent three times.

triastes–A "tripler"; used as a special title for an athlete who has won three different events at the same Olympiad.

trireme–The warship of ancient Greece. Powered by three superimposed banks of 33 oars on each side, in local races it was a means of testing the careful coordination of 198 rowers.

trochos (pl. *trochoi*)–A wheel; used to describe a hoop rolled by children. See also *krikos*

xystarches (pl. *xystarchai*)–Literally, "the leader of the *xystos*"; designates the leader of athletic guilds or unions.

xystos (pl. *xystoi*)–A covered practice track. See *gymnasion*

Zanes (s. *Zan*)–Variant of Zeus, applied to the statues of the god set up outside the stadium at Olympia and paid for by the fines levied against cheaters.

BIBLIOGRAPHY

With a few exceptions, this bibliography, organized by chapter, covers only material that has appeared since the publication of two thorough reviews of the literature on ancient athletics: Nigel B. Crowther's "Studies in Greek Athletics" (*Classical World* 78 [1984]: 497–558 and 79 [1985]: 73–135), and Thomas F. Scanlon's *Greek and Roman Athletics: A Bibliography* (Chicago, 1984). Interested readers should turn to these sources for a more complete listing of works relevant to various aspects of Greek and Roman athletics.

ABBREVIATIONS

A	Stephen G. Miller, *Arete: Greek Sports from Ancient Sources* (Berkeley, 2004)	JRA	*Journal of Roman Archaeology*
		JRS	*Journal of Roman Studies*
		JSH	*Journal of Sport History*
AA	*Archäologischer Anzeiger*	MDAI(A)	*Mitteilungen des Deutschen Archäologischen Instituts, Athenische Abteilung*
AC	*L'Antiquité classique*		
AW	*Ancient World*	OAth	*Opuscula Atheniensia*
AJA	*American Journal of Archaeology*	OJA	*Oxford Journal of Archaeology*
AJPh	*American Journal of Philology*	PCPhS	*Proceedings of the Cambridge Philological Society*
BCH	*Bulletin de correspondance hellénique*		
BSA	*Annual of the British School at Athens*	PLond	*London Papyri*
CB	*Classical Bulletin*	POxy	*Oxyrhynchus Papyri*
CID	*Corpus des Inscriptions de Delphes*	PZenon	C. C. Edgar, *Catalogue général des antiquités égyptiennes de museé du Caire, nos. 59001–59139; Zenon Papyri I* (Cairo, 1925)
CJ	*Classical Journal*		
ClAnt	*Classical Antiquity*		
CR	*Classical Review*		
ESHR	*European Sports History Review*	QUCC	*Quaderni urbinati di cultura classica*
HER	*History of Education Review*	RhM	*Rhenisches Museum*
ID	*Inscriptions de Délos*	SEG	*Supplementum Epigraphicum Graecum*
IG	*Inscriptiones Graecae*	SIFC	*Studi Italiani de filologia classica*
IJHS	*International Journal of the History of Sport*	SIG³	*Sylloge Inscriptionum Graecarum*
		SMSR	*Studi e materiali di storia delle religioni*
IvO	*Inschriften von Olympia*	TAPhA	*Transactions of the American Philological Association*
JHS	*Journal of Hellenic Studies*		
JNES	*Journal of Near Eastern Studies*	ZPE	*Zeitschrift für Papyrologie und Epigraphie*

1
Introduction

GENERAL

Bandy, Susan J., ed. *Coroebus Triumphs.* San Diego, 1988.

Bernardini, Paola Angeli. *Lo sport in Grecia.* Bari, 1988.

Bouvet-Lanselle, Violaine, cord. *Olympie: Cycle de huit conférences organisé au musée du Louvre.* Paris, 2001.

Coulson, William, and Helmut Kyrieleis, eds. *Proceedings of an International Symposium on the Olympic Games.* Athens, 1992.

Decker, Wolfgang. "Sport." *Der Neue Pauly: Enzyklopädie der Antike,* 11:847–855. Stuttgart, 2001.

Decker, Wolfgang. "Sportfeste." *Der Neue Pauly: Enzyklopädie der Antike,* 11:838–846. Stuttgart, 2001.

Decker, Wolfgang. *Sport in der griechischen Antike: Vom minoischen Wettkampf bis zu den Olympischen Spielen.* Munich, 1995.

Golden, Mark. *Sport and Society in Ancient Greece.* Cambridge, 1998.

Golden, Mark. *Sport in the Ancient World from A to Z.* New York, 2004.

Hodkinson, Stephen, and Anton Powell, eds. *Sparta: New Perspectives.* Swansea, 1999.

Olivová, Vêra. *Sports and Games in the Ancient World.* London, 1984.

Phillips, David, and David Pritchard, eds. *Sport and Festival in the Ancient Greek World.* Swansea, 2003.

Pleket, H. W. Review of Golden, *Sport and Society. Nikephoros* 13 (2000): 281–292.

Raschke, Wendy J, ed. *The Archaeology of the Olympics.* Madison, Wis., 1988.

Scanlon, Thomas F. *Eros and Greek Athletics.* Oxford, 2002.

Sweet, Waldo. *Sport and Recreation in Ancient Greece.* Oxford, 1987.

Weiler, Ingomar. "Der 'Niedergang' und das Ende der antiken Olympischen Spiele in der Forschung." *Grazer Beiträge* 12–13 (1985–1986): 235–263.

WRITTEN SOURCES

Badinou, P. *Olympiaka: Anthologie des sources grecques.* Bienne, Switzerland, n.d.

Bernardini, Paolo Angeli, ed. *Luciano: Anacarsi o sull'atletica.* Padua, 1995.

Ebert, Joachim. *Agonismata.* Stuttgart, 1997.

Fiedler, Wilfried. "Der Faustkampf in der griechischen Dichtung." *Stadion* 18 (1992): 1–67.

Langenfeld, Hans. "Artemidors Traumbuch als sporthistorische Quelle." *Stadion* 17 (1991): 1–26.

Matz, David. *Greek and Roman Sport: A Dictionary of Athletes and Events from the Eighth Century B.C. to the Third Century A.D.* Jefferson, N.C., 1991.

Miller, Stephen G. *Arete: Greek Sports from Ancient Sources.* Berkeley, 2004.

Moretti, Luigi. "Nuovo supplemento al catalogo degli Olympionikai." *Miscellanea Greca e Romana* 12 (1987): 67–91.

Weiler, Ingomar, gen. ed. *Quellendokumentation zur Gymnastik und Agonistik im Altertum.* 5 vols. (Vienna 1991–1996)

Vol. 1: *Diskos,* ed. M. Lavrencic, G. Doblhofer, and P. Mauritsch (1991)

Vol. 2: *Weitsprung,* ed. G. Doblhofer, P. Mauritsch, and M. Lavrencic (1992)

Vol. 3: *Speerwurf,* ed. G. Doblhofer, P. Mauritsch, and M. Lavrencic (1993)

Vol. 4: *Boxen,* ed. G. Doblhofer and P. Mauritsch (1995)

Vol. 5: *Pankration,* ed. G. Doblhofer and P. Mauritsch (1996).

COLLECTIONS OF ILLUSTRATIONS

Βαλαβάνης Πάνος Δ. *Παναθηναϊκοί αμφορείς από την Ερέτρια.* Athens, 1991.

Bentz, Martin, and Norbert Eschbach, eds. *Panathenaïka: Symposion zu den Panathenäischen Preisamphoren.* Mainz, 2001.

Comune di Firenze. *L'archeologia racconta lo sport nell'antichità.* Florence, 1988.

Measham, Terence, Elisabeth Spathari, and Paul Donnelly. *1,000 Years of the Olympic Games.* Sydney, 2000.

Sinn, Ulrich. *Sport in der Antike.* Würzberg, 1996.

Spathari, Elsi. *The Olympic Spirit.* Athens, 1992.

Tzachou-Alexandri, Olga, ed. *Mind and Body: Athletic Contests in Ancient Greece.* Athens, 1989.

Vanhove, Doris, curator. *Olympism in Antiquity.* 3 vols. Lausanne, 1993, 1996, 1998.

Vanhove, Doris, ed. *Le Sport dans la Grèce antique.* Brussels, 1992.

2
The World of Greek Athletics

Bassi, Karen. "Male Nudity and Disguise in the Discourse of Greek Histrionics." *Helios* 22 (1995): 3–22.

Bonfante, L. "Nudity as a Costume in Classical Art." *AJA* 93 (1989): 543–570.

Christesen, Paul. "The Emergence of Civic Nudity in Archaic Greece." Unpublished manuscript.

Crowther, Nigel B. "The Age Category of Boys at Olympia." *Phoenix* 42 (1988): 304–308.

Crowther, Nigel B., and Monika Frass. "Flogging as a Punishment in the Ancient Games." *Nikephoros* 11 (1998): 51–82.

Fiedler, Wilfried. "Sexuelle Enthaltsamkeit griechischer Athleten und ihre medizinische Begründung." *Stadion* 11 (1985): 161–162.

Goor, Asaph, and Max Nurock. *The Fruits of the Holy Land,* 89–120. Jerusalem, 1968.

Jacquemin, Anne, ed. *Delphes cent ans après la Grande fouille.* Paris, 2000.

Kotera-Feyer, Ellen. "Die Strigilis in der attisch-rotfigurigen Vasenmalerei: Bildformeln und ihre Deutung." *Nikephoros* 11 (1998): 107–136.

Leitao, David D. "The Perils of Leukippos: Initiatory Transvestism and Male Gender in the Ekdusia at Phaistos." *ClAnt* 14 (1995): 130–163.

Mayer, Clotilde. "Das Öl im Kultus der Griechen." Ph.D. diss., Universität Würzburg, 1917.

McDonnell, Myles. "Athletic Nudity Among the Greeks and Etruscans: The Evidence of the 'Perizoma Vases.' " In *Spectacles sportifs et scéniques dans le monde Etrusco-Italique*, ed. Ecole française de Rome, 395–407. Rome, 1993.

McDonnell, Myles. "The Introduction of Athletic Nudity: Thucydides, Plato, and the Vases." *JHS* 111 (1991): 182–193.

Mouratidis, John. "The Origin of Nudity in Greek Athletics." *JSH* 12 (1985): 213–232.

Papalas, Anthony J. "Boy Athletes in Ancient Greece." *Stadion* 17 (1991): 165–172.

Pemberton, Elizabeth. "Agones Hieroi: Greek Athletic Contests in Their Religious Context." *Nikephoros* 13 (2000): 111–124.

Petermandl, Werner. "Überlegungen zur Funktion der Altersklassen bei den griechischen Agonen." *Nikephoros* 10 (1997): 135–147.

Pfeijffer, Ilja Leonard. "Athletic Age Categories in Victory Odes." *Nikephoros* 11 (1998): 21–38.

Sansome, David. *Greek Athletics and the Genesis of Sport.* Berkeley, 1988.

Sweet, Waldo. "Protection of the Genitals in Greek Athletics." *AW* 11 (1985): 43–52.

Thuillier, Jean-Paul. "La nudité athlétique: Grèce, Etrurie, Rome." *Nikephoros* 1 (1988): 29–48.

Ulf, Christoph. "Die Einreibung der griechischen Athleten mit Öl." *Stadion* 5 (1979): 220–238.

3
The Origins of Greek Athletics

Brunner-Traut, Emma. "Neger- und Zergentänze im Alten Ägypten." *Nikephoros* 6 (1993): 23–32.

Carter, C. "Athletic Contests in Hittite Festivals." *JNES* 47 (1993): 185–187.

Catenacci, Carmine. "Il tiranno alle Colonne d'Eracle: L'agonistica e le tirannidi arcaiche." *Nikephoros* 5 (1992): 11–36.

Crowther, Nigel B. "Athlete as Warrior in the Ancient Greek Games: Some Reflections." *Nikephoros* 12 (1999): 121–130.

Decker, Wolfgang. "Die mykenische Herkunft der Griechischen Totenagons." *Stadion* 8–9 (1982–1983): 6–13.

Decker, Wolfgang. *Sports and Games of Ancient Egypt.* New Haven, 1992.

Decker, Wolfgang. "Zum Wagenrennen in Olympia–Probleme der Forschung." In *Proceedings of an International Symposium on the Olympic Games*, ed. William Coulson and Helmut Kyrieleis, 129–139. Athens, 1992.

Decker, Wolfgang, and Frank Förster. "Sport und interculturelle Wechselwirkung." *Annotierte Bibliographie zum Sport im Alten Ägypten II: 1978–2000. Nikephoros* Beihefte 8 (2002): 1072–1152.

Eder, Christian. "Kampfsport in der Sielelkunst der Altlevante." *Nikephoros* 7 (1994): 83–120.

Evjen, Harold D. "Competitive Athletics in Ancient Greece: The Search for Origins and Influences." *OAth* 16 (1986): 51–56.

Evjen, Harold D. "The Origins and Functions of Formal Athletic Competition in the Ancient World." In *Proceedings of an International Symposium on the Olympic Games*, ed. William Coulson and Helmut Kyrieleis, 95–104. Athens, 1992.

Günter, Wolfgang. "Ein neuer mykenischer Reiter." *Nikephoros* 8 (1995): 7–18.

Haas, Volkert. "Kompositbogen und Bogenschiessen als Wettkampf im Alten Orient." *Nikephoros* 2 (1989): 27–42.

Haider, Peter W. "Trainingsanlagen im Alten Ägypten?" *Nikephoros* 1 (1988): 1–28.

Kyle, Donald B. "Non-Competition in Homeric Sport: Spectatorship and Status." *Stadion* 10 (1984): 1–20.

Lamont, Deane Anderson. "Running Phenomena in Ancient Sumer." *JSH* 22 (1995): 207–215.

Laser, S. *Sport und Spiel. Archaeologia Homerica.* Vol. 3:T. Göttingen, 1987.

Lee, Hugh M. "The Ancient Olympic Games: Origin, Evolution, Revolution." *CB* 74 (1998): 129–141.

Mouratidis, John. "Anachronism in the Homeric Games and Sports." *Nikephoros* 3 (1990): 11–22.

Puhvel, Jaan. "Hittite Athletics as Prefigurations of Ancient Greek Games." In *The Archaeology of the Olympics*, ed. Wendy J. Raschke, 26–34. Madison, Wis., 1988.

Renfrew, Colin. "The Minoan-Mycenaean Origins of the Panhellenic Games." In *The Archaeology of the Olympics*, ed. Wendy J. Raschke, 13–25. Madison, Wis., 1988.

Rollinger, Robert. "Aspekte des Sports im Alten Sumer: Sportliche Betätigung und Herrschaftsideologie im Wechselspiel." *Nikephoros* 7 (1994): 7–64.

Scanlon, Thomas F. "Women, Bull Sports, Cults and Initiation in Minoan Crete." *Nikephoros* 12 (1999): 33–70.

Ulf, Christoph. "Die Frage nach dem Ursprung des Sports, oder: weshalf und wie menschliches Verhalten anfängt, Sport zu sein." *Nikephoros* 4 (1991): 13–20.

Vermaak, Petrus Stefanus. "Sûlgi as Sportsman in the Sumerian Self-Laudatory Royal Hymns." *Nikephoros* 6 (1993): 7–22.

Vermaak, Petrus Stefanus. "The Sumerian GES`PU-LIRU`MU-MA." *Nikephoros* 7 (1994): 65–82.

Weiler, Ingomar. "Langseitperspektiven zur Genese des Sports." *Nikephoros* 2 (1989): 7–26.

4

The Crown Competitions

THE GYMNIKOS AGON

General

Sinn, Ulrich, ed. *Sport in der Antike: Wettkampf, Spiel und Erziehung im Altertum.* Würzburg, 1996.

Swaddling, Judith, *The Ancient Olympic Games.* Austin, 1999.

The Footraces

Crowther, Nigel B. "The Finish in the Greek Foot-Race." *Nikephoros* 12 (1999): 131–142.

Kertész, István. "Schlacht und 'Lauf' dei Marathon — Legende und Wirklichkeit." *Nikephoros* 4 (1991): 155–160.

Kunze, Emil. *Beinschienen. Olympische Forschungen* 21. Berlin, 1991.

Miller, Stephen G. "Turns and Lanes in the Ancient Stadium." *AJA* 84 (1980): 159–166.

Rieger, Barbara. *Von der Linie (Gramme) zur Hysplex: Startvorrichtungen in den panhellenischen Stadien Griechenlands.* Ph.D. diss., Deutsche Sporthochschule Köln, 2002.

Siewert, Peter. "Die Namen der antiken Marathonläufer." *Nikephoros* 3 (1990): 121–126.

Tzifopoulos, Yannis Z. " 'Hemerodromoi' and Cretan 'Dromeis': Athletes or Military Personnel? The Case of the Cretan Philonides." *Nikephoros* 11 (1998): 137–170.

Valavanis, Panos D. *Hysplex: The Starting Mechanism in Ancient Stadia.* Berkeley, 1999.

Wrestling, Boxing, and the Pankration

Brophy, Robert, and Mary Brophy. "Deaths in the Pan-Hellenic Games II: All Combative Sports." *AJPh* 106 (1985): 171–198.

Campagner, Roberto. "Le mosse proibite del pancrazio in Aristofane, Aves, 441–443." *Nikephoros* 3 (1990): 141–144.

Crowther, Nigel B. "A Spartan Olympic Boxing Champion." *AC* 59 (1990): 198–202.

Lee, Hugh M. "The Later Greek Boxing Glove and the 'Roman' Caestus: A Centennial Reevaluation of Jüthner's 'Über Antike Turngeräthe.' " *Nikephoros* 10 (1997): 161–178.

Milavic, Anthony F. "Pankration and Greek Coins." *IJHS* 18 (2001): 179–192.

Papalas, Anthony J. "The Development of Greek Boxing." *AW* 11 (1984): 67–76.

Piem, Olaf. "Die Siegerstatuen von Schwerathleten in Olympia und ihre Zusammenstellung durch Pausanias." *Nikephoros* 13 (2000): 95–110.

Poliakoff, Michael B. *Combat Sports in the Ancient World: Competition, Violence, and Culture.* New Haven, 1987.

Poliakoff, Michael B. "Deaths in the Pan-hellenic Games: Addenda et Corrigenda." *AJPh* 107 (1986): 400–402.

Poliakoff, Michael B. "Melankomas, ἐκ κλίμακος, and Greek Boxing." *AJPh* 108 (1987): 511–518.

Rausa, Federico. "Μύρμηξ = ἱμὰς ὀξύς: Una proposta sull'orgine del nome." *Nikephoros* 13 (2000): 153–162.

The Pentathlon

Baitinger, Holger. *Die Angriffswaffen aus Olympia. Olympische Forschungen* 29. Berlin, 2001.

Jackson, Donald F. "Philostratos and the Pentathlon." *JHS* 111 (1991): 178–181.

Kyle, Donald G. "Philostratus, 'Repêchage,' Running and Wrestling: The Greek Pentathlon Again." *JSH* 22 (1995): 60–65.

Kyle, Donald G. "Winning and Watching the Greek Pentathlon." *JSH* 17 (1990): 291–305.

Langdon, Merle. "Scoring the Ancient Pentathlon: Final Solution?" *ZPE* 78 (1989): 117–118.

Langdon, Merle. "Throwing the Discus in Antiquity: The Literary Evidence." *Nikephoros* 3 (1990): 177–184.

Lee, Hugh M. "Yet Another Scoring System for the Ancient Pentathlon." *Nikephoros* 8 (1995): 41–55.

Maróti, Egon. "Zum Siegerepigramm des Nikoladas." *Nikephoros* 3 (1990): 133–140.

Maróti, Egon, and György Maróti. "Zur Frage des Pentathlon-Sieges." *Nikephoros* 6 (1993): 53–60.

Matthews, Victor. "The Greek Pentathlon Again." *Zeitschrift für Papyrologie und Epigraphik* 100 (1994): 129–138.

Waddell, Gene. "The Greek Pentathlon." *Greek Vases in the J. Paul Getty Museum* 5 (1991): 99–106.

THE HIPPIKOS AGON

Bell, David. "The Horse Race (κέλης) in Ancient Greece from the Pre-Classical Period to the First Century B.C." *Stadion* 15 (1989): 167–190.

Crowther, Nigel B. "Greek Equestrian Events in the Late Republic and Early Empire: Africanus and the Olympic Victory Lists." *Nikephoros* 8 (1995): 111–124.

Crowther, Nigel B. "More on 'drómos' as a Technical Term in Greek Sport." *Nikephoros* 6 (1993): 33–37.

Crowther, Nigel B. "Reflections on Greek Equestrian Events: Violence and Spectator Attitudes." *Nikephoros* 7 (1994): 121–134.

Decker, Wolfgang. "Zum Wagenrennen in Olympia–Probleme der Forschung." In *Proceedings of an International Symposium on the Olympic Games*, ed. William Coulson and Helmut Kyrieleis, 129–139. Athens, 1992.

Ebert, J. "Eine Textverderbnis bei Pindar, *Pyth.* 5.49." QUCC 38 (1991): 25–30. Reprinted in his *Agonismata*, 23–28. Stuttgart, 1997.

Ebert, J. "Neues zum Hippodrom und zu den hippischen Konkurrenzen in Olympia." *Nikephoros* 2 (1989): 89–108. Reprinted in his *Agonismata*, 336–355. Stuttgart, 1997.

Golden, Mark. "Equestrian Competition in Ancient Greece: Difference, Dissent, Democracy." *Phoenix* 51 (1997): 327–344.

Olivová, Věra. "Chariot Racing in the Ancient World." *Nikephoros* 2 (1989): 65–88.

Stefanek, Philipp. "Früher Reitagon auf einer protokorinthischen Vase von ca. 660 B.C." *Nikephoros* 2 (1989): 109–120.

THE MOUSIKOS AGON

Bélis, Annie. "Auloi grecs du Louvre." *BCH* 108 (1984): 111–122.

Larmour, David H. J. *Stage and Stadium. Nikephoros* Beihefte 4. Hildesheim, 1999.

Raschke, Wendy. "Aulos and Athlete: The Function of the Flute Player in Greek Athletics." *Arete* 2 (1985): 177–200.

Vos, M. F. "Aulodic and Auletic Contests." In *Enthousiasmos: Essays on Greek and Related Pottery Presented to J. M. Hemelrijk*, ed. H. A. G. Brijder et al., 121–130. Amsterdam, 1986.

OTHER EVENTS

Crowther, Nigel B. "The Role of Heralds and Trumpeters at Greek Athletic Festivals." *Nikephoros* 7 (1994): 135–156.

Eckstein, Felix. "Trompeter in Olympia." In *Roma Renascens: Beiträge zur Spätantike und Rezeptionsgeschichte*, ed. Michael Wissemann, 52–64. Festschrift Ilona Opelt. Frankfurt, 1988.

5
The Sites of the Crown Competitions
OLYMPIA

Antonaccio, Carla M. *An Archaeology of Ancestors*, 170–176. London, 1995.

Brulotte, Eric L. "The 'Pillar of Oinomaos' and the Location of Stadium I at Olympia." *AJA* 98 (1994): 53–64.

Buhman, Horst. "Der sakrale Charakter der antiken olympischen Spiele." *Anregung* 34 (1988): 103–108.

Ebert, Joachim. "Zur neuen Bronzeplatte mit Siegerinschriften aus Olympia. Inv. 1148." *Nikephoros* 10 (1997): 217–234. Reprinted in his *Agonismata*, 317–334. Stuttgart, 1997.

Heiden, Joachim. *Die Tondächer von Olympia*. Berlin, 1995.

Herrmann, Klaus. "Olympia: The Sanctuary and the Contests." In *Mind and Body: Athletic Contests in Ancient Greece*, ed. Olga Tzachou-Alexandri, 44–67. Athens, 1989.

Howie, Gordon. "Pindar's Account of Pelops' Contest with Oenomaus." *Nikephoros* 4 (1991): 55–120.

Knauss, J. *Olympische Studien: Herakles und der Stall des Augias: Kladeosmauer und Alpheiosdamm, die Hochwasserfreilegung von Alt-Olympia*. Munich, 1998.

Kyrieleis, Helmut, *Bericht über die Ausgrabungen in Olympia XII. 1982 bis 1999*. Berlin, 2003

Kyrieleis, Helmut, ed. *Akten des Internationalen Symposions: Olympia 1875–2000*. Berlin, 2002.

Lee, Hugh. "The 'First' Olympic Games of 776 B.C." In *The Archaeology of the Olympics*, ed. Wendy J. Raschke, 110–118. Madison, Wis., 1988.

Mallwitz, Alfred. "Cult and Competitions Locations at Olympia." In *The Archaeology of the Olympics*, ed. Wendy J. Raschke, 79–109. Madison, Wis., 1988.

Miller, Stephen G. "The Apodyterion." In his *Nemea II: The Early Hellenistic Stadium*, 190–210. Berkeley, 2001.

Morgan, Catherine. *Athletes and Oracles: The Transformation of Delphi and Olympia in the Eighth Century B.C.* Cambridge, 1990.

Nagy, Gregory. "Pindar's *Olympian* 1 and the Aetiology of the Olympic Games." *TAPhA* 116 (1986): 71–88.

Παπακωνσταντίνου Ελένη. "Ολυμπία: Στάδια εξέλιζης και οργάνωσης του χώρου. In *Proceedings of an International Symposium on the Olympic Games*, ed. William Coulson and Helmut Kyrieleis, 51–64. Athens, 1992.

Siewert, Peter. "Die frühe Verwendung und die Bedeutung des Ortsnahmens Olympia." *MDAI(A)* 106 (1991): 65–69.

Siewert, Peter. "Zum Ursprung der Olympischen Spiele." *Nikephoros* 5 (1992): 7–8.

Sinn, Ulrich. "Das Auftreten der Athleten in Olympia in Nachklassischer Zeit." In *Proceedings of an International Symposium on the Olympic Games*, ed. William Coulson and Helmut Kyrieleis, 45–50. Athens, 1992.

Sinn, Ulrich. "Bericht über das Forschungsprojekt 'Olympia während der römischen Kaiserzeit und in the Spätantike' VI. Die Arbeiten im Jahr 1996." *Nikephoros* 10 (1997): 215–216.

Sinn, Ulrich. "Olympia: Die Stellung der Wettkämpfe im Kult des Zeus Olympios." *Nikephoros* 4 (1991): 31–54.

Sinn, Ulrich. Review of Knauss, *Olympische Studien*. *Nikephoros* 12 (1999): 289–290.

Ulf, Christoph. "Die Mythen um Olympia–Politischer Gehalt und politische Intention." *Nikephoros* 10 (1997): 9–52.

Völling, Thomas. "Bericht über das Forschungsproject 'Olympia während der römischen Kaiserzeit und in the Spätantike.' IV. Die Arbeiten im Jahr 1995." *Nikephoros* 8 (1995): 161–182.

Wacker, Christian. *Das Gymnasion in Olympia: Geschichte und Funktion. Würzburger Forschungen zur Altertumskunde* 2 (1996).

DELPHI

Aupert, P. "Le Cadre des Jeux Pythiques." In *Proceedings of an International Symposium on the Olympic Games,* ed. William Coulson and Helmut Kyrieleis, 67–71. Athens, 1992.

Aupert, P. *Fouilles de Delphes.* Vol. 2: *Le Stade.* Paris, 1979.

Bommelaer, J.-F. *Guide de Delphes: Le Site.* Athens, 1991.

Brodersen, K. "Zur Datierung der ersten Pythien." *ZPE* 82 (1990): 25–31.

Fontenrose, Joseph. "The Cult of Apollo and the Games at Delphi." In *The Archaeology of the Olympics,* ed. Wendy J. Raschke, 121–140. Madison, Wis., 1988.

Guide de Delphes: Le Musée. Athens, 1991.

Jacquemin, Anne, ed. *Delphes cent ans après la grande fouille.* Paris, 2000.

Maass, Michael. *Delphi: Orakel am Nabel der Welt.* Thorbecke, Germany, 1996.

Morgan, Catherine. *Athletes and Oracles: The Transformation of Delphi and Olympia in the Eighth Century* B.C. Cambridge, 1990.

Picard, Olivier. "Delphi and the Pythian Games." In *Mind and Body: Athletic Contests in Ancient Greece,* ed. Olga Tzachou-Alexandri, 69–81. Athens, 1989.

Roux, G. *Delphes, son oracle et ses dieux.* 2d ed. Paris, 1981.

Sansone, David. "Cleobis and Biton in Delphi." *Nikephoros* 4 (1991): 121–132.

ISTHMIA

Bonnet, Corinne. "Le Culte de Leucothéa et de Mélicerte, en Grèce, au Proche-Orient et en Italie." *SMSR* 10 (1986): 53–71.

Gebhard, Elizabeth R. "The Beginnings of Panhellenic Games at the Isthmos." In *Akten des Internationalen Symposions: Olympia 1875–2000,* ed. Helmut Kyrieleis, 221–237. Berlin, 2002.

Gebhard, Elizabeth R. "The Evolution of a Pan-Hellenic Sanctuary: From Archaeology Towards History at Isthmia." In *Greek Sanctuaries, New Approaches,* ed. Nanno Marinatos and Robin Hägg, 154–177. London, 1993.

Gebhard, Elizabeth R. "The Sanctuary of Poseidon on the Isthmus of Corinth and the Isthmian Games." In *Mind and Body: Athletic Contests in Ancient Greece,* ed. Olga Tzachou-Alexandri, 82–88. Athens, 1989.

Gebhard, Elizabeth R., and Matthew W. Dickie. "Melikertes-Palaimon, Hero of the Isthmian Games." In *Ancient Greek Hero Cult,* ed. Robin Hägg, 159–65. Skrifter utgivna av Svenska institutet in 8°, 16. Jonsered, 1999.

Gebhard, Elizabeth R., and David S. Reese. "Sacrifices for Poseidon and Melikertes-Palaimon at Isthmia." In *Greek Sacrificial Ritual, Olympian and Chthonian*, ed. Robin Hägg. Proceedings of the Sixth International Seminar on Ancient Greek Cult, Göteborg, April 1997, ActaAth. in 8°, 17. Stockholm, forthcoming.

Jackson, Alistair H. "Hoplites and the Gods: The Dedication of Captured Arms and Armour." In *Hoplites: The Classical Greek Battle Experience*, ed. Victor Davis Hanson, 228–249. London, 1991.

Morgan, Catherine. "The Evolution of a Sacral 'Landscape': Isthmia, Perachora, and the Early Corinthian State." In *Placing the Gods*, ed. Susan E. Alcock and Robin Osborne, 105–142. Oxford, 1994.

Piérart, Marcel. "Panthéon et hellénisation dans la colonie romaine de Corinthe: La 'Redécouverte' du culte de Palaimon à l'Isthme." *Kernos* 11 (1998): 85–109.

Raubitschek, Isabelle K.† *Isthmia VII: The Metal Objects*. Princeton, 1998.

NEMEA

Miller, Stella G. "Excavations at the Panhellenic Site of Nemea: Cult, Politics, and Games." In *The Archaeology of the Olympics*, ed. Wendy J. Raschke, 141–154. Madison, Wis., 1988.

Miller, Stephen G. *Nemea: A Guide to the Site and Museum*. 2d ed. Athens, 2004.

Miller, Stephen G. *Nemea II: The Early Hellenistic Stadium*. Berkeley, 2001.

Miller, Stephen G. "The Shrine of Opheltes and the Earliest Stadium of Nemea." In *Akten des Internationalen Symposions: Olympia, 1875–2000*, ed. Helmut Kyrieleis, 239–250. Berlin, 2002.

6
The Olympic Games, 300 B.C.: A Reconstruction of a Festival

Blech, Michael. *Studien zum Kranz bei den Griechen*. Berlin, 1982.

Borthwick, E. Kerr. " A Phylloboia in Aristophanes' Clouds?" *Nikephoros* 2 (1989): 125–134.

Brodersen, Kai. "Heiliger Krieg und heiliger Friede in der frühen griechischen Geschichte." *Gymnasium* 98 (1991): 1–14.

Crowther, Nigel B. "Athlete and State: Qualifying for the Olympic Games in Ancient Greece." *JSH* 23 (1996): 34–43.

Crowther, Nigel B. "Numbers of Contestants in Greek Athletic Contests." *Nikephoros* 6 (1993): 39–52.

Crowther, Nigel B. "The Olympic Training Period." *Nikephoros* 4 (1991): 161–166.

Crowther, Nigel B. "Resolving an Impasse: Draws, Dead Heats and Similar Decisions in Greek Athletics." *Nikephoros* 13 (2000): 125–140.

Crowther, Nigel B. "Rounds and Byes in Greek Athletics." *Stadion* 18 (1992): 68–74.

Crowther, Nigel B. " 'Sed quis custodiet ipsos custodes?' The Impartiality of the Olympic Judges and the Case of Leon of Ambracia." *Nikephoros* 10 (1997): 149–160.

Crowther, Nigel B. "Victories Without Competition in the Greek Games." *Nikephoros* 14 (2001): 29–44.

Crowther, Nigel B. "Visiting the Olympic Games in Ancient Greece." *IJHS* 18, no. 4 (2001): 37–52.

Decker, Wolfgang. "Zur Vorbereitung und Organisation griechisher Agone." *Nikephoros* 10 (1997): 77–102.

de Ligt, L., and P. W. de Neeve. "Ancient Periodic Markets: Festivals and Fairs." *Athenaeum* n.s. 66 (1988): 391–416.

Dillon, Matthew. *Pilgrims and Pilgrimage in Ancient Greece*. London, 1997.

Dorati, Marco. "Un giudizio degli Egiziani sui giochi olimpici (Hdt. II 160)." *Nikephoros* 11 (1998): 9–20.

Himmelmann, Nikolaus. "Le View religieuse à Olympie: Fonction et typologie des offrandes." In *Olympie: Cycle de huit conférences organisé au musée du Louvre*, cord. Violaine Bouvet-Lanselle, 153–180. Paris, 2001.

Hitzel, Konrad. *Die Gewichte griechischer Zeit aus Olympia: Eine Studie zu den vorhellenistischen Gewichtssystemen in Griechenland*, esp. plate 43. *Olympische Forschungen* 25. Berlin, 1996. [See also the review by John H. Kroll in *AJA* 102 (1998): 632.]

Jacquemin, Anne. "Pausanias, témoin de la religion grecque dans le sanctuaire d'Olympie." In *Olympie: Cycle de huit conférences organisé au musée du Louvre*, cord. Violaine Bouvet-Lanselle, 181–214. Paris, 2001.

Kefalidou, Eurydice. "Ceremonies of Athletic Victory in Ancient Greece." *Nikephoros* 12 (1999): 95–119.

Κεφαλίδου, Ευρυδίκης. *ΝΙΚΗΤΗΣ: Εικονογραφική μελέτη του αρχαίου ελληνικού αθλητισμού*. Thessalonika, 1996.

Klingenberg, E. "ΔΙΑΚΩΛΥΕΙΝ ΑΝΤΑΓΩΝΙΣΤΗΝ. Eine platonische Bestimmung des griechischen Wettkampfrechts: Pl. Lg. 955A2–B4." In *Studi in onore di Arnaldo Biscardi*, 6:435–470. Milan, 1987.

Kokolakis, Minos. "Intellectual Activity on the Fringes of the Games." In *Proceedings of an International Symposium on the Olympic Games*, ed. William Coulson and Helmut Kyrieleis, 153–158. Athens, 1992.

Lee, Hugh M. "Some Changes in the Ancient Olympic Program and Schedule." In *Proceedings of an International Symposium on the Olympic Games*, ed. William Coulson and Helmut Kyrieleis, 105–111. Athens, 1992.

Lee, Hugh M. *The Program and Schedule of the Ancient Olympic Games. Nikephoros*, Beihelfte 6, 2001.

Meier, Christian. "Das grosse Fest zu Olympia im klassischen Altertum." *Nikephoros* 6 (1993): 61–74.

Miller, Stephen G. "The Organization and Functioning of the Olympic Games." In *Sport and Festival in the Ancient Greek World*, ed. David Phillips and David Pritchard, 1–40. Swansea, 2003.

Μουστάκα, Αλίκη. "Μορφή και συμβολισμός της Νίκης στην Αρχαία Ολυμπία." In *Proceedings of an International Symposium on the Olympic Games*, ed. William Coulson and Helmut Kyrieleis, 39–44. Athens, 1992.

Perlman, Paula. *City and Sanctuary in Ancient Greece: The* Theorodokia *in the Peloponnese*. Göttingen, 2000.

Perlman, Paula. "ΘΕΩΡΟΔΟΚΟΥΝΤΕΣ ΕΝ ΤΑΙΣ ΠΟΛΕΣΙΝ: Panhellenic Epangelia and Political Status." In *Sources for the Ancient Greek City-State*, ed. M. H. Hansen, 113–164. Acts of the Copenhagen Polis Centre 2. Copenhagen, 1995.

Siewert, Peter. "The Olympic Rules." In *Proceedings of an International Symposium on the Olympic Games*, ed. William Coulson and Helmut Kyrieleis, 111–117. Athens, 1992.

Sinn, Ulrich. *Olympia: Cult, Sport, and Ancient Festival*. Princeton, 2000.

Swaddling, Judith. *The Ancient Olympic Games*. Austin, Tex., 1999.

Wacker, Christian. "The Record of the Olympic Victory List." *Nikephoros* 11 (1998): 39–50.

Wacker, Christian. "Wo trainierten die Athleten in Olympia?" *Nikephoros* 10 (1997): 103–117.

Weiler, Ingomar. "Olympia—jenseits der Agonistik: Kultur und Spektakel." *Nikephoros* 10 (1997): 191–213.

7
The Money Games
GENERAL

Lavrencic, Monika. "Krieger und Athlet? Der militärische Aspekit in der Beurteilung des Wettkampfes der Antike." *Nikephoros* 4 (1991): 167–175.

Miller, Stephen G. "The Organization and Staging of the Olympic Games." In *Sport and Festival in the Ancient Greek World*, ed. David Phillips and David Pritchard, 1–40. Swansea 2003.

Scanlon, Thomas F. "Combat and Context: Athletics Metaphors for Warfare in Greek Literature." In *Coroebus Triumphs*, ed. Susan J. Bandy, 230–244. San Diego, 1988.

Yannakis, Thomas. "The Relationship Between the Underground-Chthonian World and the Sacred Panhellenic Games." *Nikephoros* 3 (1990): 23–30.

THE ASKLEPEIA

Tomlinson, Richard E. *Epidauros*. Austin, Tex., 1983.

THE PANATHENAIA

Βαλαβάνης, Πάνος Δ. *Παναθηναϊκοί αμφορείς από Ερέτρια.* Athens, 1991.

Benz, Martin. "Sport in der klassischen Polis." In *Die griechische Klassik: Idee oder Wirklichkeit,* ed. W.-D. Heilmeyer, 247–259. Mainz, 2002.

Crowther, Nigel B. "The Apobates Reconsidered (Demosthenes lxi 23–29)." *JHS* 111 (1991): 174–176.

Crowther, Nigel B. "Male 'beauty' contests in Greece: The Euandria and Euexia." *AC* 54 (1985): 285–291.

Crowther, Nigel B. "Team Sports in Ancient Greece: Some Observations." *IJHS* 12 (1995): 127–136.

Johnston, Alan W. "*IG* II² 2311 and the Number of Panathenaic Amphorae." *BSA* 82 (1987): 125–129.

Kratzmüller, Bettina. "Synoris — Apene: Zweigespannrennen an den Grossen Panathenäen." *Nikephoros* 6 (1993): 75–92.

Kyle, Donald G. *Athletics in Ancient Athens.* Leiden, 1987.

Larmour, David H. J. "Boat-Races and Swimming Contests at Hermione." *Aethlon* 7 (1990): 128–138.

Miller, Margaret C. "The *ependytes* in Classical Athens." *Hesperia* 58 (1989): 321.

Miller, Stephen G. "The Apodyterion." In his *Nemea II: The Early Hellenistic Stadium,* 210–222. Berkeley, 2001.

Miller, Stephen G. "Architecture as Evidence for the Identity of a Polis." In *Sources for the Ancient Greek City-State,* ed. M. H. Hansen, 201–244. *Acts of the Copenhagen Polis Centre* 2. Copenhagen, 1995.

Müller, Stefan. " 'Herrlicher Ruhm im Sport oder im Krieg' — Der *Apobates* und die Funktion des Sports in der griechischen Polis." *Nikephoros* 9 (1996): 41–70.

Neils, Jenifer. "The Panathenaia and Kleisthenic Ideology." In *Proceedings of an International Symposium on the Olympic Games,* ed. William Coulson and Helmut Kyrieleis, 151–160. Athens, 1992.

Neils, Jenifer, ed. *Goddess and Polis: The Panathenaic Festival in Ancient Athens.* Princeton, 1992.

Neils, Jenifer, ed. *Worshipping Athena: Panathenaia and Parthenon.* Madison, Wis., 1996.

Neils, Jenifer, and Stephen V. Tracy. *The Games at Athens.* American School of Classical Studies at Athens, 2003.

Pritchett, W. Kendrick. *The Greek State at War,* 2: 208–231. Berkeley, 1974.

Rausch, Mario. "Zeitpunkt und Anlass der Einführung der Phylenagone in Athen." *Nikephoros* 11 (1998): 95–102.

Reed, Nancy B. "A Chariot Race of Athens' Finest: The *Apobates* Contest Re-Examined." *JSH* 17 (1990): 306–317.

Reed, Nancy B. "The Euandria Competition at the Panathenaea Reconsidered." *AW* 15 (1987): 59–64.

Robertson, Noel. "The Origin of the Panathenaea." *RhM* 128 (1985): 231–295.

Tracy, Stephen V. "The Panathenaic Festival and Games: An Epigraphic Inquiry." *Nikephoros* 4 (1991): 133–154.

Tracy, Stephen V., and Christian Habicht. "New and Old Panathenaic Victor Lists." *Hesperia* 60 (1991): 187–236.

Valavanis, Panos. "La Proclamation des vainqueurs aux Panathénées." *BCH* 114 (1990): 325–359.

Valavanis, Panos. "ΤΗΝΕΛΛΑ ΚΑΛΛΙΝΙΚΕ . . . Prozessionen von Panathenäensiegern auf der Akropolis." *AA* (1991): 487–498.

Winkler, John J. "The Ephebes' Song: *Tragôidia* and *Polis*." In *Nothing to do with Dionysos?* ed. John J. Winkler and Froma Zeitlin, 20–62. Princeton, 1990.

Web site: http: / / cma.soton.ac.uk / HistShip / shlect26.htm

THE ELEUTHERIA

Gallis, Kostas J. "The Games in Ancient Larisa: An Example of Provincial Olympic Games." In *The Archaeology of the Olympics*, ed. Wendy J. Raschke, 217–235. Madison, Wis., 1988.

THE KARNEIA

Beck, F. A. "Spartan Education Revisited." *HER* 22 (1993): 16–31.

Cartledge, Paul. *Spartan Reflections*. Berkeley, 2001.

Crowther, Nigel B. "A Spartan Olympic Boxing Champion." *AC* 59 (1990): 198–202.

Hodkinson, Stephen. "An Agonistic Culture?" In *Sparta: New Perspectives*, ed. Stephen Hodkinson and Anton Powell, 147–187. Swansea, 1999.

Kennell, Nigel M. *The Gymnasium of Virtue*. Chapel Hill, N.C., 1995.

Pettersson, Michael. *Cults of Apollo at Sparta: The Hyakinthia, the Gymnopaidiai, and the Karneia*. Stockholm, 1992.

8
Women and Athletics

Arrigoni, G. "Donne e sport nel mondo greco religione e società." In *Le donne in Grecia*, ed. G. Arrigoni, 55–201. Rome, 1985.

Bérard, Claude. "L'impossibile femme athlete." *Annali archeologia e storia antica* 8 (1986): 195–202.

Bernardini, Paola Angeli. "Aspects Ludiques, rituels et sportifs de la course féminine dans la Grèce antique." *Stadion* 12–13 (1986–1987): 17–26.

Bouvrie, Synnøve des. "Gender and the Games at Olympia." In *Greece and Gender*, ed. Brit Berggreen and Nannó Marinatos, 55–74. Papers from the Norwegian Institute at Athens 2. Bergen, 1995.

Cole, S. "The Social Function of Rituals of Maturation: The Koureion and the Arkteia." *ZPE* 55 (1984): 233–244.

Dowden, Ken. *Death and the Maiden: Girls' Initiation Rites in Greek Mythology.* London, 1989.

Frass, Monika. "Gesellschaftliche Akzeptanz 'sportlicher' Frauen in der Antike." *Nikephoros* 10 (1997): 119–134.

Hamilton, Richard. "Alkman and the Athenian Arkteia." *Hesperia* 58 (1989): 449–472.

Hansen, William. "The Winning of Hippodameia." *TAPhA* 130 (2000): 19–40.

Lee, Hugh M. "Athletics and the Bikini Girls from Piazza Armerina." *Stadion* 10 (1984): 45–78.

Lee, Hugh M. "*SIG*³ 802: Did Women Compete Against Men in Greek Athletic Festivals?" *Nikephoros* 1 (1988): 103–118.

Ley, Anne. "Atalante—Von der Athletin zur Liebhaberin." *Nikephoros* 3 (1990): 31–72.

Mantas, Konstantinos. "Women and Athletics in the Roman East." *Nikephoros* 8 (1995): 125–144.

McCauly, Barbara. "The Transfer of Hippodameia's Bones: A Historical Context." *CJ* 93 (1998): 225–239.

Millender, Ellen. "Athenian Ideology and the Empowered Spartan Woman." In *Sparta: New Perspectives,* ed. Stephen Hodkinson and Anton Powell, 355–391. Swansea, 1999.

Pomeroy, Sarah B. *Spartan Women.* Oxford, 2002.

Reeder, Ellen D. *Pandora: Women in Classical Greece,* 363–373. Princeton, 1995.

Scanlon, Thomas F. "The Footrace of the Heraia at Olympia." *AW* 9 (1984): 77–90.

Scanlon, Thomas F. "Race or Chase at the Arkteia of Attica?" *Nikephoros* 3 (1990): 73–120.

Scanlon, Thomas F. "*Virgineum Gymnasium*: Spartan Females and Early Greek Athletics." In *The Archaeology of the Olympics,* ed. Wendy J. Raschke, 185–216. Madison, Wis., 1988.

Serwint, Nancy. "Female Athletic Costume at the Heraia and Prenuptial Initiation Rites." *AJA* 97 (1993): 403–422.

Sourvinou-Inwood, Christiane. *Studies in Girls' Transitions: Aspects of the Arkteia and Age Representation in Attic Iconography.* Athens, 1988.

9
Athletes and Heroes

Βαλαβάνης, Πάνος Δ. Ἆθλα, ἀθλητές καὶ ἔπαθλα. Athens, 1996.

Barron, J. P. "Pythagoras' Euthymos." In *Text and Tradition: Studies in Honor of Mortimer Chambers,* ed. R. Mellor and L. Tritle, 37–62. Claremont, Calif., 1999.

Benz, Martin, and Christian Mann. "Zur Heroisierung von Athleten." In *Konstruktionen von Wirklichkeit: Bilder im Griechenland des 5. und 4. Jhs. v. Chr.*, ed. R. von den Hoff and S. Schmidt, 215–230. Stuttgart, 2001.

Burkert, Walter. "Heros, Tod und Sport: Ritual und Mythos der olympischen Spiele in der Antike." In *Körper- und Einbildungskraf*, ed. Gunter Gebauer, 31–42. Berlin, 1988.

Burkert, Walter. *Homo Necans*, 93–103. Berkeley, 1983.

Lattimore, Steven. "The Nature of Early Greek Victor Statues." In *Coroebus Triumphs*, ed. Susan J. Bandy, 245–256. San Diego, 1988.

Lippolis, Enzo. *Gli eroi di Olimpia*. Taranto, Italy, 1992.

Taeuber, Hans. "Ein Inschriftenfragment der Pulydamas-Basis von Olympia." *Nikephoros* 10 (1997): 235–244.

Yiannakis, Thomas. "The Relationship Between the Underground-Chthonian World and the Sacred Panhellenic Games." *Nikephoros* 3 (1990): 23–30.

10
Sport and Recreation

Crowther, Nigel B. "The Ancient Greek Game of Episkyros." Stadion 23 (1997): 1–15.

Fittá, Marco. *Spiele und Spielzeug in der Antike*. Stuttgart, 1998.

Gilmour, G. H. "The Nature of Function of Astragalus Bones from Archaeological Contexts in the Levant and Eastern Mediterranean." *OJA* 16 (1997): 167–175.

Golden, M. *Children and Childhood in Classical Athens*. Baltimore, 1990.

Kurke, Leslie. *Coins, Bodies, Games, and Gold*, 247–298. Princeton, 1999.

Λάζος, Χρήστος Δ. *Παίζονταης στο Χρόνο*. Athens, 2002.

Matthews, Victor J. "*Suram dare:* A Gesture in Roman Ball Playing." *Nikephoros* 3 (1990): 185–188.

Neils, Jenifer, and John H. Oakley. *Coming of Age in Ancient Greece*. New Haven, 2003

Papadopoulos, J. K. "Παίζω ἤ χέζω? A Contextual Approach to *pessoi*." *Hesperia* 72 (2003).

Πλατή, Μαρίν. *Παίζοντας στην αρχαία Ελλάδα*. Athens, 1998.

11
Training
THE BUILDINGS

Glass, Stephen L. "The Greek Gymnasium: Some Problems." In *The Archaeology of the Olympics*, ed. Wendy J. Raschke 155–173. Madison, Wis., 1988.

Θέμελης, Πέτρος. "Το Στάδιο της Μεσσήνης." In *Proceedings of an International Symposium on the Olympic Games*, ed. William Coulson and Helmut Kyrieleis, 87–94. Athens, 1992.

Morison, William W. "Attic Gymnasia and Palaistrai: Public or Private?" *AW* 31 (2000): 140–144.

Mussche, H. "Sport et architecture." in *Le Sport dans la Grèce antique*, ed. Doris Vanhove, 43–55. Brussels, 1992.

Themelis, Petros G. *Ancient Messene: Site and Monuments*, 46–50. Athens, 1999.

Tzachou-Alexandri, Olga. "The Gymnasium. An Institution for Athletics and Education." In *Mind and Body: Athletic Contests in Ancient Greece*, ed. Olga Tzachou-Alexandri, 31–37. Athens, 1989.

Vanhove, D. "Le Gymnase." In *Le Sport dans la Grèce antique*, ed. Doris Vanhove, 57–77. Brussels, 1992.

THE PEOPLE

Albanidis, Evangelos. "The Ephebia in the Ancient Hellenic World and Its Role in the Making of Masculinity." *ESHR* 2 (2000): 4–23.

Crowther, Nigel B. "Euexia, Eutaxia, Philoponia: The Contests of the Greek Gymnasium." *ZPE* 85 (1991): 301–304.

Dickie, Matthew W. "Παλαιστρίτης/'Palaestrita': Callisthenics in the Greek and Roman Gymnasium." *Nikephoros* 6 (1993): 105–152.

Dover, Kenneth J. *Greek Homosexuality*. 2d ed. Cambridge, Mass., 1989.

Gauthier, Ph., and M. B. Hatzopoulos. *La Loi gymnasiarchique de Beroia*. ΜΕΛΕΤΗΜΑΤΑ 16. Athens, 1993.

Golden, Mark. *Children and Childhood in Classical Athens*. Baltimore, 1990.

Hall, A., and N. Milner. "Education and Athletics: Documents Illustrating the Festivals of Oenoanda." In *Studies in the History and Topography of Lycia and Pisidia in Memoriam A. S. Hall*, ed. D. French, 7–47. Oxford, 1994.

Halperin, David. *One Hundred Years of Homosexuality*. New York, 1990.

Mitchell, Stephen. "Festivals, Games, and Civic Life in Roman Asia Minor." *JRS* 80 (1990): 183–193.

Percy, William Armstrong III. *Pederasty and Pedagogy in Archaic Greece*. Urbana, Ill., 1996.

Scanlon, Thomas F. "*Gymnikê Paideia*: Greek Athletics and the Construction of Culture." *CB* 74 (1998): 143–157.

Stewart, Andrew. *Art, Desire, and the Body in Ancient Greece*. Cambridge, 1997.

12
Athletics as Entertainment in the Hellenistic and Roman Periods

Alcock, Susan E. "Nero at Play? The Emperor's Grecian Odyssey." In *Reflections of Nero: Culture, History and Representation*, ed. J. Elsner and J. Masters, 98–111. London, 1994.

Boe, Alfred F. "Sports in the Bible." In *Coroebus Triumphs*, ed. Susan J. Bandy, 218–229. San Diego, 1988.

Caldelli, M. L. *L'agon Capitolinus: Storia e protagonisti dall'istituztione domiziana al IV secolo*. Rome, 1993.

Carter, M. "The Roman Spectacles of Antiochus IV Epiphanes at Daphne, 166 B.C." *Nikephoros* 14 (2001): 45–62.

Edmondson, Jonathan C. "The Cultural Politics of Public Spectacle in Rome and the Greek East." In *The Art of Ancient Spectacle*, ed, Bettina Bergmann and Christine Kondoleon, 77–95. Washington, D.C., 1999.

Farrington, A. "Olympic Victors and the Popularity of the Olympic Games in the Imperial Period." *Tyche* 12 (1997): 15–46.

Harris, H. A. *Greek Athletics and the Jews*. Cardiff, Wales, 1976.

Herz, P. "Die Entwicklung der griechischen Agonistik in der Kaiserzeit." In *Olympische Studien*, ed. N. Müller and M. Messing, 111–131. Niedernhausen, Germany, 1988.

Herz, Peter. "Gedanken zu den Spielen der Provinz Asia in Kyzikos." *Nikephoros* 11 (1998): 171–182.

Humphrey, John H. " 'Amphitheatrical' Hippo-Stadia." In *Caesarea Maritimia: A Retrospective after Two Millennia*, ed. A. Raban and K. Holum, 121–129. New York, 1996.

Humphrey, John H. *Roman Circuses*. London, 1986.

Jones, Christopher P. "A New Lycian Dossier Establishing an Artistic Contest and Festival in the Reign of Hadrian." *JRA* 3 (1990): 484–488.

Kennell, Nigel M. "ΝΕΡΩΝ ΠΕΡΙΔΟΝΙΚΗΣ." *AJPh* 109 (1988): 239–251.

Kertész, István. "Plercs de oikos hapas stephanon." *Nikephoros* 12 (1999): 143–148.

Lee, Hugh M. "Venues for Greek Athletics in Rome." In *Rome and Her Monuments: Essays on the City and Literature of Rome in Honor of Katherine Geffcken*, ed. S. K. Dickison and Judith P. Hallett, 215–239. Wauconda, Ill., 2000.

Mehl, Andreas. "Erziehung zum Hellenen—Erziehung zum Weltbürger: Bemerkungen zum Gymnasion im hellenistichsen Osten." *Nikephoros* 5 (1992): 43–74.

Miller, Stephen G. "Society." In his *Nemea II: The Early Hellenistic Stadium*, 245–248. Berkeley, 2001.

Miller, Stephen G. "Stadiums." *The Oxford Encyclopedia of Archaeology in the Near East*, 5:74–75. Oxford, 1997.

Mitchell, Stephen. "Festivals, Games, and Civic Life in Roman Asia Minor." *JRS* 80 (1990): 183–193.

Patrich, Joseph. "The *Carceres* of the Herodian Hippodrome / Stadium at Caesarea Maritima and Connections with the Circus Maximus." *JRA* 14 (2001): 269–283.

Patrich, Joseph. "Herod's Hippodrome / Stadium at Caesarea and the Games Conducted Therein." In *What Athens Has to Do with Jerusalem: Essays in Honor of Gideon Foerster*, ed. L. Rutgers, 29–68. Louvain, 2001.

Perry, J. S. " 'Clinopale': Sport and Erotic Humor in the Roman Empire." *Nikephoros* 14 (2001): 83–90.

Poliakoff, Michael. "Jacob, Job, and Other Wrestlers: Reception of Greek Athletics by Jews and Christians in Antiquity." *JSH* 11 (1984): 48–65.

Porath, Y. "Herod's 'Amphitheatre' at Caesarea: A Multipurpose Entertainment Building." In *The Roman and Byzantine Near East,* ed. J. H. Humphrey, 15–27. *JRA* Supplement 14 (1995).

Rieger, Barbara. "Die Capitolia des Kaisers Domitian." *Nikephoros* 12 (1999): 171–204.

Rogers, Guy M. "Demosthenes of Oenoanda and Models of Euergetism." *JRS* 81 (1991): 91–100.

Spawford, A. J. "Agonistic Festivals in Roman Greece." In *The Greek Renaissance in the Roman Empire: Papers from the 10th British Museum Classical Colloguium,* ed. Susan Walker and Avril Cameron, 193–197. London, 1989.

Strasser, J.-Y. "Etudes sur les concours d'Occident." *Nikephoros* 14 (2001): 109–155.

van Nijf, Onno. "Athletics, Festivals, and Greek Identity in the Roman East." *PCPhS* 45 (1999): 176–200.

Wallner, C. "M. Ulpius Heliodors und T. Flavius Archibios. Beobachtungen zu ihren Ehreninschriften (*IG* IV 591; *I. Napoli* I,51)." *Nikephoros* 14 (2001): 91–108.

Welch, Katherine. "Greek Stadia and Roman Spectacles: Asia, Athens, and the Tomb of Herodes Atticus." *JRA* 11 (1998): 117–145.

Welch, Katherine. "Negotiating Roman Spectacle Architecture in the Greek World: Athens and Corinth." In *The Art of Ancient Spectacle,* ed. Bettina Bergmann and Christine Kondoleon, 125–148. Washington, D.C., 1999.

13
Professionals and Amateurs

Bilinski, Bronislaw. "Un pescivendolo olimpionico (Aristotles Rht. I 7 1365a — Ps. Simonides fr. 110 D)." *Nikephoros* 3 (1990): 157–176.

Fiedler, Wilfried. "Sexuelle Enthaltsamkeit griechischer Athleten und ihre medizinische Begründung." *Stadion* 11 (1985): 137–175.

Kyle, Donald G. "Solon and Athletics." *AW* 9 (1984): 91–105.

Pleket, Henri W. "The Participants in the Ancient Olympic Games: Social Background and Mentality." In *Proceedings of an International Symposium on the Olympic Games,* ed. William Coulson and Helmut Kyrieleis, 147–152. Athens, 1992.

Pleket, Henri W. "Zuer Soziologie des antiken Sports." *Nikephoros* 14 (2001): 157–212.

Renfrew, Jane M. "Food for Athletes and Gods: A Classical Diet." In *The Archaeology of the Olympics,* ed. Wendy J. Raschke, 174–184. Madison, Wis., 1988.

Young, David C. "First with the Most: Greek Athletic Records and 'Specialization.' " *Nikephoros* 9 (1996): 175–198.

Young, David C. "How the Amateurs Won the Olympics." In *The Archaeology of the Olympics*, ed. Wendy J. Raschke, 55–78. Madison, Wis., 1988.

Young, David C. *The Olympic Myth of Greek Amateur Athletics*. Chicago, 1984.

14
Politics and the Games

Crowther, Nigel B. "Athlete and State: Qualifying for the Olympic Games in Ancient Greece." *JSH* 23 (1996): 34–43.

Ioakimidou, Chrissula. "Auch wir sind Griechen! Statenreihen westgriechischer Kolonisten in Delphi und Olympia." *Nikephoros* 13 (2000): 63–94.

Miller, Stella G. "Macedonians at Delphi." In *Delphes cent ans après la grande fouille*, ed. Anne Jacquemin, 263–281. Paris, 2000.

Polignac, François de. *Cults, Territory, and the Origins of the Greek City-State*. Chicago, 1995.

Ulf, Christoph. "Die Mythen um Olympia–politischer Gehalt und politische Intention." *Nikephoros* 10 (1997): 9–52.

Weiler, Ingomar. "Korruption in der Olympischen Agoistik und die Diplomatische Mission des Hypereides in Elis." In *Achaia und Elis in der Antike*, ed. A. D. Rizakis, 87–92. ΜΕΛΕΤΗΜΑΤΑ 13. Athens, 1991.

15
Athletics and Society

Bernardini, Paola Angeli. "Olimpia e i giochi Olimpici: Le fonti letterarie tra lode e critica." *Nikephoros* 10 (1997): 179–190.

Bernardini, Paola Angeli. "*Sfairai* e *kylikes* nel simposio: Un' immagine agonistica in Dionisio Calco, fr. 2, 3–4 Gent.-Pr." *Nikephoros* 3 (1990): 127–132.

Bernardini, Paola Angeli. "La storia del'epinicio: Aspetti socio-economici." *SIFC* 10 (1992): 965–979.

Bilik, Ronald. "Die Zuverlässigkeit der frühen Olympionikenliste: Die Geschichtge eines Forschungsproblems im chronologischen Überblick." *Nikephoros* 13 (2000): 47–62.

Bravi, L. "L'epigramma simonideo per il pugile Casmilo di Rodi (XXXI Page)," *Nikephoros* 14 (2001): 11–19.

Burckhardt, Leonhard. "Vom 'Agon' zur 'Nullsummenkonkurrenz': Bemerkungen zu einigen Versuchen, die competitive Mentalität der Griechen zu erfassen." *Nikephoros* 12 (1999): 71–93.

Cairns, Francis. "Some Reflections of the Ranking of the Major Games in Fifth Century B.C. Epinician Poetry." In *Achaia und Elis in der Antike, ed.* A. D. Rizakis, 95–98. ΜΕΛΕΤΗΜΑΤΑ 13. Athens, 1991.

Campagner, Roberto. *Lessico agonistico di Aristofane*. Rome, 2001.

Crowther, Nigel B. "Cicero's Attitude to Greek Athletics." *Nikephoros* 14 (2001): 63–81.

Ebert, Joachim. *Agonismata*. Stuttgart, 1997.

Ebert, Joachim. *Griechische Epigramme auf Sieger an Gymnischen und Hippischen Agonen.* Berlin, 1972.

Ebert, Joachim. "Jahrtausendfeiern für Rom und die Olympischen Spiele." *Nikephoros* 6 (1993): 159–166.

Ebert, Joachim. "Die 'Olympische Chronik' *IG* II / III² 2326." *Archiv für Papyrusforschung* 28 (1982): 5–14. Reprinted in his *Agonismata*, 237–252. Stuttgart, 1997.

Ebert, Joachim. "Zur neuen Bronzeplatte mit Siegerinschriften aus Olympia, Inv. 1148." *Nikephoros* 10 (1997): 217–234. Reprinted in his *Agonismata*, 317–335. Stuttgart, 1997.

Franciò, Marcello. "Per un lessico agonistico-sportivo greco: Analisi di Polluce tra testi e intertesti." *Nikephoros* 13 (2000): 163–186.

García Romero, Fernando. "῎Ερως Ἀθλητής: Les Métaphores érotico-sportives dans les comédies d'Aristophane." *Nikephoros* 8 (1995): 57–76.

Geominy, Wilfred, and Stegan Lehman. "Zum Bronzebild des sitzenden Faustkämpfers im Museo Nazionale Romano." *Stadion* 15 (1989): 139–166.

Γιαλούρης, Νικος. "Το ιδαντικό της ἁμίλλας: Η συμβολη των αγώνων στην ανάπτυξη των τεχνών και των γραμμάτων." In *Proceedings of an International Symposium on the Olympic Games,* ed. William Coulson and Helmut Kyrieleis, 159–165. Athens, 1992.

Herrmann, Fritz Gregor. "Wrestling Metaphors in Plato's 'Theaetetus.'" *Nikephoros* 8 (1995): 77–110.

Herrmann, Hans-Volkmar. "Die Siegerstatuen von Olympia: Schriftliche Überlieferung und archäologischer Befund." *Nikephoros* 1 (1988): 119–184.

Hollein, Heinz-Günter. *Bürgerbild und Bildwelt der attischen Demokratie auf den rotfigurern Vasen des 6.–4. Jahrhunders v. Chr.* Frankfurt, 1988.

Hyde, W. W. *Olympic Victor Monuments and Greek Athletic Art.* Washington, D.C., 1921.

Kurke, Leslie. "The Economy of *Kudos*." In *Cultural Poetics in Archaic Greece,* ed. C. Dougherty and L. Kurke, 131–163. Cambridge, 1993.

Kurke, Leslie. *The Traffic in Praise: Pindar and the Poetics of Social Economy.* Ithaca, 1991.

Kyle, Donald G. "The First Hundred Olympiads: A Process of Decline or Democratization?" *Nikephoros* 10 (1997): 53–76.

Lattimore, Steven. "The Nature of Early Greek Victor Statues." In *Coroebus Triumphs,* ed. Susan J. Bandy, 245–256. San Diego, 1988.

Lomiento, Liana. "Semantica agonistica: *Kylindein* in Pind. *Nem.* 4, v. 40 e Nonn. *Dionys.* 48, vv. 134–154." *Nikephoros* 3 (1990): 145–156.

Lorenz, Thuri. "Der Doryphoros des Polyklet: Athlet, Musterfigur, politisches Denkmal oder mythischer Held?" *Nikephoros* 4 (1991): 177–190.

Merker, Irwin L. "Cheilon *Periodonikes*." AW 22 (1991): 43–48.

Miller, Stephen G. "Naked Democracy." In *Polis and Politics*. Festschrift M. H. Hansen, ed. P. Flensted-Jensen, T. H. Nielsen, and L. Rubinstein, 277–296. Copenhagen, 2000.

Myrick, L. "The Way Up and Down: Trace Horse and Turning Imagery in the Orestes Plays." *CJ* 89 (1994): 131–148.

Peiser, Benny. "The Crime of Hippias of Elis: Zur Kontroverse um die Olympionikenliste." *Stadion* 16 (1990): 37–66.

Raschke, Wendy J. "Images of Victory: Some New Considerations of Athletics Monuments." In *The Archaeology of the Olympics*, ed. Wendy J. Raschke, 38–54. Madison, Wis., 1988.

Raschke, Wendy J. "A Red-Figure Kyklix in Malibu: The Iconographty of Female Charioteers." *Nikephoros* 7 (1994): 157–180.

Rausa, Federico. *L'immagine del vincitore: L'athleta nella statuaria greca dall'età arcaiaca all'ellenismo*. Treviso, Italy, 1994.

Robinson, Eric W. *The First Democracies: Early Popular Government Outside Athens. Historia Einzelschriften* 107 (1997).

Scanlon, Thomas F. "Combat and Context: Athletics Metaphors for Warfare in Greek Literature." In *Coroebus Triumphs*, ed. Susan J. Bandy, 230–244. San Diego, 1988.

Steiner, Deborah. "Moving Images: Fifth-Century Victory Monuments and the Athlete's Allure." *ClAnt* 17 (1998): 123–149.

Tarrant, Harold. "Athletics, Competition and the Intellectual." *In Sport and Festival in the Ancient Greek World*, ed. David Phillips and David Pritchard, 353–365. Swansea, 2003.

16
Arete

Martínková, I. "Kalokagathia—How to Understand the Harmony of a Human Being." *Nikephoros* 14 (2001): 21–28.

Müller, Stefan. *Das Volk der Athleten: Untersuchungen zur Ideologie und Kritik des Sports in der griechisch-römischen Antike*. Trier, Germany, 1995.

O'Sullivan, Patrick. "Victory Song, Victory Statue: Pindar's Agonistic Imagery and Its Legacy." In *Sport and Festival in the Ancient Greek World, ed.* David Phillips and David Pritchard, 75–100. Swansea, 2003.

GENERAL INDEX

Words preceded by an asterisk (*) appear in the glossary.

INDEX OF WRITTEN SOURCES

Epigraphical/Papyrological